In Pursuit of Happiness:

American Conceptions of Property

from the Seventeenth

to the Twentieth Century

In Pursuit of Happiness: American Conceptions of Property from the Seventeenth to the Twentieth Century

WILLIAM B. SCOTT

Indiana University Press Bloomington and London

Burg.

HB
701
.S36
1977

Published in Canada by Fitzhenry & Whiteside Limited, Don Mills, Ontario

Manufactured in the United States of America

Library of Congress Cataloging in Publication Data
Scott, William B   1945–
    In pursuit of happiness.
    Includes index.
    1. Property—United States—History. I. Title.
HB701.S36   1977   333.3'0973   77–74435
ISBN 0–253–32930–2   1   2   3   4   5   81   80   79   78   77

For my mother and father

Contents

Preface   ix

PART I : AGRARIAN HERITAGE

1 Colonial America: Socialized Individualism   5
2 Life, Liberty, and Estate: Harrington and Locke   24
3 Life, Liberty, and the Pursuit of Happiness:
   The Creation of the Agrarian Republic   36

PART II : AN AGE OF GROWTH AND DIVERSITY

4 Every Man Under His Own Vine and Fig Tree:
   Agrarian Republicanism   53
5 The Pursuit of Plenty: Wages as Property   71
6 Bearers of Water and Hewers of Wood: Men
   as Property   94
7 Private Right versus Public Good: Property
   and Antebellum Law   114

PART III : THE COLLECTIVIST AGE

8 Private Property and Free Enterprise: Stephen
   Field, William Graham Sumner, and
   Raymond Moley   137
9 New Individualism: Four American Collectivists   159
10 Latter-Day Jeffersonians: Agrarian
   Republicanism in Industrial America   181

Conclusion: The Lingering World of Thomas Jefferson   200

Notes   207

Index   239

Preface

When I undertook this project six years ago I set out to determine "the American conception of property" and how that conception had changed through time. Very quickly I learned the first axiom of intellectual history. Literary sources only reveal the ideas of the particular person involved and do not necessarily mirror wider views. Furthermore, only rarely have Americans seen fit to reflect at length on their notion of property. Property, like water, has for the most part been one of those facts of life which seldom needed explanation or justification. Consequently, I have focused my attention on those individuals who gave some thought to the concept of ownership and whose thought was either significant or particularly perceptive. Thus, this is not a study of the "American mind" or even a study of "representative" samples of such a mind, although at times I considered and tried to assess the views of Americans generally. Instead, it is a study of a number of different American minds and their differing conceptions of property.

Among commentators on American society it has become almost ritualistic to point out Americans' general commitment to "private property." Such an observation has validity. Americans, in the past, do seem to have supported some notion of private ownership. Yet, despite general agreement, Americans have not all agreed as to the exact meaning of property rights or the ends they should serve. Jefferson and Hamilton, for instance, both endorsed pri-

vate ownership, but each defined property rights differently just as their preferred models of society were different. I have tried to clarify the various meanings Americans
have attached to the image of property and how those
images changed as historical circumstances changed. Hopefully, this analysis will contribute to the understanding of
this important concept which has helped shape our decep-
tively complex society. Notwithstanding our underlying
unity, Americans have not shared a common idea of what
America should be and some of these differences can best
be understood by examining our varying conceptions of
property.

Despite the diversity the most pervasive and persistent
conception of property has been that of opportunity or, as
Jefferson so suggestively put it, the right to "pursue happiness." Since the seventeenth century, Americans have
viewed access to and control over productive resources as
a primary right of citizenship. Eighteenth-century Americans so valued this idea of property that American revolutionaries described the right of property as inalienable and
its security one of government's chief ends. Today, even
though the opportunity to own and control productive
property is no longer feasible for most persons, Americans
generally continue to honor, at least sentimentally, the
eighteenth-century concept. Americans still believe that individual property rights are essential to personal liberty
and their right to "pursue happiness." This book is an
effort to answer why this is so.

In writing this book I have accumulated a number of
debts. H. Larry Ingle of the University of Tennessee at
Chattanooga and David L. Smiley of Wake Forest University as teachers and friends made my work possible in
ways they probably do not realize. Edward S. Shapiro of
Seton Hall University kindly read a portion of the manuscript and saved me from several errors in respect to the
"decentralist" intellectuals in the 1920s and 1930s. Daniel

T. Rodgers and Stanley I. Kutler of the University of Wisconsin and Richard Schlatter of Rutgers University each read an early draft and offered helpful and encouraging comments. Paul Conkin of the University of Wisconsin as advisor, critic, and teacher set standards of excellence which I have only partially been able to meet. Without his suggestions and patience this book would never have been. He personifies all that I value in a teacher and a scholar and which I have come to associate with the Department of History at the University of Wisconsin, Madison. At Kenyon Lee Wilson delayed her vacation two weeks to complete the typing of the final manuscript. Finally, my wife, Donna, provided the constant help, reassurance, and companionship which acknowledgment tends to trivialize.

Gambier, Ohio   William B. Scott

Part I

THE AGRARIAN HERITAGE

THE settlement of British North America offered venturesome Englishmen an exciting prospect. America contained a virtually limitless expanse of land. It held out to Englishmen unprecedented opportunity. Except for technologically primitive aboriginal tribes, the land stood unoccupied, inviting settlement. It contained no social structure and no coercive government. English settlement in the early decades changed this. The English crown claimed dominion over the land, and the King proceeded to parcel out his holdings to royal favorites and various chartered companies. At first, settlement was tightly organized as chartered companies controlled settlement, established municipal regulations, and monopolized economic enterprise. In most instances the governors of the new colonies sought to establish societies similar to that of England —complete with social hierarchy, economic regulation, and restricted political participation. But in all cases these efforts failed. The distance from imperial authority, the failure of the English aristocracy to transplant itself, and the easy availability of inexpensive land all worked to relax restrictions on individual enterprise and aspiration. By the middle of the eighteenth century British North Americans had already become the richest, freest, and most egalitarian people in the West. This unique circumstance exerted a profound influence on American conceptions of ownership. Since land was plentiful, all limitations as to use and amount seemed unduly restrictive and anachronistic. Furthermore, only rarely would a free person become the tenant of another. Virtually anyone willing to work or move westward could secure sufficient land to support himself and his family—and most persons did. In time Americans came to believe that all men should own land, and that widespread ownership of land was characteristic of a virtuous society. St. John de Crèvecoeur in his now famous *Letters from an American Farmer*, written just prior to the American Revolution, exemplified these attitudes. "The instant I enter on my own land," wrote Crèvecoeur, "the bright idea of property, of exclusive right, of independence, exalt my mind. Precious soil, I say to myself, by what singular custom of law is it that thou wast made to constitute the riches of the freeholder? What should we American farmers be without the distinct possession of that soil?" He added: "No wonder we should thus cherish its possession; no wonder that so many Europeans who have never been able to say that such portion of land was theirs cross the Atlantic to realize that happiness. This formerly rude soil has established all our rights; on it is founded our rank, our freedom, our power as citizens, our importance as inhabitants of such a district. This image, I must confess, I always behold with pleasure and extend them as far as my imagination can reach; for this is what may be called the true and only philosophy of an American farmer."[1]

Colonial New England ministers even found Biblical sanction for universal freeholding, as they frequently quoted in their election day sermons the famous lines from Micah 4:3–4:

> And he shall judge among many people, and rebuke strong nations afar off; and they shall beat their swords

into plowshares, and their spears into pruninghooks: Nation shall not lift up a sword against nation, neither shall they learn war any more.

But they shall sit every man under his vine and under his fig tree; and none shall make them afraid: For the Lord of hosts hath spoken it.

So pervasive were such ideas that in 1776 when Americans established their own governments they declared that all men enjoyed certain inherent rights among which was the individual's right to acquire and possess property—the right to be a freeholder, to be a man of property and standing.

CHAPTER 1

Colonial America:
Socialized Individualism

From first settlement Americans have valued the "right of property." Colonial Americans included the "right of property" under the "rights of Englishmen." As a "right of Englishmen" property derived from feudal law. Property rights were privileges bestowed on an individual by his sovereign. Once granted an individual's property right could not legally be abridged or annulled except in the words of the Magna Carta "by the lawful judgment of his peers or by the law of the land." In this sense the "right of property" symbolized the right of the English nobility to secure their possessions from arbitrary executive power.[1] American colonials also associated property rights with a work ethic, a labor theory of value, and the medieval Christian idea of a "just price." Because of the easy availability of land and the failure of the English nobility to transplant itself in the New World, the "rights of Englishmen" gradually lost their aristocratic implications in colonial America. When combined with a labor theory of value, the ancient feudal rights to property came to mean all men's right to exclusive ownership of productive resources and to the fruits of their labor free from arbitrary governmental action.

For colonial Americans land ownership represented the primary avenue of economic opportunity. In nearly every colony land was also the prerequisite for political participation. A man could neither vote nor hold public office if

5

he owned no land. For instance, at age twenty-five John Adams had graduated from Harvard and secured a license to practice law, but he could not vote, hold office, or even consider marriage. Not until age twenty-six when he inherited his father's land did Adams qualify as a freeholder and feel secure enough to marry. Not all colonial towns were as strict as Adams' hometown of Braintree, Massachusetts, but as a rule in colonial America landownership was of greatest importance—for the economic security it provided, the political power it conferred, and the opportunity it promised.[2]

In America landownership had not always been considered a right. At Jamestown the Virginia Company insisted that all land remain under company ownership as accorded by its royal charter. The Virginia Company required all of its employees to contribute "the fruits of their labor" to the common storehouse. The company distributed food and supplied to each according to his needs. After several years of near starvation the company abandoned its policy of corporate ownership and gave to each settler a three-acre garden to support himself. This seemed to work. "For formerly when our people were fed out of the common store and labored jointly in the manuring of the ground and planting corn," noted a visitor, "glad was that man that could slip from his labor, nay, the most honest of them in a general business, would not take so much faithful and true pains, in a week, as now he will do in a day, neither cared they for the increase, presuming that howsoever their harvest prospered, the general store must maintain them, by which means we reaped not so much corn from the labors of 30 men as three men have done for themselves . . ." since the private allotment of land.[3]

What began as an expedient soon was elevated to a principle. The company made a virtue of necessity and began to distribute land to its settlers. For the most part the grants were of "free and common socage" or "fee simple" tenures which were free from all feudal burdens except for a nominal annual quitrent. Very quickly the company found that the most effective way to attract new colonists was to offer all comers the opportunity to own land. It proposed to do this through a "headright" system which allowed a certain amount of land to each person upon entry into the colony. But before the company fully instituted the policy it lost its charter and Virginia became a royal colony. Nonetheless, the crown put into effect the company's plans. The Virginia headright law varied through the years, but in 1700 it provided fifty acres for anyone who paid their own or another person's passage and fifty acres for indentured servants at the expiration of their service. In an effort to prevent cheating and to guarantee that the purposes of the headright system were achieved, the Virginia law included a clause which required the grantee to build a house on the land and to plant a crop on it within three years or forfeit his claim.[4]

Virginia was not the only colony to use headrights to encourage immigration. At one time or another during the colonial period all of the colonies outside New England offered headrights. The amount varied from colony to colony. In 1663 Carolina offered one hundred acres to each free settler and fifty acres for each male servant and thirty for each female that a man might bring to the colony. When the male's service expired, the law entitled him to ten acres of land, the female six. The miserly grant to servants undoubtedly reflected an early inducement for the importation of slaves into Carolina. Maryland held out a more liberal offer to indentured servants of fifty acres of land at the end of service plus a year's supply of corn, three suits of clothes, and the necessary tools to begin farming. By far the most appealing proposition came from Pennsylvania. Under the influence of William Penn, the Quaker colony allowed persons with money to buy land outright with no quitrents or, if a settler had no money, he could acquire a hundred-acre estate for one penny per acre per year. If a prospective settler had neither the money for land or passage, Penn allowed him to indenture himself to someone else for passage and upon completion of his service he would receive fifty acres of land from Penn. In addition the colony provided the free but indigent settler with seeds, tools, stock, and other supplies if at the end of seven years the man agreed to buy the land he had worked. All that Penn demanded was hard work.[5]

In New England a similar development toward freeholding occurred. As in all other facets of their life colonial New Englanders' attitudes toward ownership were profoundly influenced by their religious beliefs—beliefs frequently shared by other colonials. In John Winthrop's famous phrase New Englanders had come to the new world to found a "city on a hill" for all other Christians to emulate. They hoped to separate themselves from the corruption of England and Europe to create a "purified" society both just and godly. For the pious Puritan ownership could never simply be a means for personal fulfillment or gain. It must also contribute to communal well-being as well as provide the individual the means to serve and worship God. "Here then we must in generall know," admonished the English Puritan divine William Perkins, "that he abuseth his calling, whosoever he be that against the end thereof, employes it for himself, seeking wholly his own, and not the common good. And that common saying, 'Every man for himself, and God for us all,' is wicked and is directly against the end of every calling or honest kinde of life."[6]

Despite their emphasis on the communal, Puritan New Englanders rejected much of the medieval conception of property. Influenced by Augustine, the medieval church had adopted the Stoic notion that God had originally given nature to all men in common, and all men enjoyed an equal claim to nature. Since nature provided the means to sustain life, this doctrine was basically an affirmation of the right of all persons to life. Because of man's sinful nature God, through the church and king, distributed to each according to his and society's needs. Otherwise there would be disorder as each individual would seek to assert his claim to nature at the expense of all others. Thus, while everyone enjoyed some claim to nature, no one held exclusive title over any land. Property in medieval Europe meant obligations and conditional ownership, not rights and economic freedom.

The feudal class system demanded servile labor of some, but not of others. All men held land under conditions which, if violated, would forfeit their right to its use. In theory the church, king, and community controlled economic activity for the good of the whole through regulation of wages, prices, quality of workmanship, hours, and profits; they discouraged competition, usury, exploitation, and shabby goods. Neither peasant nor artisan was encouraged to try new methods or through industry to enlarge his wealth or to improve his social status. The medieval political economy asked the individual to sacrifice himself for the good of the whole. For those satisfied with a life of material and spiritual security—usually those at the bottom and very top of the feudal hierarchy—the social order worked well. And if one assumed that there existed a fixed amount of wealth and that productivity could not be increased through invention and industry, as most medieval persons did, such a system seemed both appropriate and just.[7]

But not everyone accepted the medieval ideal. Towns, commerce, and in some instances freehold farming provided outlets for a limited number of ambitious and independent men who could not accept their appointed position in society. For such persons the feudal restrictions on property and enterprise seemed burdensome. In the sixteenth century large numbers of these entrepreneurial persons gravitated toward the Protestantism of John Calvin with its emphasis on the moral responsibility of individuals and the virtue of work. Gradually Calvinists so redefined property as to free it from nearly all feudal restrictions. Still, they remained faithful to the strong moral emphasis of medieval Christianity. Calvinists acknowledged that property, like all else, came from God, and that the individual's relationship to property was one of stewardship. They argued that an industrious and creative citizenry, if given free access to productive resources and the right to enjoy the fruits of their labor, would produce an abundance from which the entire society would benefit. Ownership and management of productive resources became for Calvinists a means for individuals to serve God and society. Property provided men a calling.[8]

Colonial New Englanders honored these Calvinist beliefs. Foreshadowing John Locke, New Englanders glorified work, defended the individual's rights to pursue a calling, and recognized a person's claim to the full product of his labor. Together, the work ethic, the idea of a calling, and the labor theory of value justified acquisitive behavior and the accumulation of wealth. Furthermore, because New Englanders assumed that God rewarded the righteous, they tended to honor those persons who obtained material success. Nonetheless, throughout the colonial period Calvinist New Englanders insisted that personal acquisition in the last instance should serve social ends. Harking back to medieval ideas of Christian stewardship and a "just price," colonial New Englanders, like so many other American colonials, generally agreed that society had the right and the obligation to insure individual property contributed to the general welfare.[9]

New England Puritans' adherence to this strain of socialized individualism was particularly evident in the first few precarious years of development. While en route to the New World, John Winthrop, leader of the Massachusetts Bay Puritans, gave eloquent expression to these ideals in his sermon, "A Model of Christian Charity," delivered on board the *Arabella*. Winthrop wanted to forestall the development of a selfish individualism which he feared might destroy the community and its mission. Although

God had not distributed his blessings to all men equally, he explained to the congregation, that did not mean that one man because of greater wealth or intelligence was morally superior to other less well-endowed men. God, said Winthrop, had provided different talents to equip men for the different tasks of the community. All gold, all silver, all wealth, was not any one man's but God's to be used for the benefit of the entire community. "In such cases as this," lectured Winthrop, "the care of the publique must oversway all private respects, by which not only conscience, but meare civill pollicy doth binde us; for it is a true rule that perticuler estates cannott subsist in the ruine of the publique." Winthrop warned that there might even be a time when each citizen would be asked to give all that he owned to insure the success of the holy experiment.[10]

That the Puritans placed a high value on individual ownership is obvious; otherwise there would have been no need for Winthrop's sermon. The 1641 Massachusetts Body of Liberties specifically guaranteed to an individual the right to own cattle, goods, and estates. Drawing upon English common law, the Body of Liberties forbade the confiscation of private property "unless it is by virtue of equity or some express law of the Country." If it became necessary to take or destroy a person's property for "public use or service," the Body of Liberties required that the public pay the injured person fair and reasonable compensation. But it also insisted that all private possessions be used consistent with the needs and interests of the general welfare. Accordingly, under what might be called "police powers," New Englanders tried to regulate wages, prices, and interest rates, and they passed laws to insure the quality of workmanship and goods. Public officials scrutinized the regulation of weights and measures as well as ferries, mills, and inns. In 1639 when several persons accused an important and well-to-do Boston merchant, John Keaynes, of charging inordinately high prices, the Massachusetts government fined Keaynes, and his congregation censored his behavior. Deeply hurt, Keaynes nonetheless on his death left his fortune to the people of Massachusetts.[11]

Seventeenth-century Puritan New Englanders always seemed to have assumed individual ownership of personal goods, livestock, and real estate. But in the founding of the separatist colony of Plymouth in 1620 individual ownership of land was not at first permitted. As in Jamestown the authorities of Plymouth faced the chronic problem of a new colony—how to motivate its people to do the planting necessary for survival? At the start, because of their contract with their backers, the Plymouth settlers tried communal farming. Everyone worked on the same fields and shared supplies from a common storehouse. But demands far exceeded yields and the colony faced starvation. The colonists resolved the problem by ending communal labor and making it clear that only those who planted and successfully harvested would eat. "This had very good success," explained Governor William Bradford, "for it made all hands industrious, so as much more corn was planted than otherwise would have been by any means the Governor or any other could use, and saved him a great deal of trouble, and gave for better content. The women now went willingly into the fields, and took their little ones with them to set corn; which before would have alleged weakness and inability; when to have compelled would have been thought great tyranny and oppression."[12]

For seventeenth-century New Englanders individual ownership of land seemed preferable to collective ownership for several reasons. First, as Bradford pointed out, it apparently increased productivity. One New Englander expressed a common belief: "Well understanding that one acre enclosed is much beneficial that [sic] 5 falling to his share in common."[13] Freehold farming also seemed well suited to the Calvinist idea of calling as well as New Englanders' commitment to a labor theory of value. New England Calvinists believed that God had called everyone to a task. Therefore everyone had a moral obligation to work for the glory of God. If all assumed their God-appointed tasks, then all the necessary work in a community would be completed and the community would prosper. If, on the other hand, someone shirked his obligation either the community would suffer or someone else would be forced to shoulder an inequitable share of the work. New Englanders, John Cotton declared, like "Bees will not suffer drones among them if they lay up anything, it shall be for them that cannot work."[14] Individual landownership provided the logical solution. It not only gave men a necessary calling—the production of food, but it also insured that each person would be rewarded in proportion to his industry. As Bradford had said, only the industrious would eat. Lastly, individual ownership of land acted as a bond between generations. If children expected to inherit their parents' farm, they had to respect their parents' wishes as well as provide for their elders in old age. Landownership thus provided a freeholder moral purpose, economic security, and individual autonomy.

New Englanders' wholesale adoption of freehold farming during the seventeenth century was a testament to its compatibility with their values. During the first several decades following settlement a number of New England villages sought to establish a system of "open field" farming characteristic of the English villages many had left. Villagers sowed and harvested their fields in common, and everyone grazed livestock together in general pastures. But by the eighteenth century in every known instance New Englanders abandoned "open field" farming in favor of individual farmsteads or freeholds. Furthermore, among the North American British colonies, only those in New England were free from quitrents—the annual rent feudal law required an inferior to pay his superior. Whatever vestigial medieval ideas on collective land ownership New Englanders might have brought with them, clearly by the eighteenth century they had exorcised them. By 1700 New

England had assumed the character of a region dominated by small, independent, freehold farmers—a reputation it retained until the mid-nineteenth century. What was true of New England was generally the case in British North America as a whole. Only the tidewater South with its slave plantations and upstate New York with its leasehold system diverged from the prevailing American pattern of freehold farming.[15]

Consequently, from the very beginning America appeared to Europeans as a land where enterprising and industrious persons could expect to become landed men of property. An eighteenth-century immigrant tract, typical of a whole body of similar literature, made this clear. America is a land where "a man of small substance, if upon precarious footing at home can, at once, secure to himself a handsome, independent living and do well for himself and posterity." "The poorest man," the writer continued, "if he can but work, procures at once plenty of subsistence which grows yearly upon his hands until by gentle and agreeable labor he arrives, at last, at a state of affluence and ease." All should hasten across the Atlantic, he urged, "that here each may sit safe, and at ease under his own fig-tree, indulging himself in the natural bent of his genious, in patronizing the useful arts of life, and in practicing the virtues of humanity."[16] Promotional literature of this sort established a level of expectation in the minds of immigrants and residents alike. In a vague and informal manner it established the economic conditions which the colonizers of America believed government should provide.

The promotional literature was not illusionary. Colonial America offered men wide opportunity to acquire land. From north to south, on the frontier and in the cities, the vast majority of white adult males owned land. Most families lived on farms producing small surpluses for the commercial market of England or American cities, and in the large seaports most men ran their own shops and owned their own homes. In cities like Boston only 29 percent of adult males hired themselves out to other men, and many of these dependent laborers were either young unmarried men or they owned enough personal goods to qualify for voting. By 1763 the unpropertied or dependent laboring force in the colonies, exclusive of slaves, was no more than 20 to 30 percent of the population. This is not to say that everyone who came to the North American colonies became a self-sufficient man of property. He did not. In fact, almost none of the slaves secured independence or property and perhaps less than 10 percent of the convicts and indentured servants attained the rank of freeholder. But most colonial Americans by 1750 did own land or other forms of productive property, and the opportunity for the indigents to secure land was great, particularly in newly settled areas.[17]

On the surface, freeholding seemed to reconcile colonial Americans' acquisitive habits with the moral affirmation of a labor theory of value. Even so, a labor theory of value proved a two-edged sword. New Englanders' rationalization of their seizure of Indian land provides an excellent example of how Americans used a labor theory of value to justify their acquisitions, and then, when their own possessions seemed inconsistent with it, their qualification of the theory. The Indians presented New England Calvinists with a difficult moral problem. How could they as Christians justify their occupation of the land if someone else already occupied it? Their fervent religiosity restricted the range of possible rationalizations. They defined all men as descendants of Adam, and one group of God's children had no right to steal from another. For this reason colonists could not declare the Indians without human or property rights. And being moral men, believing in right and wrong, in law and legal process, they could not justify taking the land simply on grounds of superior strength or might makes right.[18]

A labor theory of value provided an out. Anticipating Locke, Winthrop argued that in a "state of nature" all property had been held in common. But God had given men a mandate to "increase and multiply, replenish the earth and subdue it." God had not provided men with the earth to let it lie fallow. He had given the earth to men to labor on and to glorify Him through their work and improvements. All unimproved land, Winthrop declared, remained the possession of no one, and whoever labored on unimproved or unclaimed land made it his own. Land became private property only through cultivation, manuring, and enclosing. Therefore anyone had the right to appropriate any unimproved land by enclosing and cultivating. Since by English standards the Indians had not noticeably improved the land or enclosed it, it was not theirs but lay in an unclaimed "state of nature." Far from stealing the Indian's land, Winthrop described British colonials as land reformers.[19]

Not everyone accepted Winthrop's interpretation of the righteousness of colonial land claims. Roger Williams, the volatile founder of Rhode Island, argued that the Indians did not live in a state of nature but had improved the land by burning the underbrush and that their woodlands were no less useful than the king's parks in England. Instead of simply claiming the land based on enclosure and improvement, Williams demanded that the colonists first purchase the rights to the land from its original owners, the Indians.[20]

John Cotton rebutted Williams' accusations. Cotton argued that although the number of the king's parks seemed more than he needed, the king, because he was the king, had greater needs than other men. Also, the king allowed tame animals to graze in the forest and tenants to live on the land as well as to gather wood from the forest. Cotton denied that the Indians' burning improved the land and suggested that they had done so only as a pastime. Besides, he explained, the Massachusetts authorities had paid the Indians for the land, thereby establishing both a "natural" (labor) and a "legal" (payment) right to the land.[21]

Although to Williams the difference between his and the Massachusetts position seemed of gravest importance, it did not provide much of an alternative for the Indians. As long as the white settlers continued to occupy the Indians' land the aboriginal way of life was doomed, no matter how alienation took place. Furthermore, by emphasizing legal purchase Williams ignored any other claim the Indians had to the land. Cotton's willingness to accept Williams' "bill of sale" argument illustrated how legally documented claims could replace the moral conditions of "need and use" when one's interest dictated. Williams' separation of property rights from labor defused a potentially effective moral weapon against land speculation and profiteering. A legalistic conception of property rights made it possible for men to accumulate wealth without worrying whether it had been earned, whether it deprived others of the opportunity to own, or whether it was in the public interest.[22]

In 1722 Solomon Stoddard illustrated the importance of emphasizing legal claims and the playing down of right based on "need and use." Stoddard, in response to a pamphlet which had suggested that all unused, privately owned land be redistributed to persons without land, insisted that "need and use" applied only to Indian land. He accepted Winthrop's "subdued and improved" theory to justify New England titles, but he also realized that taken to its logical conclusion a criterion of "need and use" threatened many existing landholdings. Taking his cue from John Cotton, Stoddard declared that in addition to subduing and improving the land, the Puritan fathers had paid the Indians to secure clear legal title. Thus no man, he warned, should presume a right to confiscate another man's land with the excuse that it was unused and unimproved. According to Stoddard, the bill of sale from the Indians superseded any claims based on "need and use." Stoddard distinguished between moral and legal rights in such a way as to legitimatize almost any accumulation of private wealth.[23]

Because of the general availability of cheap land in colonial America only occasionally did a situation arise when a vested land title seem to frustrate another individual's right to acquire. But when such a situation occurred, invariably someone would raise the moral criterion of "need and use." One such person was Joseph Morgan—the target of Stoddard's pamphlet. Early in the eighteenth century Boston suffered from inflated land values which made it difficult for farmers to remain on their land. Morgan, a Congregational minister and close friend of Cotton Mather, believed that all of Boston's problems could be traced to land monopoly. In a pamphlet entitled *The Original Rights of Mankind* (1722) Morgan attacked all landownership which exceeded "need and use" as a violation of natural justice. "Then it is," he explained, "unscriptural and contrary to our reasonable nature, that the earth and the creatures thereof should be sold, or by laws, deeds, grants, or any other color or manner of device whatsoever, be made the property of particular persons who exact all the fruits of the sweat of the poor husband and his family's labors and thereby make their families, if not the province, to be their slaves."[24] Morgan believed that unused, privately owned tracts produced an artificial shortage which drove up the price of land. As a result, landowners were able to engross huge, unearned profits, profits produced by the labor of the enterprising and industrious members of the community. Anticipating Henry George, Morgan called for the taxation of all dormant land until none remained so that everyone might "be supplied with farms, according to the donation of God freely, without price or purchase for it is their birthright as they are men."[25]

Undoubtedly the most extreme example of land monopoly in colonial America occurred in New York. Ever since the English takeover of the Dutch colony, New York had been plagued with a series of governors who had systematically depleted the state's land reserves by allowing generous and often illegal land grants to friends and favorites.

As a result, by the first decade of the eighteenth century the colony was saddled with a land system in which a few men owned most of the land, leaving little for newcomers. Land prices in New York ran as high as ten to twenty pounds an acre, with some men owning as much as two hundred thousand acres "entirely desolate and useless both to the King and his people." High land prices meant that prospective farmers had either to become the tenants of large landowners or to move to Connecticut or Pennsylvania.[26]

Cadwallader Colden, surveyer-general and lieutenant-governor of New York, recognized the problem and on several occasions tried to deprive the large landowners of their unutilized holdings. In 1732 he proposed a 2s. 3d. quitrent per hundred acres. He admitted that this would not redistribute the land as needed, but he noted that at least the quitrent would make estates larger than twenty thousand acres unprofitable. The owners would be forced either to sell their land or to surrender their grants. This would allow landowners to keep their productive land, but force them to give up the unused land which they held for speculative purposes. At one time the arrangement provided a more equitable basis of taxation and the opportunity for the landless to acquire land. Colden's motives were not unmixed, or entirely linked to the public interest. There is strong evidence that he wanted to dispossess the existing landlords so that he and his friends could assume title to the repossessed land. Motives aside, it is revealing that Colden used arguments which he thought would appeal to a large segment of New Yorkers. Further, at no time did Colden think that his suggestions for land reform threatened property rights. Rather, he argued, the policies would guarantee to more men the chance to own land.[27]

In 1746 in New Jersey a much more radical argument in favor of land reform appeared. A New Jersey resident in an anonymous letter published in the *New York Weekly*

Post Boy noted, in regard to proprietary grants, that all men had an equal claim to nature, and any man could make that part his own with which he mixed his labor. Therefore, he declared, uncultivated land in the new world lay "as free and as common for all to settle upon as the waters of the rivers are to all to drink." But in parceling out the land the government had given to a few men the best land in such exorbitant quantities "that the rest of the subjects have been obliged to buy it for their use, at an extravagant price; a hardship, that seems as great as if they had been put under the necessity of buying the waters of the rivers."[28] These remarks may have been too radical for Colden's tastes, but the two did agree that legal claims to land in excess of what a person needed or used could be abridged or taxed in order to keep open for every one the opportunity to own the means of subsistence.

The best example of a colonial assembly actually using "need and use" to attack large landholdings occurred in Pennsylvania during the French and Indian War (Seven Years' War in Europe). The Penn family retained proprietary title to Pennsylvania until the end of the colonial period. Penn's sons lacked their father's magnanimity towards the colonists. The younger Penns seemed to be holding on to the colony not to serve it, as their father had, but to earn money from quitrents. With the outbreak of the French and Indian War colonial legislatures began to appropriate money for defense. In Pennsylvania this took the form of a land tax. Since the Penns owned more land than anyone else, a land tax was a popular means to raise revenue. To make the tax even more palatable, the legislature drew up its tax bill in such a way as to insure that the Penns would pay more per acre than anyone else. The Penns opposed the land tax through their governor, who vetoed all such money bills because they included what the Penns felt were illegal attacks on their property.[29]

The assembly responded that since the Penns owned more land than anyone else in the colony and the money would be used to protect their property it was only fair for the Penns to pay the discriminatory taxes. The assembly thought that to tax the proprietors' unused and vacant land especially just, since high taxes would force the proprietors to sell their land and thereby encourage more settlers. Besides, they noted, the vacant lands had increased in value through no merit of the Penns, but as a result of the labor and industry of the people of Pennsylvania. The Penns, reacting to parliamentary pressure, finally resolved the issue by allowing the tax on their lands so long as it was general and nondiscriminatory. Thus, given the right circumstances, such as an absentee landlord like the Penn family, American colonials were quite willing to impose discriminatory taxes on unearned and unused landholdings in behalf of social equity and individual opportunity.[30]

Benjamin Franklin in many ways epitomized the curious mixture of acquisitiveness and moral sensitivity that characterized so many of his contemporary Americans. Born in New England, Franklin left home at an early age and in Philadelphia established himself as a printer, inventor, and civic leader. In his writings Franklin presented himself as an archtypical American—a man of simple but practical virtues. A child of Puritan upbringing, he considered all legally held private possessions morally justified. Still, Franklin insisted that all private possessions must be subject to community control. "All property, indeed, except the savage's temporary cabin, his matchcoat, and other little acquisitions, absolutely necessary for his subsistence," declared Franklin, "seems to me to be the creature of public convention. Hence the public has the right to regulate descents, and all other conveyances of property, and even of limiting the quantity and uses of it." The only inviolate right of property which Franklin allowed an individual was to the productive resources necessary for subsistence. "But all property superfluous to such purposes," he argued, "is the property of the public, who by their laws, have created it, and who may therefore by other laws dispose of it, whenever the welfare of the public shall demand such disposition. He that does not like civil society on these terms," asserted Franklin, "let him retire and live among savages."[31]

Franklin valued private ownership and was instrumental in creating the romanticized image of the small American freeholder. Landownership allowed a man to be free and autonomous and to reap the full fruit of his labor. He attributed the differences between American farmers and European peasants to the widespread ownership of land in America. The American farmer, observed Franklin, did not have to "pay rack'd rents" to landlords or support a wealthy, parasitic gentry. Once while in Europe he wrote home, "I thought often of the happiness of New England where every man is a freeholder, has a vote in public affairs, lives in a tidy, warm house, has plenty of food and fuel, with whole clothes from head to foot, the manufacture perhaps of his own family."[32] Even so, like many other colonial Americans, Franklin was not disturbed by wealth and luxury. He firmly believed that an individual's pursuit of luxury often worked to the community's benefit. "A vain silly fellow," he wrote, "builds a fine house, furnishes it richly, lives in it expensively, and in a few years ruins himself." But in the process the fool's silly extravagences supported other more sensible and thrifty men. Furthermore, the pursuit of wealth provided the indolent an incentive to labor. "Is not the hope of one day being able to purchase and enjoy luxuries," he asked his countrymen, "a great spur to labor and industry?"[33]

Franklin embodied almost the entire range of colonial American attitudes toward ownership. He placed special value on landownership and the right of individuals to the resources necessary for subsistence. He identified with the hard-working freeholder who demanded a full day's work for a full day's pay. And he understood Americans' acquisitive appetites and often indulged his own. Accumulated wealth did not bother Franklin as long as opportunity remained open for others. But in the final analysis he insisted that the community must be able to control its resources and the economic activities of its citizens. The right to the product of one's labor, the right to acquire, and the idea that the individual and his possessions must finally be subject to society—all reflected views common among colonial Americans. Franklin's very complex conception of individual ownership encompassed much of eighteenth-century debate over private property. However, only rarely did anyone manage to restrain so successfully the inherent tension between individual right and community need or between acquisitiveness and scarcity as Franklin. Almost entirely devoid of religiosity, Franklin still remained faithful to the Calvinist ideal of socialized individualism.

CHAPTER 2

Life, Liberty, and Estate: Harrington and Locke

For a variety of reasons by 1750 Americans had come to view themselves as a uniquely favored people—a people morally superior to Europeans. America lacked the unpropertied masses of Europe as well as a decadent class of aristocrats. Americans often described themselves as a nation of virtuous middle-class farmers, merchants, and artisans both frugal and hard working. Seemingly in America position and power were based on ability not privilege or birth. Furthermore, Americans believed that colonial politics were far less corrupt than European politics. Americans elected most of their public officials and insisted on efficient and honest government. Politicians supposedly took office to serve their constituents, not to line their pockets or gain easy jobs for their friends and relations. In the eighteenth century this sense of American "exceptionalism" was reinforced and given definition in England by certain antiestablishment intellectuals who had been influenced strongly by the political theories of James Harrington and John Locke. Mid-eighteenth-century Americans found in Locke's and Harrington's ideas on liberty and property a justification and an explanation for their unique superiority.[1]

The English Civil War had driven James Harrington to political philosophy. For him seventeenth-century English politics provided a classic example of the failure of government and the triumph of chaos. In the absence of a stable and disinterested government English society had turned on itself; power not right, men not law, dictated public policy. Harrington looked to history and political philosophy for an answer to England's political disorder, as he readily adopted the classical and renaissance view that change usually meant change for the worse. He considered change a symptom of civil corruption and an indication of the decline of civic virtue. While stability was a necessary attribute of a good government, a virtuous polity must also govern in the interest of its entire citizenry. A society that allowed class or personal interest to determine public policy lacked virtue and suffered from corruption.[2] Government, wrote Harrington, "is an act whereby a civil society is instituted and preserved upon a common foundation of right or interest . . . an empire of laws, and not of men."[3] A virtuous commonwealth must be both stable and just.

After lengthy study Harrington concluded that property was the decisive factor of politics. The individual or social class that controlled the preponderance of wealth in a particular society also controlled its government. The reason was simple. Political power rested on military might, and soldiers fought for those who fed and housed them. As Harrington put it, "But an army is a beast that has a great belly and must be fed."[4] An army could be "fed" by any form of wealth, but the most permanent and dependable source was land. Harrington believed that a shortage of land had caused the downfall of the Stuart kings. They had tried to exercise absolute power over England at a time when the English monarchy no longer controlled most of the nation's land. Parliament, representing the landed classes of England, resisted the authority of the crown. During the Civil War Parliament prevailed precisely because its larger landholdings allowed it to raise and support a larger army. But parliamentary victory did not necessarily assure England a stable and just government. Quite the contrary. Following Parliament's victory, Oliver

Cromwell, backed by his New Model Army, assumed power. Because Cromwell, like the Stuarts, did not own a preponderance of the land in England, his regime could not last. Inevitably the landed classes of England would rise up against their Protector and thrust England into renewed civil war. According to Harrington, England would not secure political stability until a single social class held an overwhelming majority of the land and that class also dominated policy making.

Harrington thought that in England both justice and stability were obtainable. In 1656 he published *The Common-wealth of Oceana* in which he set out in minute detail the necessary steps. Adopting the renaissance concept of civic humanism, he assumed that man, being a social creature, could only fulfill his individual strivings through service to society, and such responsible citizenship depended on individual autonomy. Unless the citizen was economically free, he could not act with disinterested virtue. Instead, he entered politics to serve the interests of those who controlled him.[5]

Like most seventeenth-century Englishmen, Harrington defined freedom in terms of landownership. A landless person depended on another for his subsistence. Landless men were by definition servile because they were compelled to obey their master's will or starve. For this reason a landless person could not be politically virtuous. A virtuous political community necessarily excluded all dependent men whether they were servants, employees, or bureaucrats. And since a virtuous polity depended on a virtuous citizenry, the fewer servile men a society contained the greater its virtue. Conversely, the fewer free men a society contained the greater its corruption. Harrington reasoned that society should seek to maximize the number of its independent men and minimize dependent men. The ideal society would be one in which all citizens were propertied and therefore free. In such a commonwealth no social class would possess the resources necessary to maintain a private army. Instead national defense would depend on a militia of armed and free citizens. "A commonwealth," declared Harrington, "that is internally equal, has no internal cause of commotion, and therefore can have no such effect but from without. A common-wealth internally inequal has no internal cause of quiet, and therefore can have no such effect but by diversion."[6] For Harrington, the obvious solution was an "agrarian law" which placed limits on landholding.

Harrington did not intend his "agrarian law" to create a commonwealth of equal men. Equality was not an important value to him. He cared more about virtue and accepted as desirable hierarchy and social classes. Social classes reflected the real differences between men, and if properly balanced, classes helped stabilize society. Harrington viewed an "agrarian law" as the best means to prevent any single class from monopolizing landholding. If either the nobility or the common people monopolized landholding to the exclusion of the other, that class would dominate policy making and legislate in the interest of its own class rather than in the interest of the whole commonwealth. But if each class possessed some land, then each would share in policy making. By checking one another's selfish tendencies, both classes would insist that all legislation served the general welfare. Class interests would be muted as each property-holding citizen would find his interest inextricably tied to the common interest.

Harrington believed that his "agrarian law" would achieve two different but complementary ends. First, by returning surplus land to the marketplace all citizens would gain an opportunity to acquire the land necessary for autonomy. Freeholding became an ever-realizable possibility, thereby increasing the total number of citizens capable of political virtue. Secondly, by limiting the amount of land any single person could own, an "agrarian law" would insure that small freeholders owned the overwhelming majority of the land and consequently the balance of power. The king and the nobility, in order to retain their own property, would have to serve the interests of the commonwealth as a whole since rebellion against a "numerous and armed" citizenry was out of the question. Harrington insisted that his agrarian commonwealth of independent freeholders would be stable, virtuous, and strong. It need not fear civic corruption, internal division, or external enemies.

In 1656 Harrington respectfully dedicated *The Commonwealth of Oceana* to Oliver Cromwell in the hope that Cromwell might introduce the desired reforms. For the most part Harrington's ideas fell on deaf ears. It is doubtful that Cromwell ever read *The Common-wealth*. Within four years of the book's publication Cromwell had died, his son and successor Richard had been deposed, and the Stuart monarchy under Charles II had been restored. Superficially English politics had returned to its pre-Civil War forms. Suddenly, republican theories, such as Harrington's which had seemed innocuous under Cromwell's regime, assumed radical implications under the restored monarchy. To persist in advocating the overthrow of the monarchy in favor of a republic was to invite persecution, imprisonment, or, as in the case of Algernon Sidney, execution.

Men like Sidney were exceptional. Most opponents of the restoration either kept their peace or accommodated themselves to the changed political climate by adopting the role of the loyal opposition. After Charles II's death in 1685 accommodation became more difficult. Charles' successor James II was much more insistent in exercising the prerogatives of the crown. James also refused to hide his loyalty to the Roman Catholic faith. Once it became clear that James would have a male Catholic heir a large number of his political opponents decided that the Stuart monarchy must be deposed. To justify their revolutionary action, many of the opponents of James turned to earlier republican theories. John Locke found the older republi-

can ideas inadequate, and he set about developing a new
and more comprehensive theory of government and revolution. Sometime prior to 1688 Locke completed his project, which he entitled *Two Treatises of Government*. Locke
based his argument on Harrington's theory of political
power, a labor theory of value, and natural rights philosophy.[7]

One of the difficulties in understanding the *Two Treatises
of Government* is that Locke used the key words "property" and "people" differently than we generally do today.
For him "property" did not simply mean possessions. It
included life, liberty, and estate. Self-possession or liberty
comes close to Locke's use of the term "property." Locke
claimed that the individual possessed a natural and unalienable right to his life, the freedom to control his life,
and control over those things he had created with his life.
An individual joined society and accepted government "to
better preserve himself, his Liberty and Property."[8] Only
through organized society and orderly government could
an individual assure himself the security necessary to exercise his God-given right to freedom. "Freedom of men
under Government," he declared, "is to have a standing
rule to live by, common to every one of that society, and
made by the legislative power erected in it; a liberty to
follow in all things where the rule prescribes not and not
to be subject to the inconstant, uncertain, unknown, arbitrary will of another man."[9] Even as Locke insisted that
the right of property derived from God, he always allowed
that the liberty to exercise the right derived from social
order—an order established and determined by society.

Locke's use of the term "people" also varied from present usage. In one sense Locke used "people" in its inclu-
sive sense to mean all men. All humans, he affirmed, have
a right to life which no one, not even they themselves, had a
right to destroy. When he referred to the "state of nature,"
Locke almost always used "people" in its universal sense.
Consistent with this pattern, he asserted that every man

enjoyed a "natural right" to property. In a state of nature God had given the earth to all men in common and all men possessed a natural right of access to nature. Without such a right an individual might starve. Locke's right to property was really the right to subsistence—the Christian idea of each person's right to life. When he referred to the state of "society" and "politics," Locke narrowed the meaning of "people" to include only "free persons" in the Harringtonian use of the term. According to Locke, if a person voluntarily sold his labor to another, he became a servant. Or if he lost his freedom during a "just war," he became a slave. In either case, servant or slave, the individual had lost his autonomy. He depended on another for his livelihood. He was not self-possessed. Another person owned and controlled him. While a servile person retained his life, he had lost or given up his liberty. Locke, like Harrington, insisted that only free men could participate in government, and, since government's chief end was to protect liberty and property, only free men had any interest in government. In effect, he limited government to freeholders.[10]

Locke's entire theory of government rested on the implicit assumption that freedom was a consequence of landholding and only free men were eligible to participate in government. Throughout the *Two Treatises* he concerned himself, not with liberty of man in the abstract, but the liberty of freeholders. He wished to confer on the traditional property rights of English freeholders abstract and universal qualities. For this he turned to ancient, but increasingly fashionable, natural rights theory. A central doctrine of natural rights theory was the idea that God had given the earth to all men in common. If this was so, Locke was obligated to explain why some men ended up with large amounts of land and others owned none. How could some men claim a "natural right" of property to that which God had given to all men? Locke did not challenge the ancient convention. Instead, he argued that this situation was only temporary. God intended men to enjoy His bounty and this could only be accomplished if individuals took parts of nature for their own. After all, if men had not taken food from nature's common store and eaten it, they would have died.

It was clear to Locke that from the very start individuals through their labor had possessed portions of nature and made it their own. Labor, therefore, gave to the individual a rightful title to nature. Labor justified individual ownership since no man could claim a property in another person's labor without consent. In time men learned that by tilling and improving the land they could mulitiply God's original gift. Purposeful labor increased the productive capacity of nature—particularly land. By mixing their labor with the land, Locke asserted, men made it their own. Equally important, individual ownership of land did not deplete what God had given to men in common; it actually augmented the sum of human wealth. In privatizing nature individuals had not taken from others. Rather, they had claimed as property only what they themselves had added, and in the process they had dramatically increased the productive capacity of nature and made possible a more comfortable and secure existence for all mankind.[11]

Through a labor theory of value Locke had explained and justified individual ownership of produce. But the land itself, apart from any improvements, remained a gift of nature and not the product of anyone's labor. Locke did not repudiate medieval moral theory which placed strict limitations on individual landownership. In fact, he acknowledged quite severe limitations. First, he limited natural rights claims to that land with which an individual or his servant had mixed their labor. Next, he restricted ownership to the land that an individual needed and could use. Nature or its spoilable bounty must not be wasted. An individual by right could not claim, and then not utilize, what other men needed. Finally, Locke stipulated that an individual could freely appropriate land only as long as there remained as much and as good as he had taken. As long as land remained for others, one person's ownership of land did not deprive others of their natural right to own land.

If enforced, these limitations would have eliminated most claims to landownership in seventeenth-century England. But as Locke explained, most men no longer lived in a state of nature. Men who lived in society relied on government to regulate all ownership, including land. Even so, society while it might extend or add to natural right, could not abridge natural rights without an individual's consent—to do so would violate God's law. Consent was the key word. Locke suggested that even before men formed societies they had implicitly consented to the use of money to facilitate exchange. The introduction of money made the natural limits of "need and use" obsolete. Now an individual could cultivate as much land as he wished without fear of wasting nature's produce—as long as he could find a buyer. Money allowed an individual to exchange his spoilable produce for unspoilable money. Since Locke accepted hired, indentured, and enslaved labor as meeting the labor qualification of ownership, the only remaining natural rights qualification on landownership was the necessity to leave "as much and as good" for others. Locke met this restriction by pointing out that in America great quantities of land remained in an unclaimed state of nature. If any person living in a civil state wished to exercise his natural right to land, he only had to remove himself from society and assert his natural rights in America. But if an individual chose to remain in society and enjoy its immense benefits, he had to accept the necessity of having his person and property "subject to the Government and Dominion of that Commonwealth, as long as it hath being."[12]

Two things should be noted. First, notwithstanding Locke's theory of money, the limitation of "need and use" still applied to unutilized land. Any land an individual held for purely speculative purposes lacked, according to Locke, natural right sanctions. By acknowledging the Biblical commandment to "subdue and conquer," Locke limited natural right claims to land in productive use. To meet his natural rights criteria, individual landownership had to increase the sum of human wealth. Secondly, Locke did not make at all clear the status of individual landownership after all of the earth's land had been claimed by organized societies. Once men could no longer leave society to exercise their natural right to own land, all individual claims to land seemed in violation of natural law. In a situation of land monopoly Locke's theory of ownership could provide a strong moral argument to abrogate all individual claims to land.

Throughout the *Two Treatises* Locke emphasized the limitations of government and the liberty of individuals. Clearly his primary concern was the security of individual liberty and property. Nonetheless, Locke seemed more concerned that government act in an orderly and predictable manner than that it be bound by any absolute limits on its power. He considered society the final authority in all political disputes, and while he placed rigorous restraints on executive power, he granted enormous discretionary power to an elected legislature. He described an elected legislature as the direct representative of "the People" and therefore the "Supream Power of the Commonwealth." The "first and fundamental natural Law," wrote Locke, "which is to govern even the Legislative it self, is the preservation of the Society, and (as far as will consist with the publick good) of every person in it . . . the fundamental law of Nature being the preservation of Mankind, no Humane Sanction can be good or valid against it."[13] All considerations, including individual persons and their property, were secondary to this primary obligation of government. This did not mean that a legislature should act arbitrarily and willfully. Locke insisted that the legislature's enormous power was limited by its obligation to act in an orderly manner consistent with standing law. He conceded to the legislature the authority to regulate the means by which its citizens exercised their right to life, liberty, and estate but only so long as their substantive rights were not violated. As he put it, a legislature could not "destroy, enslave, or designedly impoverish" its citizens.[14]

Locke's definition of government's taxing powers illustrates just how broadly he construed legislative power: "Tis fit everyone who enjoys his share of the protection should pay out of his estate his proportion for the maintenance of it. But still it must be with his consent."[15] By "consent" Locke did not mean each property holder's direct consent. He only required the consent of a majority of a properly elected and apportioned legislature. An individual could oppose a tax levy, elect a representative who voted against the levy, and still, according to Locke, be rightfully taxed. The only limitations he placed on legislative taxing power was that any tax must be for the "publick good," it could not transfer the property of one person to another, and it must apply equally to all persons.

If government exceeded these limitations, even with legislative sanction, Locke believed it violated natural law. In that situation the individual, asserted Locke, could rightfully revolt against his government. And in the case of long-standing tyranny "the people" had the right to dissolve their government and elect a new legislature. But, he argued, as long as a government lasted its citizens must obey its authority. Likewise, once an individual formally entered society, he must thereafter conform to the will of society and its elected representatives. Thus Locke's vaunted right of revolution was the limited right of the individual to exercise his liberty and to enjoy property consistent with the will of a majority in his society. "The People shall be Judge," declared Locke, "if any Men find themselves aggrieved, and think the Prince acts contrary to, or beyond that Trust, who so proper to Judge as the

Body of the People." In the case of the dissolution of government "the People have a Right to act as Supreme, and continue the Legislative in themselves, or erect a new Form, or under the old Form place it in new hands, as they think good."[16]

Because Locke assumed that political participation would always be limited to property holders, he could hardly imagine the "people" violating their own property rights. Despite the strikingly democratic tone of the *Two Treatises of Government*, it was not in substance democratic. Instead, it was a carefully worked out theory of government which sought to justify the liberty of "free" Englishmen and the resistance of anti-Stuart landholders to what they considered the usurpations of the king. But in the American colonies Locke's ideas, combined with those of Harrington, took on new implications. In America Locke's use of "the people" as synonymous with freeholders lost its restrictive character. While in England less than 10 percent of the adult males held enough real estate to qualify as freeholders, in the American colonies most of the white population qualified. Similarly, in a society in which as many as 70 percent of the adult white males owned enough land to qualify as freeholders Harrington's agrarian republic no longer seemed quaint or visionary. It appeared descriptive of American reality. Here was a country where men could labor, acquire land, pursue their happiness, and still not preclude latecomers from the same opportunity. Locke's labor theory of value, his ideas of the consent of the governed, and his defense of the right of revolution defined and justified the colonial political economy. Likewise, Harrington's agrarian republic seemed prophetically to anticipate the freeholding republic endorsed by Franklin, Jefferson, Crèvecoeur, and countless other eighteenth-century Americans. For over a hundred years, for significant numbers of influential and articulate Americans the ideas of Harrington, Locke, and other English writers offered beguiling possibilities.

CHAPTER 3

❁

Life, Liberty, and the Pursuit of Happiness: The Creation of the Agrarian Republic

On July 4, 1776, the "Thirteen United States of America" under the authority of the "laws of Nature and Nature's God" declared their independence of the British empire. American revolutionaries accused George III of a "long train of abuses and usurpations," but it was his taxing them without representation which finally drove them to revolution. They argued that the king had violated their rights as freeholders to control the disposition of their property and the produce of their labor. The king had treated Americans as servile dependents, not autonomous freeholders. If such actions were allowed to continue unchecked, American freeholders would no longer be free, or as one expressed it, "We must admit at once we are absolute Slaves" for we "have no property of our own."[1] Rather than allow that to happen large numbers of Americans revolted and established a republican government to protect their rights. "Res populi, and the original meaning of the word republic," wrote John Adams, "could be no other than a government in which the property of the people predominated and governed; and it had more relation to property than to liberty."[2]

In 1763 when British imperial authorities began to assert their authority over the colonies, many American colonials viewed the action as a deliberate assault on their liberty. "Taxation without representation" seemed to threaten their autonomy as freeholders. Many Americans accepted the ideas of Harrington and Locke and believed that only economically autonomous men were free. For such persons the imperial authorities threatened the continued existence of Americans as free men. The only hope to retain their freedom seemed to be revolution. In 1774 George Washington expressed this sentiment in a letter to a friend, "The crisis is arrived when we must assert our rights, or submit to every imposition, that can be heaped upon us, till custom and use shall make us as tame and abject slaves, as the blacks we rule over with such arbitrary sway."[3]

American colonials' defense of their property rights relied heavily on Lockean natural rights arguments. In 1764 James Otis, one of the first colonials to openly oppose parliamentary policies, criticized Parliament for overstepping the bounds of right by taxing the American colonies without their consent. "If such a proceeding is a breach of the law of nature, no law of society can make it just." The very act of taxing, said Otis, "exercised over those who are not represented, appears to me to be depriving them of one of their most essential rights as freemen; and if continued, seems to be in effect an entire disenfranchisement of every civil right. For what one civil right is worth a rush, after a man's property is subject to be taken from him at pleasure, without his consent."[4] Five years later, Otis clarified somewhat the meaning he attached to the word "property." More than most colonials Otis seemed to be aware of some of the ambiguities contained in the natural rights concept of property. "The rights of men are natural and civil; both of these are divisible into absolute and relative," said Otis. He then described civil laws as those made by social convention which could not conflict with an individual's natural rights of personal liberty, private property, and personal security. Otis differentiated between natural and civil rights, and defended Americans' rights as natural because they did not derive from English charter grants, but from natural equity or right reason. Otis implied that property claims dependent on special, publicly vested privilege differed qualitatively from those acquired through enterprise and labor.[5]

Samuel Adams, Otis's fellow Bostonian and revolutionary, adhered to a similar distinction between natural and vested property. He too assumed that legitimate property derived from labor and therefore came under the sanctions of natural rights. "It is acknowledged to be an unalterable law of nature," said Adams, "that a man should have the free use and sole disposal of the fruit of his honest industry, subject to no control."[6] His definition of property included every imaginable type of possession. "The bow, the arrow, and the tomahawk; the hunting and the fishing ground," explained Adams, "are species of property, as important to an American savage, as pearls, rubies, and diamonds are to the mogul, or a nabob in the East, or the lands, tenements, hereditaments, messuages, or gold and silver of the Europeans."[7] Adams's easy, unqualified use of the word "property" seemed to make him a vigorous defender even of vested privilege, but the appearance was misleading. The only men in Adams's eyes who did not support themselves and who lived off unearned wealth were the British bureaucrats, men for whom he had nothing but scorn. The parliamentary enactments were unjust, declared Adams, because they took the "earnings and industry of the honest yeomen, merchants, and tradesmen, of this continent" without their consent and used it to support such nonproducers as "standing armies and ships of war; episcopates and their numerous ecclesiastical retinue; pensioners, placemen and other jobbers, for an abandoned and shameless ministry of hirelings, pimps, parasites, panders, prostitutes and whores."[8] Adams drew the line between legitimate and illegitimate property at the place of origin. If the wealth derived from a special, government privilege, it was illegitimate. Colonial America contained little wealth rooted in such special political privileges. What accumulated wealth there was presented no great threat to the society since, as yet, it did not de-

prive other men of the opportunity to acquire property—
with the obvious exception of Negro slaves. For most people, America remained a land of opportunity, and Adams
was one of its most faithful spokesmen.[9]

A number of Americans interpreted the new intrusions
into colonial affairs by the English government as an effort
to reduce them to servile, feudal dependents and to destroy their status as freeholders. For men like John and
Sam Adams, John Dickinson, Benjamin Franklin, Alexander Hamilton, and Thomas Jefferson, England remained a
largely feudal society still entwined with subservient relationships in contrast to the autonomous freeholders of
America. They played upon the difference between the
landlordism of Europe where status and wealth rested on
unearned privilege and the freeholding of America where
wealth and power depended on talent and labor. To them
such a feudal order precluded private property and the
possibility of individual liberty. Only independence from
British control could free American society from the feu-
dalization which the newly aggressive imperial system
threatened.[10]

Feudalism versus freeholding also figured in the debate
over the origin of colonial land titles. Many revolutionaries
found that natural rights arguments undercut their own
land claims, which were based on English charter grants
or, in Otis's words, vested privilege. Martin Howard, a
Rhode Island loyalist, used just this issue to counter arguments in favor of colonial disobedience to imperial legislation. Howard pointed out that the colonial legislators'
right to govern derived directly from the king and Parliament, and not from their rights as freeholders. He based
his argument on colonial land tenure. The colonists held
their land by "common socage," explained Howard, a feudal tenure which required of the holder fealty and obedience to the crown. Far from having any inherent or inalienable rights as freeholders, said Howard, American
colonials' liberty and property depended upon their obe-

dience to royal authority and on the good will of the English government.[11]

Howard's position was not shared by dissident colonials. Still they found their feudal tenures embarrassing. They had no intention of acknowledging the feudal obligations implied by their land titles and lost no time explaining them away. Jefferson suggested that colonial land titles rested on "allodial" tenure free from any feudal restraints. He insisted that Saxon land had always been "allodial" and the only English land subject to feudal tenure and held in "common socage" was conquered by William I. William had not conquered North America. Instead the colonials' forebears had conquered and subdued the land and improved it with their labor. Jefferson explained that the reason colonial charters specified "free and common socage" was that the colonials' ancestors, being farmers and not lawyers, had not understood the difference between the two types of tenure. As a result, the king's lawyers were able to trick them into accepting "common socage" instead of "allodial" tenure.[12] John Adams offered a different but more plausible interpretation. Adams argued that the lands of the new world had never been vacant and the Indians had not been conquered. Thus, colonial tenure could not be feudal. Instead of conquest, colonial title derived from the honest purchase by American colonials from the Indians. Therefore, colonial title did not depend on charter grants at all, but rested on the blood, toil, and money expended to purchase and improve the land. Since it had not been a free gift of the crown, declared Adams, the British government could not arbitrarily deprive the colonists of their land or any other of their rights as freeholders without violating natural law.[13]

For obvious reasons, most of the revolutionary debate touching on property rights revolved around the protection of existing property rights, not the right or opportunity to acquire property, which British policy rarely threatened and even on occasion abetted. Influenced by

Harrington, a number of American political leaders believed that landholding determined political power, and if America were to remain a free society, it must insure a wide distribution of land. "The only possible way then," declared John Adams, "of preserving the balance of power on the side of equal liberty and public virtue, is to make the acquisition of land easy to every member of society; to make a division of land into small quantities, so that the multitude may be possessed of landed estates." For, he continued, "if the multitude is possessed of real estate, the multitude will take care of the liberty, virtue, and interest of the multitude in all acts of government."[14] The desirability of maintaining widespread landholding in America manifested itself in the constitutions of several of the new state governments. The 1776 Virginia Declaration of Rights declared that "all men are born equally free and independent, and have certain natural, inherent rights of which they cannot, by any compact, deprive or divest their posterity; among which are the enjoyment of life, liberty, with the means of possessing property and pursuing and obtaining happiness and safety."[15] The constitutions of Massachusetts, New Hampshire, New York, Pennsylvania, and Vermont all contained the "right to acquire" clause, a phrase that provided for more than simply the protection of private wealth from the claims of society. In this way these new revolutionary governments affirmed some of the most radical implications of Harrington and Locke. American governments were charged with the responsibility to keep open the opportunity for all their citizens to acquire property.[16]

The advocates of the colonial cause often asserted the right of every man to life, liberty, and property without pausing before the ambiguities inherent in the words. Possibly Thomas Jefferson, in the Declaration of Independence, revealed his awareness of ambiguity when he altered "life, liberty, and estate" to "Life, Liberty, and the pursuit of Happiness." Jefferson never explained why he amended Locke's phrase to the "pursuit of Happiness," but later in his career he expressed serious doubts concerning the moral justification of certain forms of property. Thus, it is tempting to conclude, but impossible to prove, that in 1776 Jefferson sensed the disparity between certain contemporary forms of private property and Locke's idealized "natural property" and that in an effort to restore the old moral content to the concept of individual property, Jefferson substituted in its stead the more suggestive phrase "pursuit of Happiness."[17]

While ambassador to France from 1785 to 1789, Jefferson became disturbed over the large numbers of French peasants deprived of useful work while large amounts of land remained uncultivated. He saw that in prerevolutionary France a few large landholders had acquired so much land that they could not use it all, and rather than let someone farm it the owners turned the unused land into vast hunting preserves. Jefferson argued that a redistribution of land would make it possible for almost all Frenchmen to find gainful employment. The fact that the French nobility deprived other men of the opportunity for useful work on the basis of their land titles drove Jefferson to question the moral basis of some property claims. "Whenever there is in any country, uncultivated lands and unemployed poor," he wrote, "it is clear that the laws of property have been so extended as to violate natural rights." And if this condition continued, Jefferson suggested, the unemployed would be morally justified in asserting their natural rights to employment by appropriating for their own use any uncultivated land.[18]

Jefferson dreaded such a situation because it would throw into disarray all land titles and other property settlements on which the social order depended. Nonetheless, he believed that some property claims so violated natural justice as to justify an appropriation of private wealth. To forestall the calamitous situation of land monopoly in the United States, Jefferson recommended legislative regula-

tion of inheritances and a progressive tax schedule which
exempted men with property holdings below a certain
level and taxed larger property owners in geometric pro-
gression as their holdings increased in size.[19] Even so, Jefferson consistently opposed the destruction of property
rights by agents of government, even with majoritarian
support. But he made a distinction between property which
allowed men "to satisfy their natural wants" and property
which lay unused depriving other men of the opportunity
to own land. According to Jefferson, government had no
moral obligation to protect all legally vested property.
Rather its highest moral obligation was to guarantee that
every man had the opportunity to seek happiness as he
saw fit, and as long as one person's pursuit of happiness
did not restrict other men's equal right to pursue happiness, governments, even backed by overwhelming majorities, should consider an individual's property inalienable.[20]

During the Revolution it had been easy for American
political leaders to speak optimistically of the ability of
Americans to govern themselves. After all most Americans
were freeholders—men who could be trusted to act with
restraint and to respect property rights. But, for many
men, the reality of independence proved disappointing.
To men like John Adams, George Washington, John Jay,
and James Madison independence seemed to have had a
loosening effect on the American social fabric. They soon
lost any confidence that the widespread ownership of land
alone would secure everyone's liberty and property. In the
words of John Jay, too many people harbored "a reluctance
to pay taxes, an impatience of government, a taste for
property and little regard to the means of acquiring it,
together with a desire of equality in all things." Added
to this fear of majoritarian government, even one composed of freeholders, was the prospect that in the future
the United States, like Europe, would find itself with most
of its people landless. Accordingly, critics of post-Revolu-
tionary America singled out the faults of the weak and

decentralized government under the Articles of Confederation and set about to reform the national government in a manner that would enable it to "repress the evils which naturally flow from such copious sources of injustice and evil."[21]

Since the cessation of hostilities James Madison had concerned himself with the threat which popular government posed to property rights. He did not feel that the Congress under the Articles of Confederation could cope with the immediate problems of the young republic much less those of a future America not made up of freeholding farmers. An expanding population limited to a fixed amount of land inevitably would force Americans to turn to manufacturing. This would necessitate the growth of cities populated by large numbers of unstable, dependent men. Although he agreed with Jefferson that a redistribution of land would alleviate many of the immediate problems of declining landholding, Madison suggested that land redistribution could never include everyone, and that in the long run the United States could not count on land reform to spare it from the trauma of class conflict and aristocratic tyranny which Madison associated with European society. The only hope lay in organizing government in such a way that even in the absence of widespread landholding popular control could be retained without endangering personal liberty or property. The time to act, Madison wrote Jefferson, "is at the first forming of the constitution and in the present state of population when the bulk of the people have a sufficient interest in possession or its prospect to be attached to the rights of property, without being insufficiently attached to the rights of persons."[22]

Madison, like a number of other Americans, viewed society in terms of the "propertied" and the "unpropertied." Society to him consisted of distinct classes and interests and not virtuous citizens seeking to serve the common interest. A federal republic promised to solve for Madison

the problems which declining landholding threatened—
tyranny by the unpropertied masses over the propertied
minority or the despotism of the propertied few over the
mass of the unpropertied population. Under a federal system the unpropertied would be divided into as many separate groups as there were states so that they would have
little opportunity to form themselves into an effective
majority. Even if the unpropertied succeeded in gaining
control over any one state, their power to violate individuals' rights and to deprive the wealthy of their possessions would be limited by a strengthened federal government which could enforce limitations on the powers of
state governments. At the same time, argued Madison, the
great diversity of economic interests (such as those of
slaveowners, freehold farmers, merchants, financiers) and
the country's geographical differences would prevent an
elite from acting in concert to impose its will on the
unpropertied. For Madison liberty and popular government
no longer need depend on the widespread ownership of
land. A properly federalized system of government would
achieve the same ends at least at the federal level. Without
forsaking popular control, Madison believed that a federal
constitution would preserve the liberties Harrington had
associated with agrarian societies in a nonagrarian context. In so doing Madison rejected the notion of "civic
virtue" for one of "balanced interests."[23]

In May 1787 the constitutional debate began in earnest
when delegates from every state except Rhode Island assembled in Philadelphia to amend the Articles of Confederation. The delegates represented many of the diverse
facets of American life. The Convention contained farmers,
merchants, bankers, planters, speculators, and professional
men. The delegates unanimously agreed on the utility of
"property" and the necessity of government to secure individuals in their possessions, but not on the word's precise
meaning. Each delegate defended the type of ownership
most crucial to himself and his constituents—paper money,

commercial paper, freehold farms, chattel slaves, or personal goods—and each sought constitutional sanction for his particular form of wealth. The Convention also considered the need for property qualifications for voting and office holding.[24]

During the Confederation period several states had enacted legislation which had disrupted the normal channels of economic enterprise. A few legislatures had issued large quantities of paper currency causing price inflation, while some had passed laws which either stayed the collection of debts or altered the terms of contractual agreements. The holders of debts viewed these policies as confiscatory of their honestly earned wealth and argued that the legislatures had in effect destroyed their "property." In response to these pleas the Philadelphia Convention prohibited states from coining money, emitting bills of credit, making anything but gold and silver legal tender, and impairing contracts (Article I, Section 8). It placed no specific restrictions on the federal government's power to enact debtor legislation or adopt paper tender, although it did not specifically delegate such powers to the federal government.[25]

Real estate enjoyed a preferred status. Despite the frequent use during the constitutional debates of the word "property" to mean any form of wealth or possession, land remained, for most delegates, the politically significant form of property. It was usually landholding which qualified a man for political participation. Even the lawyer and financier, Gouverneur Morris, indicated his preference for landed property as a prerequisite for voting. A freehold restriction, said Morris, would keep the government from ever falling under the influence of "mechanics and manufactures" who receive "their bread from their employers." Further, since most Americans already owned land, a freehold qualification would make the new government more popular. Not all the participants in the Federal Convention believed that the property qualifications characteristic of colonial politics should be continued in the new republic, but those who did frequently relied on arguments similar to those put forth by Harrington. They declared that an individual who did not control landed property was subject to the demands of those on whom he depended for support or employment. To enfranchise the unpropertied would only invite the rich or demagogic to use their wealth and influence to gain control of government and divert it from its proper ends. A freehold qualification assured that the enfranchised was self-supporting and thus possessed a will of his own. And, in free government, only men with wills of their own could be trusted with political power.[26]

Other members of the Federal Convention adopted the "stake in society" principle as expressed by William Blackstone in his *Commentaries on English Law*. Blackstone argued that only those persons with a "stake in society" were concerned enough with the social well-being to govern prudently. For Blackstone the importance of property holding was not, as Harrington believed, that freeholding made possible disinterested "civic virtue," but that a freehold indicated a person's vested interest in political stability. George Mason logically extended Blackstone's "stake in society" dictum when he asked the Convention to broaden the concept from land ownership to any "attachment to and permanent interest with society." Mason suggested that the "merchant, the monied man, the parent of a number of children" all should be trusted with political power. Madison readily agreed with Mason and offered to strike the word "landed" from the proposed clause on property restrictions. Even this did not satisfy Benjamin Franklin, who felt that no property restrictions at all should be allowed. Franklin contended that all men, propertied and unpropertied, had fought equally for independence and deserved the right to participate in its government. Others pointed out that in many parts of the country a freehold restriction had never been enforced and to enforce one now would be unwise. Faced with such a diversity of opinion the delegates avoided the issue by leaving it to the discretion of each state. In Maryland, Massachusetts, New Jersey, North Carolina, and Virginia this meant the continuation of a freehold or an equivalent qualification on voting and office holding. Delaware, Georgia, New Hampshire, New York, and South Carolina allowed all taxpayers to vote, but limited office holding to a fifty-pound freehold or more. Connecticut and Pennsylvania allowed all taxpayers to hold office and vote.[27]

A few American political leaders, such as Madison and Morris, had accepted the likelihood that in the future large numbers, even a majority, of Americans would be landless wage earners or tenants. Nonetheless, the constitutional deliberations disclosed that most participants remained convinced that into the indefinite future the United States would and should remain a republic of landed freeholders. Charles Pinckney expressed this widely held and often-voiced sentiment when he said, as long as the "means of subsistence are so much within every man's power" America need not worry about the future of republican government. "The owners and cultivators of the soil make up the great body of the people," said Pinckney, and "here rest, and I hope ever will continue, all the authority of the government."[28] Thus, despite the ambiguous use of the word "property" which often made it nearly synonymous with all forms of wealth, Americans following Harrington continued to attach special meaning to landed property. "Life, Liberty, and Property" generally implied that every white man would enjoy the right to acquire and hold land.

The constitutional changes of 1787 did not go unchallenged. The Antifederalists, a mixed group of men united primarily by their opposition to the Federal Constitution, argued that the Constitution had resurrected an even greater danger to property rights and individual liberties —a powerful centralized government. The Antifederalists denied that Congress, under the Articles of Confederation, had failed to protect individuals' property as the supporters of constitutional change had charged. The real threat to personal liberty and private property lay not in mob rule but in a strong central government which had the power to levy taxes on men's industry and enforce its edicts with hordes of tax gatherers and a standing army. The Antifederalists particularly criticized the Federal Constitution's lack of a bill of rights. To remedy these shortcomings they suggested amendments which would return the balance of power to the states, prohibit unlawful search and seizure, and protect the freedoms of assembly, speech, religion, and press from federal encroachment. In many ways the charges leveled by the Antifederalists against the Federal Constitution brought the debate on the rights of property full circle. The Revolutionary crisis had centered around the issue of the tyranny of a centralized bureaucracy over individual liberty and property. The supporters of the Federal Constitution had altered the Articles of Confederation because they were convinced that liberty and property had more to fear from majorities than from strong government. And now, the Antifederalists argued that the Federal Constitution had gone too far and established a new centralized bureaucracy, not unlike the British imperial system. They accused the supporters of the Federal Constitution of abandoning the purposes of the Revolution.[29]

In response to the Antifederalists' charges the new federal Congress initiated amendments which affirmed the residual powers of state government and specifically prohibited federal infringement upon many of the liberties so dear to the Antifederalists. But the Bill of Rights did not include a positive statement affirming the federal government's obligation to secure for all of its citizens a viable opportunity to acquire and control a share of the society's productive resources. It only contained the Fifth Amendment prohibition against the federal government's abridging any person's "life, liberty, or property, without due process of law." Thus Jefferson's phrase in the Declaration of Independence asserting every man's inalienable right "to Life, Liberty, and pursuit of Happiness" stood as the most important national expression of American commitment to Harrington's vision of an agrarian republic.[30]

Part II

AN AGE OF GROWTH AND DIVERSITY

AMERICAN society in the decades between the adoption of the Federal Constitution and the outbreak of the Civil War underwent significant changes. The two most apparent were the startling economic growth and the marked diversification of the economy. Following the Revolution, the trans-Appalachian West was opened to settlement. This not only made available a vast new expanse of land for agriculture, but also stimulated the development of transportation, banking, and manufacturing. Moreover, the technical breakthroughs in textile manufacturing and processing of short-staple cotton invigorated slavery in the South. Thus, while the West offered American farmers unprecedented opportunity, it also accelerated the development of all other sectors of the economy. During the antebellum period the United States was transformed from a relatively homogeneous republic of farmers, artisans, merchants, slaveholders, and slaves into a complex nation composed of a wide range of economic interests. Never before had there been so many Americans engaged in so many different occupations.

These changes introduced a degree of heterogeneity and social stratification America had heretofore lacked. Freehold farmers no longer dominated American economic and political life. Slaveholders, factory and railroad workers, bankers, and wage earners all began to challenge many of the assumptions of agrarian republicanism. The revival of slavery and the emergence of the wage-labor system compelled many persons to reformulate, and in the case of some southern slaveholders reject entirely, the agrarian-natural rights conception of property. Nonetheless, Americans generally persisted in using traditional natural rights language to affirm their belief in the ideals of agrarian republicanism, even as their policy choices indicated new preferences.

CHAPTER 4

Every Man Under His Own Vine and Fig Tree: Agrarian Republicanism

The agrarian republicanism that derived from Harrington and Locke provided Americans an explanation and a justification for their Revolution. Natural rights theory became especially popular in the decades immediately following the ratification of the Federal Constitution, as the trans-Appalachian West offered Americans almost unlimited opportunity to acquire land. By the beginning of the nineteenth century it had become commonplace for Americans to speak of the right to property as a "natural right," by which they frequently meant a natural right to become a freehold farmer. Nonetheless, Americans used the term "natural right to property" in several different ways. In a strictly legal context an individual's "natural right" to property was generally taken to mean a procedural check on arbitrary government. In the words of the Fifth Amendment: "No person shall be . . . deprived of life, liberty, or property without due process of law; nor shall private property be taken for public use, without just compensation." In a political context the concept came to mean a citizen's right to participate in politics. If only economically autonomous men could be entrusted with government, then all property holders, however defined, should be entrusted with political power. Finally, the natural right of property also could mean the individual's right to access to productive resources and a full claim to the fruit of his labor. In this sense access to productive resources freed the individual from economic exploitation.

While those Americans committed to an agrarian republic generally used the concept of natural rights in all three senses, they emphasized the third. Like Harrington, they believed that liberty was impossible without landholding. Landownership was necessary for responsible citizenship; it was the best means to guarantee an individual a full return on his labor; and it was the most effective check on arbitrary government. Landownership made possible individual liberty—procedural, political, and economic. Consequently, agrarian republicans viewed government's chief end as the assurance that each citizen enjoyed the opportunity to exercise his "natural right" to acquire land. As a rule, they opposed large and centralized government because invariably government fell into the hands of special interest groups. When that happened, taxation and political privilege no longer served socially useful purposes but simply became the means of transferring the earned wealth of producers to the nonproducers who controlled government. In the words of Thomas Paine, "Government even in its best state is but a necessary evil."[1] For this reason agrarians were ambivalent toward government. They believed government must be strong enough to keep the opportunity open for everyone to own land as well as to prevent individuals from monopolizing the available land. At the same time they feared that if government became too strong it would violate its trust and destroy all private property and therefore individual liberty.

Nathaniel Chipman understood the multiple meanings Americans attached to the "natural rights" concept of property. In 1793 Chipman, a prominent Vermont jurist, in his important *Sketches of the Principles of Government* sought to clarify some of the ambiguities. Paraphrasing the Virginia Declaration of Rights, Chipman asserted that all men were born equal in their right to acquire property, to exclusive enjoyment of it, and to dispose of it as they saw fit. The right of property implied two things—the right to acquire and the right to hold. Of the two, Chipman believed, the right to hold was secondary, for it might have to be abridged to honor another's more important right to acquire.[2] He perceived two threats to private property—monopoly by the few and leveling by the many— each discouraged industry and creativity. Chipman thought that all property rights should be based on labor. For that reason he opposed monopolies and other special privileges because they allowed selected individuals to profit, not from their own labor, but from unearned advantages. Monopolies also deprived other, less advantaged, persons of the opportunity to labor and acquire property. Monopolies restricted enterprise. For similar reasons he opposed efforts to equalize wealth. Chipman thought that the equalization of wealth violated all men's primary right, the right to excel. If government equalized property, it would rob the industrious of the fruits of their labor and reward the indolent. It would condemn society to a state of peaceful but tasteless enjoyment of stupid inactivity. Extreme equality, Chipman asserted, meant extreme tyranny.[3]

John Taylor of Caroline in his defense of agrarian republicanism opposed more vehemently than even Chipman all publicly derived privileges. Taylor, a Virginia planter, slaveowner, and close friend of Jefferson, believed that government had a moral obligation to protect individual property. He defined private property as that portion of an individual's honest earnings which the public good could spare. The right to property was the freedom that an individual enjoyed in disposing of his earnings as he saw fit. Taylor argued that wealth and property should be distributed according to men's productiveness and a government which distributed the wealth of producers to nonproducers destroyed private property and became tyrannical. Taylor allowed only one exception. He believed American realities prevented black men from sharing in an American republic of property holders, although he supported their colonization in African republics.[4]

Taylor associated special privilege with factory manufacturing. He did not think factory manufacturing could succeed in the United States without governmental support. Thus, if the United States opted for a factory system, it would have to grant tariff subsidies and special corporate privileges. To Taylor all of these policies had one damning effect. They transferred the earned property of farmers and artisans to parasitic factory owners and bankers. He feared that a collusion between factory owners, bankers, and governmental bureaucrats would raise taxes and prices to such an extent that producers would be left with almost no control over their earnings and lose all choice in the disposition of their wealth. Taylor particularly feared a strong national government, because he thought it would be less subject to popular control than state governments and more susceptible to the blandishments of special interests. Further, large government meant a large bureaucracy and high taxes. Taylor was concerned with the tendency of strong national governments to build large armies and engage in wars which provided an excuse for even more taxes which would be spent to further subsidize factory owners.[5]

Taylor addressed his appeal to mechanics and craftsmen as well as to farmers. He believed that only if they acted in concert could they hope to prevent nonproducers from using government to despoil producers of their earnings. If government granted subsidies and special corporate privileges to factory owners, said Taylor, it would make it impossible for independent craftsmen and mechanics to compete successfully. The previously free and independent mechanic would be forced to seek employment in the factory and become dependent on the owner for all his basic needs. Taylor argued that the factory owner would receive even more of the factory worker's hard-earned money by means of the high tariff-supported prices which increased the living expenses of the worker. For Taylor, a factory system, supported by a strong national government and its concomitant network of special unearned privileges, doomed any hope of widespread property holding in the

United States, and in the process destroyed all hope of republican government.[6]

Of the many spokesmen for rural life in the early nation Thomas Jefferson stands out because of his immediate political influence, his impact on American thought, and as an enduring symbol of agrarian republicanism. Widespread ownership of land was central to Jefferson's idea of a good society. Landowning made a man economically and politically independent. With it an individual did not have to depend on another for his living or vote according to the demands of his employer. Landownership also developed in men a consideration of others' possessions. It gave them a vested interest in civil order. Jefferson opposed the factory and wage system because he believed it would result in a large class of unpropertied wage earners. Factories conjured up in his mind images of unstable, dependent masses controlled and exploited by a privileged ruling class. He recognized that the nation's independence demanded the development of manufacturing, but he hoped to avoid the problems of a wage-earning class by encouraging household industries. "Let our workshops remain in Europe," urged Jefferson.[7]

Jefferson believed government should play a limited role in protecting private property, in opening up opportunity for individuals to acquire landed property, and in insuring that the marketplace remained accessible to all. He saw no reason for an elaborate bureaucracy, since farmers needed little that they could not provide for themselves. Large government meant large taxes, and like Taylor, he believed taxation had been the traditional device by which nonproducers had transferred to themselves the hard-earned property of producers. Although Jefferson did not challenge or begrudge the taxes necessary for publicly desirable projects that benefited the entire society, he wanted to be certain that tax revenues were not used to support parasitic bureaucracies or, even worse, to subsidize anyone's economic interest. He believed that the best way to insure that government continued to serve the needs of the governed, instead of special interests, was to keep it close to the people. Thus, he preferred state over national power because state government could be better scrutinized by its constituents than a distant national government.[8]

Jefferson's views revealed the lasting influence of older moral concepts that were still attached to the word "property." He emphasized the artful without denying the acquisitive ends of ownership. For him, ownership remained the means by which an individual retained control over his work and thus over the opportunity to labor creatively as well as the means to participate in government responsibly. Throughout the antebellum period a conspicuous number of persons shared Jefferson's emphatically moralistic conception of property as the means of self-employment. This was most evident in discussions of land policy. In the young republic, land and property were almost synonymous terms. Not only was land the most important resource of the United States, it was also the most important form of productive property which most men could hope to own. Until the end of the nineteenth century a majority of Americans continued to derive their living from agriculture, and freeholding remained the easiest means of upward mobility for persons of low status and income. For these Americans, as in the colonial period, opportunity meant access to land.[9]

In the nineteenth century, Harringtonian ideas continued to influence a number of important political leaders who believed that the future of the republic depended on widespread ownership of land. They therefore demanded basic changes in federal land policy. Thomas Hart Benton, United States Senator from Missouri and an early advocate of land for the poor, expressed such feelings. "We are a republic, and [if] we wish to continue so," said Benton, "then [we must] multiply the class of freeholders; pass the public lands cheaply and easily into the hands of the people; sell for a reasonable price to those who are able to pay; give without price to those who are not."[10] In 1832 President Andrew Jackson joined Benton. "It cannot be doubted that the speedy settlement of these lands constitutes the true interests of the Republic," Jackson declared. "The wealth and strength of the country are its population, and the best part of the population are cultivators of the soil. Independent farmers are everywhere the basis of society and true friends of liberty." Jackson denied the justice of any longer using the public lands for revenue purposes, and suggested that public land be sold to settlers in small parcels at nominal prices. The goal of federal land policy, said Jackson, should be "to afford every American citizen of enterprise the opportunity of securing an independent freehold."[11]

Advocates of land reform focused on two plans—preemption and graduation. Throughout the period from 1790 to 1820 settlers sent petition after petition to Congress asking for the right to preempt certain lands from the general land auction. The procedure for selling federal land was that the government first surveyed the land and then offered it at public auction to the highest bidder. Preemption allowed an adult male or widow to settle on public land before the survey, and at the time of the auction the preemptor would have the right to buy a certain amount of land (usually 160 acres) at the minimum government price (usually $1.25 per acre) on the condition that he or she had improved the land. By giving the actual settler an advantage over land speculators, supporters of preemption hoped that most of the land would be sold to persons interested in settling and farming the land themselves. Graduation provided for the disposal of all land left unbought after the public auction. Benton suggested that after five years any land remaining unsold at the minimum price be annually reduced in price until either someone bought it or, after a specified period, it would be granted free to any landless person or turned over to the state in which it lay. Like preemption, the amount of land a person could acquire at graduated prices would be limited in amount and confined to actual settlers.

Supporters of both graduation and preemption relied heavily on natural rights theories. Several quoted or paraphrased directly from Locke's *Two Treatises*, and nearly all the land reformers implicitly accepted the principle that access to land should be based on a person's willingness to work, not on how much he could afford to pay. Congressman Arphaxed Loomis of New York declared, "It is but a common right, common honesty; it originates in the principle which is above law itself, and which always should be followed by laws—common right, the title which every man has to what he earns by the sweat of his brow." The reformers frequently quoted the Declaration of Independence and insisted that all men's right to pursue happiness was directly related to their ability to acquire a farmstead. If congressional debate was indicative of national sentiment, by 1840 a popular consensus agreed that the federal government should dispose of its land in a manner that guaranteed everyone willing to work the opportunity to own productive land.[12]

As a rule most of the impetus for land reform came from the trans-Appalachian West where settlers often saw themselves as the victims of absentee land speculators. But beginning in the late 1820s the most vocal and best organized agitation for land reform came from the skilled craftsmen of the eastern cities who sensed that the factory wage system was displacing them. The crippling impact of the Panic of 1837 on the movement to organize labor convinced a number of workingmen of the futility of trying to raise wages and improve working conditions when such a surplus of labor existed in the cities. Around 1840 a group of ex-Locofocos, the labor wing of the New York Democratic Party, led by George Henry Evans organized the National Reform Association. The association published several newspapers and books as well as numerous pamphlets and petitions to carry their message of "vote yourself a farm" to eastern working men. Never a broad-based movement, National Reform was largely restricted to its half-dozen leaders and the indeterminable number of subscribers to its newspaper.[13]

The National Reformers were the self-proclaimed spokesmen for those skilled, independent craftsmen whom the wage system was rapidly replacing. They considered themselves the true sons of Thomas Jefferson and articulated the naive rationalism characteristic of Thomas Paine's *Rights of Man*. The factory system appeared to them as a diabolical force which threatened to destroy the autonomy of independent craftsmen. Factory owners, they declared, exploited the labor of women and children and forced formerly self-supporting men to become mere hirelings. Evans compared the wage system to southern slavery and concluded that while wage earners could choose their own master and slaves could count on support in sickness and old age, in all other respects the two labor systems were similar. He argued that both systems denied men the possibility of the "real" freedom derived from self-employment. For Evans, "hireling" and "slave" were interchangeable terms. One National Reformer argued, in forceful rhetoric and unorthodox spelling and grammar, that any man who sold his labor to another forfeited "every prerogative which constitutes the *Man*! Aye, give up your very manhood, and become a pliant, abject, crouching, cringing slaves to all absorbing, monopolizing, gormandizing, all consuming *Capital*, whose ever lasting cry is *income, income*, more *income*."[14]

The National Reformers concluded that the problem lay in the monopolization of land and other productive resources. They believed that, given a choice, no man would work for another. Land speculators had acquired large amounts of land and driven land prices higher than most men could afford. Consequently, large numbers of persons involuntarily left their land and hired themselves out to other men as tenants on farms or as laborers in the cities. These landless people swelled the cities and drove wages down. The condition of surplus labor made it impossible for wage earners to make a decent living. No labor organization, the reformers argued, could cope successfully with such a problem. The only hope lay in getting people back on land of their own and out of the labor market.[15]

Led by Evans, the land reformers saw the public domain as the ready-made solution to all of the nation's troubles. The reformers called on the federal government to grant public land to settlers in lots of 160 acres and to cease altogether selling land to speculators or nonsettlers. This would have the immediate effect of making it possible for anyone to leave the city and become a proprietor on his own land. And, even if a person preferred to remain in the city, he could anticipate the increasing scarcity of labor to raise wage scales. Evans wanted land distributed in fee simple title with the single qualification that no one could sell his land to someone who already owned land. A person could sell or give his land only to his children or to someone without any land. By making land nontransferable, Evans believed that land would remain in the hands of producers, and not become a speculative commodity for securing unearned gain. He recognized that in the future the public land would run out. At that time, he accepted as necessary government regulation of the amount of land any one person could own in order that all men could own some land. Evans expected to achieve this not through appropriation of existing land claims, but through inheritance laws. One of the National Reformers, Lewis Masquerier, suggested that sexual abstention or at least moderation might obviate the need to reduce holdings below 160 acres. But Evans, who valued the right to procreate as much as the right to own, foresaw a time when landholdings might have to be reduced to as little as ten acres per family.[16]

The initial land grants represented only the first step in what Evans and other National Reformers anticipated would be a complete restructuring of American life. They envisioned the nation divided into townships six miles square with a mile-square park in the center to be used for recreation, public buildings, and schools, and the park to be surrounded by small owner-operated commercial and manufacturing shops. In this way the National Reformers hoped to integrate manufacturing, farming, education, residential, and political activities into a single, closely knit, rural village. Ideally, a man would divide his time between farming, manufacturing, intellectual inquiry, and politics. And best of all, there would be no capitalists, no factories, and no cities—only free men, free enterprise, and ports of entry. America would be a series of contiguous New England villages, and all men would be landed, self-employed, and independent.[17]

All of the associates in the National Reform movement supported private property and adhered to a labor theory of value, but only one, John Pickering, tried systematically to work out a political economy based on universal landholding. In *The Working Man's Political Economy* (1847) Pickering asserted that initially the earth had been given to all men in common and no man could morally claim more than his share of nature. All men possessed an equal claim to the land and all other "elements of nature," said Pickering, but claims to productive resources could only be made by occupation and use. In Pickering's model society a man could establish a title to a specific piece of land, but he could not transfer his title to another person. Land could be claimed, occupied, used, and profited from, but it could not be bought and sold or even given away.[18]

Pickering drew a distinction between private claims over productive resources and claims over produce resulting from the utilization of those resources. He limited individual control over resources by occupation and use, but he placed no restrictions on produce. Pickering refused to call land or any productive resource "private property," since to him private property referred only to commodities. "Property, wealth, and riches we consider as synonymous," wrote Pickering, and as long as men's claim to commodities derived from their own labor they were free to dispose of their "private property" as they saw fit. He interpreted the phrase "every man's right to life, liberty, and property" as referring only to commodities or money. Pickering felt that by removing productive resources from the market place he could safely allow the individual to accumulate money or nonessential commodities without jeopardizing other men's right to work and acquire property of their own. He made one qualification on commodity exchange. He wanted the government to compile a commodity price list which reflected the labor expended to produce particular items. This, he believed, would prevent unscrupulous men from defrauding the ignorant of their earned "property," and at the same time would encourage efficiency and industry by providing a bonus for those people who managed to produce commodities with less labor than the commodity list provided.[19]

Pickering and the other National Reformers hoped that land reform would solve the problems caused by the factory system. They expected it to preserve individual proprietorship and retard the wage system. The National Reformers opted for an economy which assured individual autonomy, but in the process they denied themselves the potential material blessings of a collectivized economy. They contented themselves with a society of relative equality and modest wealth where no man worked for another and where no one controlled another—a utopia based on private ownership.

Evans and his colleagues influenced more moderate men. Several congressional supporters of homestead legislation lifted their proposals directly from the National Reform program and more than one congressman specifically referred to National Reform in their speeches. But National Reform's most important convert was Horace Greeley. Born in 1811 in New Hampshire, Greeley began his newspaper career in 1821. In 1841 he founded the influential *New York Tribune*, which many contemporaries considered the best newspaper in New York City. The *Weekly* and *Semi-Weekly* editions became the widest circulated newpaper in the nonslaveholding West. Throughout his life Greeley supported reform causes which ranged from the temperance movement to antislavery. He involved himself actively in politics, serving terms in the New York legislature as well as the United States Congress. In 1872 he ran unsuccessfully as the Liberal Republican nominee for president. He died following his 1872 presidential campaign.[20]

In 1845 Greeley began supporting land reform and pushed it openly in his newspapers. His position coincided with his basic sympathy for working people and his personal commitment to a labor theory of value. "In short," wrote Greeley, "the terrestrial Man, possessed of the well-known properties of matter as well as of spirit can only in truth enjoy the rights of 'life, liberty, and the pursuit of happiness' by being guaranteed some *place* in which to enjoy them. He who has no clear, inherent right to live *somewhere* has no right to live at all." All men have a natural right to labor on a portion of the earth, continued Greeley, and without the right of access to land all other rights had no meaning. Greeley believed that God had given the earth to all men for them to enjoy and that no one could morally claim more of the earth than he could cultivate himself. Otherwise, some men's landownership would deprive others of the means to support themselves and force the landless to become the employee or tenant of the landed.[21]

By restricting the ownership of land, said Greeley, the United States could insure that all its citizens would be able to own some land and that no one would be forced to work for someone else. Landownership limited to "need and use" would force everyone to work for a living and prevent anyone from living off the involuntary labor of another. Thus Greeley did not view land reform as a boon for the lazy or improvident. To the contrary, he wrote, "not to transfer the toiler's earnings to the idler, but to *prevent* such transfer, is the object of land reform." Greeley emphasized that he did not advocate equality, but opportunity. Making the same distinction between productive resources and commodities that Pickering had made, Greeley was willing to allow men to accumulate all the wealth they wanted, but he would carefully limit the amount of land a person could legally own.[22]

Like the National Reformers, Greeley blamed the unemployment and low wages of American working people on land monopoly, and believed that until government placed the price of land within the reach of everyone, wage scales and working conditions in factories would remain deplorable. Only when every man had the option of either working at a particular wage or supporting himself on his own land would American producers reap the full rewards of their labor. Self-employment, said Greeley, was the only real assurance that one person would not be exploited by another. Greeley wanted the federal government to provide free to any person the land necessary to give him a 160-acre homestead. "Man has a natural right to such portion of the earth not already improved by others as he can cultivate and make fruitful," declared Greeley. "The act of government is simply officious and impertinent which assumes to give him [less than] this, and it is a gross usurpation and moral nullity to undertake to give him more." He did not challenge existing land and property claims. Again, like the National Reformers, Greeley wanted inheritance laws revised to limit the amount of land a person could inherit and land laws amended to limit the amount a person could hold legal title to. He also supported legislation to make homesteads inalienable from involuntary seizure for debts or taxes.[23]

Greeley's infatuation with land reform paralleled a revival of popular interest in land reform which climaxed in the enactment of the 1859 Homestead Act, which President James Buchanan vetoed. With the South out of the Union, Congress in 1862 reenacted the bill and Lincoln signed it into law. Land reformers also sought to include in state constitutions homestead exemption clauses which prohibited the taking of homesteads for debts or taxes. Before the Civil War only Michigan adopted such an amendment. The Michigan constitution exempted forty acres of homestead or $500 worth of property from debt and tax collection except in the case of a mortgage. And even the mortgager could not lay claim to the homestead if the wife had failed to cosign the mortgage. In the case of the owner's death, the Michigan constitution disallowed all debt collection on the exempted homestead during the minority of the children or as long as the widow lived. During reconstruction under Radical Republican influence nine southern states included similar provisions in their constitutions.[24]

During the 1858–1862 congressional debate over homestead legislation a handful of men desperately sought to enact legislation to halt the national trend towards urbanization and wage earning. The most conspicuous of these were Greeley, Andrew Johnson of Tennessee, Galusha A. Grow and Thaddeus Stevens of Pennsylvania, and George W. Julian of Indiana. These men and several of their closest supporters espoused a program not markedly different from the National Reformers. Not only did they advocate that the federal government provide settlers with a 160-acre homestead, but they wanted all homesteads secured from debt and tax collection. They also demanded that all public land sales to nonsettlers be ended. This meant no more grants to railroads, mining companies, or other similar enterprises. In addition, their speeches implied, but did not openly advocate, that these same policies should apply, not just to public lands, but to all lands in the nation.[25]

The radical congressional land reformers denied the moral legitimacy of landowning based on anything other than use and occupation. In a fashion typical of his colleagues, Galusha Grow declared that all men have the right to life and happiness "and each may, by right, appropriate to his own use so much as is necessary for his support." The land reformers argued that to declare men's "right to life, liberty, and the pursuit of happiness" without providing them the means to obtain that right was mockery. A government which denied its citizens access to land shirked its moral responsibilities. If society denied to anyone of its citizens the right to own land, insisted one radical reformer, it in effect had denied the moral basis for all individual title to land. For if government could deprive one person of his natural and inalienable right to own land, then it could with as much justice abolish all property rights in society. The radicals believed that the Homestead Act would make it possible for the eastern factory worker to acquire a farm of his own in the West and to reap the full reward of his labors. It would discourage those who lived off other men's labors and prevent the engrossment of the public domain by land monopolists and corporations. Free homesteads would deliver American producers from the hands of both the land speculator and the factory owner.[26]

The opponents of homesteading disagreed with the land reformers on almost all these points. They argued that homesteading represented class legislation designed to benefit only the indigent. And far from upholding all men's right to property, it actually destroyed the property of eastern land owners by lowering land values. Furthermore, homesteading threatened national progress by giving away the nation's landed resources which could be better used to underwrite education, railroads, canals, and other internal improvements. They believed that the nation's future greatness depended on large-scale manufacturing, and that homesteading encouraged workers to forsake the factories for farming. Government, they said, by fostering subsistence homesteading not only dissipated the national wealth but also hindered economic development by depriving manufacturers of their labor force.[27]

It was on this last point that the land reformers and the opponents of homestead legislation agreed in substance but disagreed as to methods. Both accepted the desirability of economic development, but while one group believed that homesteading promoted it, the other felt it inhibited development. The land reformers hoped to reserve the national domain exclusively for settlers, and although they never denied the need for economic development, they placed a higher value on widespread landholding than on national wealth and power. But even a majority of those who voted for the Homestead Act had no intention of reserving the public domain for settlers only. For the majority, rapid settlement and cultivation of the land represented one means of developing the nation's resources. Internal improvements, manufacturing, and mining were other, just as desirable, means of increasing the nation's wealth and power. For this reason, while most congressmen supported homesteading, they also endorsed using public land to subsidize all other forms of national development. Thus, in many ways the values of most of those who voted for the Homestead Act were closer to the opponents of homestead legislation than to the more radical land reformers.[28]

When James Buchanan vetoed the 1859 Homestead Act, he described the bill as class legislation which benefited only one class of Americans—the farmers. Buchanan pointed out that laborers could not hope to profit from homesteading, because they lacked both the skills and the resources to take advantage of its provisions. He was right. Despite all the hope expressed by land reformers that the

Homestead Act would give laborers the opportunity to become freeholders, it did not. Only a limited number of people could avail themselves of the opportunities opened up by the Homestead Act. The act did not insure that in the future most Americans would own productive property and be self-employed. By 1870 only 45 percent of the American working force remained self-employed.[29] The Homestead Act of 1862 represented the most concerted effort by American policy makers to redeem the Jeffersonian dream of universal freeholding. But even in 1862 it seemed an almost quaint and quixotic effort. It did not come close to dealing with the magnitude of the changes taking place in American life.

In 1861 Abraham Lincoln made the point that most Americans were neither slaveowners nor capitalists, employers nor employees. Most Americans, said Lincoln, were self-employed. "This is the just and prosperous system which opens the way to all, gives hope to all, and consequently energy and progress and improvement of condition to all."[30] But even as Lincoln spoke, if the discussion of the Homestead Act was indicative of the national temper, large numbers of Americans had begun to define national progress, not in terms of how many people owned land or were self-employed, but how rapidly the economy developed. The debate over homesteading made it clear that, while a broad consensus accepted the desirability of landholding and individual proprietorship, they also accepted the necessity for some Americans to be wage earners in the factories and other enterprises on which they believed national progress depended.[31] Buchanan's disparaging description of American farmers as merely an interest group was far more accurate than Lincoln's affirmation of the Jeffersonian ideal. Buchanan's realistic assessment of the mid-nineteenth-century American political economy also revealed the contrast between Americans' expectations in 1860 and the ideals of the founders of the republic.

CHAPTER 5

❀

The Pursuit of Plenty:
Wages as Property

As long as most men derived their living from the land or from small shops, the conception of a property holder as an owner-operator presented no difficulties. But by the late eighteenth century two related developments—mechanization and division of labor—threatened to separate ownership from production. Mechanization required large capital outlays which few men individually could afford, and operators could use the machinery most efficiently when they performed only small, specialized tasks. While agriculture seemed most profitable when the functions of ownership, management, and labor were combined in a single person, factory-organized manufacturing appeared to demand separate categories of owners, managers, and laborers. The Jeffersonian concept of proprietorship seemed anachronistic.

In 1776 Adam Smith published *The Wealth of Nations* in which he sought to explain these new industrial developments as well as advise policy makers of the best means to achieve national prosperity. Smith's ideas in support of specialized labor and an economy of growth forced him to depart from traditional attitudes toward private property. To him the right of property amounted to a right to the return on one's own labor. Smith divided productive enterprise into separate categories of labor, management, and ownership. He argued that the smaller and simpler a man's task the more efficient his labor. Landlords could oversee land best if they only oversaw land; farmers could farm best if they only farmed; factory workers would manufacture best if they only did simple tasks; and managers could manage best if they only managed. Smith described the owner as an overseer of productive resources and the profits of ownership as wages for custodial duties. In a Jeffersonian sense, Smith's economic order contained no property holders, only wage earners of differing types performing various but necessary functions.[1]

Smith emphasized men's economic needs and assumed that most men achieved happiness through consumption. Committed to a labor theory of value, he identified public well-being with the well-being of laborers. He believed that a society was morally deficient if it failed to guarantee its laboring classes a standard of living which exceeded subsistence. Prosperity, Smith argued, could only be achieved through constant and high wages which in turn depended on a constant and high demand for labor. This required an expanding economy, which alone insured a demand for labor in excess of the supply. Smith broke with medieval economic thinkers by endorsing competition, individual mobility, and limited government interference in economic decision-making. He argued that properly policed economic freedom would assure everyone his deserved place and reward. The vicissitudes of supply and demand would also insure the best utilization of resources and labor. Only when the most productive laborer was free to seek the highest wage and the most efficient producer the best market would a society prosper and producers receive a just return on their labor. Smith believed the market, not political privilege, should determine an individual's wage or profit.[2]

Smith's *Wealth of Nations* offered American policy makers a tempting grab bag from which they could selectively extract those ideas which reinforced their own values. Americans dedicated to an agricultural society, such as

Thomas Jefferson, shared Smith's views on limited government and opposition to special privilege. Paradoxically, those Americans who initially rejected Smith's work were the advocates of factory-organized manufacturing. While men, such as Alexander Hamilton, agreed with Smith on the need for constant economic growth and a division of labor, they disagreed with his ideas of free trade and limited government. Nonetheless, Smith's insistence that national prosperity depended on a division of labor had a profound impact on American ideas concerning the relationship between ownership and labor, and helped break down eighteenth-century notions of ownership.

Despite the popularity and appeal of agrarian thought during the early years of the republic, a large and influential group of men situated for the most part in the nation's major cities rejected the agrarian image of a good society. Jefferson's archrival, Alexander Hamilton, opted instead for a nation of mixed economic interests bolstered by large-scale manufacturing. Hamilton forecast economic prosperity if the federal government actively encouraged the nation's economic development through bounties to manufacturers and support of centralized banking facilities. With an economy balanced between manufacturing, commerce, and agriculture, the United States would no longer be forced to spend its currency on foreign products or depend on other nations for vital goods and markets. Using many of Adam Smith's arguments, Hamilton insisted that the development of manufacturing meant economic prosperity for all segments of society. The United States would be able to produce the manufactures it had been buying from Europe and at the same time provide farmers with an enlarged domestic market for their produce. Further, the availability of jobs would encourage European laborers to emigrate to the United States as well as utilize America's otherwise idle women, children, and unemployed. Factories would make America more populous, wealthier, and militarily stronger.[3]

Hamilton did not place a high value on widespread ownership of productive resources. He defended private property to the degree that it assured rapid economic development of the new nation. He did not expect factory workers as a group to assume property-owning status and thus political power since he, like Jefferson, supported property restrictions on voting and office holding. Rather, Hamilton offered factory laborers the prospect of high wages, which in many of his writings he identified as their "property." For him the prospect of owning and managing productive resources was the carrot by which a society induced its most talented citizens to venture their wealth and energy in productive enterprise. If this meant granting special incorporation privileges, subsidizing desirable enterprises, or protecting men in speculative gains, so be it. Hamilton insisted that policy makers must free themselves from their myopic fear that a strong national government might be used to secure profits for nonproducers. He believed that politicians too often allowed their concern for individual equity to obscure the more important issue of national welfare. If the federal government did not secure men in their profits, with small regard for how they came by them, then no one would be willing to engage in the enterprises on which national prosperity and power depended. He believed that private ownership buttressed by favorable government policy and economic incentive would provide the nation with unprecedented wealth and power. He assumed that national wealth, not universal property holding, insured the greatest happiness to the greatest number.[4]

When Hamilton died in 1804, the United States remained predominantly a nation of small farmers. Although economic changes were already underway, there was little at the time to indicate the dramatic alteration which took place following the War of 1812. From 1815 to 1860 city dwellers increased from 6.1 percent to 20 percent of the population. By 1860 the nation had developed an economy based on an extensive transportation network, commercial agriculture, extractive industry, and factory manufacturing. In short, the United States had taken its place among the great industrial nations of the world.[5]

One of the paradoxes of the half century before the Civil War was that during this "Age of the Common Man," when American politics assumed a decidedly democratic character, unprecedented economic stratification occurred. By 1860, despite the doubling of per capita income between 1815 and 1860, the distance separating the nation's wealthiest and poorest had sharply widened. The United States had more paupers making up a larger percentage of the population than ever before. But just as important as absolute economic well-being was the decline in status of the large and growing class of wage earners. Even though many of these wage earners enjoyed higher incomes than many of Jefferson's idealized yeomen, their dependent status represented a qualitative decline for those who believed that political self-determination must be undergirded by economic self-determination. By the standards of the nation's founders these employed men, who operated the nation's factories, mines, transportation networks, and urban enterprises did not qualify for political participation because of their dependent status. For those who accepted the view that propertied men differed in kind from unpropertied men, the burgeoning class of wage earners signified a distinct group of men unfit for self-government.[6]

At the 1820 Massachusetts and 1821 New York constitutional conventions the delegates dealt with the problem of increasing numbers of wage earners. These two conventions were especially significant because they convened near the beginning of these economic changes. They were also the first states, along with Pennsylvania, to feel the impact of urbanization and the factory system.[7] In both the Massachusetts and New York constitutional conventions the issue of property qualifications for voting and office holding divided the participants into two groups. The conservatives held fast to the Blackstonian principle that only men with a stake in society could be entrusted with political power. The suffrage reformers on the other hand declared in favor of ending all but minimum restrictions on voting and office holding. The conservatives claimed to represent the values of the old republic, while the reformers spoke in behalf of a government of "men and not of property."[8]

The Massachusetts and New York conservatives numbered among their ranks such able men as Chancellor James Kent, Supreme Court Justice Joseph Story, and Daniel Webster. They argued that only men of property, and preferably small farmers, could be counted on to exercise the moderation necessary for the preservation of individual rights and property. They feared that in the future large numbers of Americans, perhaps a majority, would be dependent wage earners. These rootless men might fall prey to the machinations of either employers or unprincipled demagogues and use their vote to destroy private property and personal liberty. "The disproportion between the men of property, and the men of no property, will be in every society in a ratio to its commerce, wealth, and population," declared Chancellor Kent. The time when America was a republic of virtuous farmers was past, he continued. "We are fast becoming a great nation, with great commerce, manufactures, population, wealth, luxuries, and with the vices and miseries that they engender." Large manufacturing would mean large numbers of dependent workers, predicted Kent, "and one master capitalist with his one hundred apprentices, and journeymen, and agents, and dependents, will bear down at the polls" and destroy the property and liberties of everyone.[9]

Kent and his fellow conservatives did not question the desirability of the economic development which they claimed threatened the republic of small property holders. In fact, most of them, like Hamilton, embraced economic development as the means to national wealth and power. Instead, they sought to stem the influence of the rising class of unpropertied wage earners and thereby employers by imposing property restrictions on political participation. These measures, they argued, would secure farmers and other men of property a continued hegemony over state government, even if a majority of the population were unpropertied. Thus, despite the conservatives' insight that economic development posed a serious threat to traditional American ideas of republicanism and their avowed loyalty to the idea of a nation of yeomen freeholders, many, such as Kent, accepted with open arms the new economic order. Kent chose to reserve political power for the fortunate remnant of property holders and accepted the possibility of a large class of unpropertied men locked out of any participation in government as an undesirable, but necessary, by-product of economic development.[10]

If the conservatives at the Massachusetts and New York conventions failed to conserve, it can be said with equal justification that the reformers failed to reform. If nothing else, the defenders of property qualifications had understood the implications of contemporary changes. The reformers, however, denied the importance of widespread property holding and concerned themselves with the abstract liberty and equality of all men. They argued that participation in government should not reflect the amount of property a man owned. In the words of one delegate, suffrage, not property holding, was the "only true badge of the freeman." They ignored the conservatives' argument that personal liberty depended on economic independence. A Massachusetts reform delegate suggested that if property qualifications were based on the assumption that they steadied men's habits, then an educational qualification would be more appropriate. Furthermore, he argued, if a large factory class developed in Massachusetts it would be far better to include them in the political process because "by refusing this right to them you array them against the laws; but give them the rights of citizens—mix them with the good part of society, and you disarm them."[11]

By emphasizing the liberty and equality of all men, the reformers in the Massachusetts and New York conventions in effect denied the significant difference between wage earners and employers. Further, political enfranchisement of unpropertied wage earners seemed to preempt any redress of grievances that these men might have voiced in protest of their position in American society. Instead of recognizing the significance of increased wage earning and seeking to remedy it by extending ownership into the new economic relationships developed by the factory system, the reformers, in the name of liberty and equality, simply denied the importance of self-employment as a factor of individual autonomy and liberty. Their assertion of all men's right to political participation ignored the reality of economic passivity on the part of large numbers of men. Giving everyone a vote implied that a factory owner with one hundred employees exercised no more political power than his most humble employee, who happened to enjoy the same voting privilege on election day. Universal suffrage and claims of theoretical equality might also have obscured wage earners' self-image as subservient laborers. The right to vote perhaps inhibited them, as the delegate from Massachusetts suggested it might, from assuming a group identity that would have allowed them to act consciously to secure for themselves some managerial control over their labor or to gain a larger stake in American society than a distant promise of good wages, decent working conditions, and relatively high levels of consumption.

Jacksonian politicians as a rule also played down or ignored the impact of the wage system on American society. On a national level the Democratic Party, under the leadership of Andrew Jackson, attacked monopolies and special privileges—dramatically symbolized by the "Bank War." Jackson and Democratic politicians indulged in what from hindsight appears to have been appeals to a type of class consciousness. But instead of dividing society between the employed and the employers, the Jacksonians generally divided society between the producers and the nonproducers or the special privileged versus the unprivileged. The reason they did so is obvious. Any contemporary political party which based its political future solely on wage-earner support could not have hoped to win an election since most voters at the time were either self-employed or employers. The Jacksonian ploy of setting the producers against the nonproducers had the decided political advantage of appealing to everyone who worked for a living, a category which included farmers, shopkeepers, wage earners, teachers, newspapermen, bankers without special charter privileges, slave and factory owners, or just about every adult male in the United States.[12]

Even the more radical Jacksonian Democrats in New York, the Locofocos, who could appeal to a fairly large wage-earner constituency, directed most of their rhetoric against exclusive bank and corporate charters. The Locofocos for the most part accepted the wage system. Their solution to large economic enterprise was enactment of a general incorporation law which would give every man the equal opportunity to secure a corporate charter, as well as such demands as a ten-hour working day, higher wages, and free public education. Few prominent politicians in either major party challenged the legitimacy of the wage system itself or suggested alternate ways to organize labor in large-scale enterprise which would extend to the individual worker control over his labor and resources.[13]

Yet, Jacksonian America produced a rich crop of persons who raised basic questions about the direction of American economic development. Many of these dissenters offered far-reaching and often fantastic solutions to the new problems arising out of urbanization and factory manufacturing. These radical intellectuals exerted no perceptible influence on American industrial relationships and in retrospect it is difficult to take all of their schemes seriously. Nonetheless, the radicals deserve some attention if only because of their willingness to deal with the difficult problems produced by American economic development.[14]

One of the first men to suggest to Americans an alternate road to economic development was not an American at all, but a Welshman, Robert Owen. Of the myriad of nonreligious reformers of the period Owen was one of the very few who completely rejected the desirability of any individual ownership of the means of production. Born in 1771 in Wales, Owen amassed a modest fortune, first as a manager and then as a partner, in the New Lanark textile mills in Scotland. Owen's work as a pioneer in British textile manufacturing apparently instilled in him a dislike for traditional social patterns and a naive confidence in the possibilities of "rational" ordering of human activity. He considered the family, individual ownership, religion, commerce, armies, and bureaucracies all archaic anachronisms which hindered industrial efficiency and productive organization of society. Faddish new ideas on education, social planning, and technology fascinated Owen. He hoped to establish a series of industrial communities which utilized the latest ideas and techniques to produce unprecedented prosperity and thus human happiness.[15]

The apparently irrational and wasteful development of the British factory system appalled Owen. He sought to remedy its worst abuses in his paternally run factory at New Lanark. With the experience he gained at New Lanark, Owen set out to establish model factory communities throughout England and the United States. Owen never clarified how he intended to reorder society—even in his American commune at New Harmony, Indiana, he failed to work out any detailed ideas on community organization. A few things were clear though. He wanted to end all individual ownership of productive resources, because he felt it encouraged shortsighted self-interest that pitted one person against another to the economic detriment of everyone. Also, he expected to organize all work—manufacturing and agriculture—on a collective or factory basis which utilized to the maximum machinery and expert management.[16]

Owen believed that maximum productivity could be achieved through collective action, and that men would find their fulfillment not in their work, but in their off-hours when they could enjoy the superior rewards of efficient production and the leisure time afforded by machinery and collective action. Owen harbored no sentimental attachment for old forms of proprietorship or freehold farming, and in this way he stood almost alone as one of the few unequivocal champions of the factory system to receive a hearing in the United States. In other ways his ideas paralleled many prominent American economic writers—particularly his assertion that prosperity depended on specialization of labor and the maximum use of machinery as well as his belief that workers would be rewarded, not by an intrinsic enjoyment derived from their work, but from the consumptive privileges it provided them.[17]

Owen's ideas fostered several experiments in factory communalism in the United States. But by 1830 most Americans disenchanted with contemporary society turned either to more religious-oriented activities or to another secular communalist, Charles Fourier, and his American popularizer, Albert Brisbane. Born in 1809, Brisbane spent several years in Europe. While there he studied for two years with Fourier, the French originator of the "association" idea. In 1834 Brisbane returned to the United States to promote Fourier's ideas. He struck up an initial friendship with Horace Greeley, who supported "association" in the columns of the *New York Tribune*. In addition to Greeley's help, Brisbane publicized Fourierism in three books—*The Social Destiny* (1840), *Association* (1843), and *General Introduction to Social Sciences* (1876). It is difficult to measure the relative influence of the Fourierist movement, but in actual numbers of communities established Fourierist numbered twenty-seven and Owenite only ten. The most famous of the Fourier experiments in community life was George Ripley's Brook Farm.[18]

The economic dependence caused by the growth of large economic enterprise disturbed Albert Brisbane. He foresaw a time when in the United States the owners of commercial banks and corporations would through indirect means gain control over most of the nation's productive property, thereby dispossessing farmers and forcing them into dependent relationships as employees. Brisbane described wage earning as a form of servitude similar to chattel slavery or convict labor, because the worker had no interest in his work, no alternative except starvation, and was denied a full return on his labor. He scorned universal suffrage and political liberties as a mockery of real liberty. Only "industrial liberty" was meaningful, argued Brisbane. A man only possessed real liberty when he had a choice of occupation and an assured income that would support him comfortably.[19]

Following Fourier's ideas, Brisbane proposed to make work more attractive and rewarding by organizing men and women into "phalanxes" or large collective families of about four hundred persons. By pooling their resources, he felt that small property owners could compete successfully with large corporations. The members of the phalanx would live together in large apartment-like buildings and farm their land collectively (Brisbane preferred agriculture to manufacturing because of its "greater charm"). Collective enterprise would allow the phalanx to buy expensive machinery, rationalize land use, and eliminate the wasteful duplication when the farmers were on a hundred different farms (e.g., one large dairy barn instead of one hundred small ones). Collective enterprise would allow efficiency, increase production, and make it possible for the members to receive a maximum return on their labors so that they could afford the goods they desired and have the time for a happy and fulfilling life. "We assert, and will prove," promised Brisbane, "that labor, which is now monotonous, repugnant and degrading, can be ennobled, elevated and made honorable . . ."[20]

In the organization of labor the Fourier phalanxes resembled Owen's factories of "rationalized industry," with one significant difference. While Owen deplored all forms of individual ownership, the Fourierists based their community on collective labor, but individual ownership. A proprietor will work twice as hard and more efficiently than a hired man, said Brisbane. Therefore, to achieve maximum production all wage earners also must be proprietors. But individual ownership of productive resources did not mean individual enterprise to Brisbane; he was committed to collective labor. He advocated a labor system in which all participants owned stock. At the end of the accounting period each shareholder-worker would be paid according to a formula based on the amount of stock he owned (4/12), the time and quality of his work (5/12), and for any useful ideas he might propose (3/12). It was a joint-stock, profit-sharing corporation. Brisbane also differed from Owen in his commitment to the individual's right to uncontested control over his wage-profits.[21]

In effect, individual property for Brisbane entailed the right of the individual to determine his consumptive habits as well as to participate in the collective management of the community's resources. Large-scale, mechanized industry, in his opinion, could not afford the luxury of individuals making independent decisions on how to utilize their labor and productive resources. Neither he nor Owen challenged the factory organization of labor; rather they demanded a larger return of the profits to the laborer and more leisure—or in more prosaic terms higher wages, better working conditions, and shorter hours. Additionally, Brisbane insisted upon worker participation in management and control over his wages.

In sharp contrast to Brisbane's and Owen's infatuation with the factory system was Thomas Skidmore. Of those Americans disturbed about the inequities and changes resulting from the development of the wage system, probably no one offered a more radical solution. Born in Connecticut at the turn of the century, Skidmore as a youth moved from place to place until finally, in 1818, he settled in New York City, where as a mechanic and jack-of-many-trades in the late 1820s, he became involved in that city's nascent labor movement. In 1829 he helped found the Working Men's Party. At the party's first meeting Skidmore managed to have the assembly endorse his economic program. A few days later a more conservative group in the party called a new meeting to exorcise "Skidmorism" from the party platform and disassociate the Working Men's Party from him. Driven from his own party, Skidmore ran for the New York state assembly and nearly won. As a result of his speeches, the publication of his book *Rights of Man to Property!* (1829), and his near-win in the state assembly race, Skidmore became the chief boogyman of the conservative press and less radical labor leaders. They severely maligned him and his ideas to the point that "Skidmorism" became synonymous with "agrarianism"—the contemporary equivalent to the present use of "communism." In 1832, still a young man, Skidmore died of cholera.[22]

Although Skidmore directed his criticism more at the unequal distribution of wealth than at the wage system, his proposals directly challenged the idea of wage labor. Skidmore argued that American society had become divided between proprietors and nonproprietors with the number of proprietors steadily declining. He blamed this decrease on the malapportionment of wealth caused by inheritances. Inherited wealth gave some men unfair and unearned advantages over other men and made it possible for the heir of a rich man to enter business with a head start. As a result, the sons of poor men were forced by necessity to work for the rich man's son, which allowed the rich man to exploit the poor man and deny him a full return on his labor. Inherited wealth also made it possible for the formation of a leisure class that did not have to work for a living. Since the world had been given to men in common, said Skidmore, and no man had a larger claim to the common property than another, if natural justice were to prevail, each person at birth should receive a claim to an equal amount of the community's resources.[23]

Not one to be caught without a plan, Skidmore worked out an elaborate scheme to implement his program. The first step was the calling of a constituent assembly to amend all property laws. Then a thorough survey had to be taken of all the community's resources and each man's and woman's share of the common wealth computed— Skidmore was primarily concerned with landed property. Next, the assembly would abolish all existing titles to property and at the same time issue to each adult citizen (male and female, black, white, and red) a dividend representing each one's equal share of society's property. The state would then hold a public auction at which each citizen would have the opportunity to buy whatever property he wanted or could afford with his dividend. The property that each person acquired would be held in absolute fee simple title, and the individual could do anything he wanted with it. He could support himself on it or he could sell it to someone else and become a wage earner. If the person proved to be unable to support himself, then he could turn in his dividend or property to the state and become a public ward. But whatever a person decided he would have to live with the decision.[24]

Each man's claim to his property ended at death when it reverted to the state to be distributed by auction to maturing generations. As a result, even though a man could buy, sell, or trade titles to property as he saw fit, the title expired with the original property owner no matter who might own it at the time of his death. Thus property buyers bought at their own risk. To prevent men from

engrossing the property of their wives Skidmore suggested
that each person regardless of sex be given a separate
allotment. For married couples, at one or the other's death,
only one share would return to the common store. Skidmore, recognizing the important relationship between education and economic opportunity, wanted the state to give
to parents an annual allowance to support and educate
their children in an effort to mitigate the disadvantages
accruing to the children of improvident parents.[25]

Skidmore's plan of universal property holding seemed
more suited to a society of small farmers and mechanics
than one containing large manufacturing and commercial
enterprises. But Skidmore thought not. To meet this criticism, he suggested that if a number of persons preferred
to use their property as a share of a larger enterprise they
could "associate." Each person would then be an owner
and have a voice in the management. The association as a
group would decide wage rates to pay its members
and each member would be paid out of the association's
profits. To prevent monopoly, Skidmore would have prohibited anyone from sharing in more than one association,
and restricted membership to those who worked in the
association. An individual would be able to leave the association by selling or trading his shares to the association
or to outsiders who wanted in. In this way Skidmore
hoped that everyone would have the opportunity to be
either a completely independent proprietor or an associated one.[26]

Skidmore carried many of Jefferson's beliefs to their
logical conclusion. He believed that personal liberty was
meaningful only if the individual owned enough productive property to make himself economically independent.
To him the right to own property inherently included the
right of self-employment or the individual's direct control
over his work as well as his consumptive habits. Of the
many economic thinkers of the period Skidmore was one
of the few who tried to retain in large-scale enterprise the

bond between ownership, management, and labor which characterized freehold farming. Interestingly enough, for all his radical proposals, Skidmore believed they were necessary if such traditional concepts as the family, fee simple farming, parental control over children, and individual choice were to be preserved. But most importantly, Skidmore hoped to insure that every person in society could become a proprietor so that everyone, not just the fortunate few, could enjoy the prerogatives and liberty of self-employment.

Radicals in the antebellum period were in a distinct minority. Three writers on economics, Theodore Sedgwick, Francis Wayland, and Francis Bowen, reflected more widely held views on private property and wage earning. These men represented major political parties and articulated what might be called the conventional wisdom of the time. Sedgwick participated actively in Democratic Party activities and styled himself a reformer and champion of the poor. Wayland held the professorship of moral philosophy and the presidency of Brown University, and Bowen taught at Harvard. The ideas of these mainstream intellectuals on private ownership and their attitudes toward the factory system provide an insight into the changes that the wage system wrought in American values.

Born in 1780 in Sheffield, Massachusetts, Theodore Sedgwick grew up in a Federalist family and attended college at Yale. A lawyer by trade and politician by choice, Sedgwick supported Andrew Jackson, the Democratic Party, and railroads. He possessed a genuine sympathy for the poor and backed a number of reform causes. In 1836 he published one of the first books in the United States delineating the nation's poverty-stricken classes. In *Public and Private Economy* Sedgwick also set forth his views on economics and individual property. His attitudes toward individual ownership reflected his divided loyalties between the older, simpler agrarian economy of his boyhood in Sheffield and the expansive and developing Massachusetts

of his adulthood. Sedgwick rejected neither. He hoped
that most men would be able to own their own farms because land, more than any other form of ownership, provided men with economic independence, security, and
personal liberty. A person who owned his own farm not
only worked harder and produced more, according to
Sedgwick, but he also enjoyed it more because he made
the managerial decisions and was free to exercise his creative impulses.[27]

But not all men could be self-employed farmers. The
prosperity of the nation depended on large-scale factory
production and this meant large numbers of wage earners.
Even so, Sedgwick believed that the wage earner could
enjoy some of the pleasures of freeholding. He argued that
high wages provided men a degree of economic independence, particularly if workers bought their own homes. If
a laborer lived modestly and saved his earnings (at least
half), Sedgwick felt that in time anyone could accumulate
enough money to tide himself over most emergencies and
provide for his old age. He might even be able to save a
surplus and buy a farm or small business. But if not, high
wage scales, ten-hour workdays, and no work on Sunday
would allow the wage earner the time and money to par-
take of some of the good things in life. Sedgwick expected
laborers to vent their creative energies, denied by their
work, through after-hour activities of self-education and
cultural enrichment. Furthermore, by making possible
home ownership and savings accounts, high wages produced the same virtues as proprietorship—frugality, so-
briety, industry, and dependability.[28]

Sedgwick used the word "property" interchangeably
with wealth. Although he placed greater value on proprietorship, he considered the wage earner who owned a
house or a savings account as much a property owner as
the farmer who owned his own farm. In both cases the
individual held a "stake in society" and controlled his consumption. In this way Sedgwick blurred the distinction

between proprietorship and wage earning. Property holding became dissociated from proprietorship, and in the
process the Jeffersonian ideal which Sedgwick rhetorically
supported might as easily mean every man a wage earner
as every man a proprietor.[29]

Even more clearly than Sedgwick, Francis Wayland
revealed the changes taking place in the meaning mid-
nineteenth-century Americans gave to the word "property." Wayland, long-time president of Brown University,
clarified his views on property and wage labor in his popular college textbooks *Elements of Moral Science* (1835)
and *Elements of Political Economy* (1837). Wayland lacked
the divided loyalties that Sedgwick had shown in his preference for an agrarian society and only limited acceptance
of the wage system. Wayland believed that prosperity
could only be achieved through large-scale, factory-organized production, and that the high productivity resulting
from the division of labor promised the greatest good for
the greatest number. Not only did Wayland unequivocally
accept wage earning, but like Adam Smith, he defined
every productive member of society as a wage earner.
Wayland denied any qualitative difference between an employer and his employee. They both performed necessary
functions and received remuneration for their labor based
on their skill and industry—the employee in the form of
wages and the employer in profits.[30]

Wayland usually relied on utilitarian arguments to make
his case for individual ownership. Individual property
served two important functions. It provided laborers an
incentive to work efficiently and industriously and made
possible the accumulation of wealth necessary to finance
the expensive equipment on which factory production depended. For these two functions alone, Wayland believed
society should foster and protect individual ownership.
Nevertheless, Wayland also used natural rights language
to defend individual ownership. He believed that all men
enjoyed a God-given right to the profits from their labor.

But this did not entail access to and control over productive resources. It only required that all men receive an equitable return on their labor and have exclusive control over the disposal of their earnings.[31]

Francis Bowen possessed a more sophisticated understanding of the workings of the modern economy than had Wayland, and for this reason his writings provide added depth to Wayland's basic ideas. Bowen personified northern economic wisdom. As a student he attended Harvard, taught mathematics for two years at Phillips Exeter Academy, and then returned to Harvard to tutor four years. Later he became editor and owner of the prestigious *North American Review* and finally professor of moral philosophy at Harvard. Bowen expressed his views on property in a number of articles in the *North American Review* and in a textbook *The Principles of Political Economy* (1856). His ideas did not conflict with Wayland's in any significant degree; both men shared common assumptions on the desirability of economic development and the necessity of a division of labor. Bowen, like Wayland, used the right of individual property as primarily the right to control consumption, not production. He justified individual ownership on the grounds that it stimulated industry and encouraged capital accumulation, and he too based property rights more on utility than on natural right. Finally, he agreed with Wayland's analysis that wage earners differed from their employers only in the skills they possessed and the amount of pay they received.[32]

But Bowen went beyond Wayland in several ways, or at least expressed ideas that Wayland had only implied. First of all, Bowen insisted that cooperation and collective action, not competition and individual action, were fundamental to factory-organized production. Although Bowen argued in favor of competition, he limited its utility to the marketing of labor and goods. He continually emphasized the cooperative nature of modern production and used the interdependency of factory production to deny any conflict of interest between the employer and the employed. The modern factory could not be segregated into wage earners and owners, said Bowen, rather everyone connected with factory production were workers busy at different levels of production and with different wage scales that reflected different skills. No one person exercised complete responsibility for the production of goods, but rather a long chain of interdependent and cooperating specialized workers controlled production.[33]

Bowen had no desire to extend individual proprietorship into the factory itself; such ownership would hinder productivity. But he understood the menial nature of factory work and its tendency to dwarf operator's minds. "The successful pursuit of a single art or of the fragmenting of a single science," said Bowen, "is but poor compensation for the loss of all versatility and alertness of mind, and for allowing most of the faculties to rust by disuse." He hoped that high wages and the opportunity to buy a farm or small business in the future would compensate wage earners for their loss. Also, he thought that corporate stock issues might serve the same end by giving workers a sensation of ownership and the feeling that they shared in the management and profits of the enterprise.[34]

Bowen's attitude toward inherited wealth revealed the strong utilitarian bent of his ideas of ownership. He agreed that individuals had a right to the exclusive control over all the wealth or property they had accumulated through their labor. Bowen believed this exclusive claim ended at death; no man had a right to control the uses of his property after he died. "There is an implied contract between society and the individual, that he shall be protected in the exclusive enjoyment of his earnings, the fruits of his labors, so long as he is capable of enjoying them," wrote Bowen, but when he dies "the control is dissolved, the obligations of society have been fulfilled and what is left behind without a natural owner comes into the common stock, to be distributed, or appropriated in mass, solely

from regard to the greatest good of the greatest number."
Bowen did not advocate an end to inherited wealth. As
long as inheritances served socially desirable ends, he saw
no reason for society to interfere with an individual's
bequests. But he insisted that society allowed its citizens
to determine who inherited their wealth only as a matter
of policy and not in recognition of a right.[35]

For Bowen, property claims justified themselves only if
they contributed to economic productivity. Thus, even
though he defended large accumulations of wealth and
defended individuals' right to use their property or wages
as they saw fit, he never defended or tried to protect wealth
for the sake of any private, selfish interest. Instead, he
made property rights conditional on whether or not they
contributed to economic growth. He believed that maximum human happiness depended on high levels of consumption, and property rights were justified because of
their tendency to foster economic growth which benefited
the entire society. And again like Wayland, Bowen primarily justified the right because it promoted prosperity, not
because it insured individual autonomy and liberty. Without directly repudiating natural rights theories, Bowen
based all claims of ownership on social utility, not individual right. The only right an individual retained was his
right to an equitable return on his labor or a fair wage.

In the antebellum period, if politicians and economic
writers reflected widely held views, Americans managed
to accommodate themselves to the emerging wage system
without radically altering their political institutions or
their value system. Almost all states eliminated property
restrictions on political participation and, in theory at
least, on election day wage earners stood on equal footing
with proprietors. New ideas about the basis of liberty and
equality partially supplanted those of the founding fathers,
who had made economic autonomy and freedom synonymous and had tied political participation to economic
competence. Not only were wage earners admitted into

the political arena, but the meaning attached to individual property shifted away from productive resources toward the products secured from wages. While a labor theory of value continued to provide the moral justification for private ownership, and while men still believed that productivity and economic freedom depended on the sanctity of private possessions, the right of private property no longer necessarily included the individual's right of access to and control over the means of production. Now high wages and wage purchases had acquired some of the respectability formerly reserved exclusively for proprietorship. The shift in meaning had been subtle. None of the old values and meanings had been denied; on the contrary, nearly everyone affirmed them. The primary change was the expanded importance of wages.[36]

As insignificant as the change may seem, the assimilation of wage earning with proprietorship represented an important step in the Americanization of the factory system. Since wage earning and factory labor were now compatible with individual ownership, men could argue that factory-organized labor was not an alien intrusion into the agrarian republic, but the desirable agent of progress to national wealth and power. Finally, and perhaps more importantly, the shift in meaning from control of production to use of wages provided a psychic illusion that old values and old notions of liberty were being honored in the new economic environment. Wage earners found themselves incorporated into the republic of property holders. In this way, an expanded meaning of the word "property" helped mute class conflict even as it reinforced the decline of political deference in the face of increased economic stratification.

CHAPTER 6

Bearers of Water and Hewers of Wood: Men as Property

The same natural rights arguments which Americans used to defend freehold property also provided the most potent critique of slavery. The struggle for independence led many persons to conclude that slavery was incompatible with their vision of America as a republic of freeholders. Thus, while American political leaders accused British authorities of depriving the colonists of their property, they never considered slavery a morally legitimate form of ownership. When remonstrators demanded the recognition of all men's inalienable rights of life, liberty, and property, no one included property in slaves as one of the natural rights which a just government should recognize. The labor theory of value, which Locke had used to justify enclosure, conflicted with a slave system that enabled an owner to deprive his nonconsenting slave of the product of his labor.[1]

Locke's *Two Treatises of Government* has proven to be an extremely ambiguous legacy. Locke, in associating property rights with individual liberty may not have intended to undermine chattel slavery, just as he had not intended his theory of government to justify democratic revolution. Locke apparently saw nothing wrong with Negro slavery as he owned stock in the Royal African Company which specialized in slave trading, and in 1669 he helped draft the Fundamental Constitution of Carolina which included a provision for slavery. Nonetheless, Locke's ideas led in another direction. No person, he argued, could own another without explicit consent. Thus, whatever his personal preferences, Locke in the *Two Treatises* brought together in a well-reasoned and compelling manner most of the strands of seventeenth-century libertarian thought and in so doing completely undercut traditional defenses of slavery. In this instance Locke's ideas proved more important than his actions.[2]

Locke insisted that all men by nature enjoyed certain morally inalienable rights. The individual's most important right was to the fruit of his labor, for this made all other rights meaningful possibilities. Just as a government could not claim a right over an individual's life, liberty or property, so no person could rightfully claim ownership over another person, for this would deprive that person of the fruits of his labor and amount to legalized stealing. Since no one could claim the product of another person's labor unless the laborer freely consented to the bargain, said Locke, it could not be assumed that any man would freely consent to slavery. Slavery was a "vile and miserable" institution which was "directly opposite to the generous temper and courage" of Englishmen. If society sanctioned slavery, it denied individual rights and sanctioned a relationship based on power and tradition rather than on right and consent.[3]

Locke allowed slavery under two circumstances—captives taken in a just war and men condemned for capital crimes. In these situations men willingly accepted slavery in exchange for their lives. But slavery for any other reason violated the slave's natural rights as an individual. Therefore, according to Locke, any person unjustly enslaved had every moral right to kill his oppressor. He only cautioned that the injured be certain of the unrighteousness of his enslavement because heaven was his judge. Locke's sanctioning of slave revolts provided little practical aid for the enslaved person, for the rebellious slave, as Locke admitted, would more than likely be killed for his action—morally justified or not. Nonetheless, Locke placed God squarely on the side of the enslaved and did not morally obligate the slave to accept passively his fate.[4]

Antislavery advocates relied heavily on such natural rights ideas as evidenced by their frequent use of the phrase in the Declaration of Independence: "all men are created equal, that they are endowed by their Creator with certain unalienable rights, that among these are Life, Liberty, and the pursuit of Happiness." In his 1776 *Dialogue Concerning the Slavery of Africans*, Samuel Hopkins, Congregational minister and disciple of Jonathan Edwards, declared that "The benevolent creator and father of men, having given to them all an equal right to life, liberty and property, no sovereign power on earth can justly deprive them of either.'" Hopkins exhorted his fellow Americans as free men and as Christians to abolish property in men because it deprived slaves "of all liberty and property, and their children after them to the latest posterity, subjected to the will of those who appear to have no feeling of their misery." Thomas Paine not only wanted Americans to end slavery, but also to provide the freed slaves with land "so all may have some property, and the fruits of their labors at their own disposal, and be encouraged to industry; the family may live together, and enjoy the natural satisfaction of exercising relative affections and duties, with civil protection, and other advantages, like fellow men."[5]

The disparity between the stated ideals in the Declaration of Independence and human slavery intruded itself into the debates over the Federal Constitution. With near unanimity the delegates accepted the natural rights assumption that slaves were not a legitimate form of property, but southern delegates made it clear that they had no intention of entering into a "more perfect union" if it threatened slavery. For many Southerners, slaves represented their most important possession, and they demanded constitutional assurance that their slave "property"—immoral as it might be—would be protected with the same diligence as other private possessions. The Convention resolved the issue by giving the slaveholders practical guarantees for their "peculiar property." The slave states received representation for three out of every five slaves and a fugitive slave clause which authorized the federal government to capture and return escaped slaves. Men, North and South, who opposed slavery and supported the movement for constitutional reform, seemed to recognize the practical impossibility of securing southern ratification of any constitution that prohibited slavery.[6]

The libertarian ideas of the Revolution had an impact on some men whose personal interest was tied to slavery. St. George Tucker, a justice of the Virginia Supreme Court and later a federal district judge, exemplified southern slaveholders who opposed slavery. In 1796 Tucker published *A Dissertation on Slavery* in which he argued that slavery violated the basic principle of American government that all men should be equally free. It prevented slaves from exercising those rights for which governments were created—the right to work, acquire, and enjoy property. He refused to give any credence to the argument that governmental efforts to emancipate slaves violated slaveholders' property rights. No one, said Tucker, could rightfully claim a property in other men. The right of all men to life, liberty, and property exceeded in importance slaveowners' rights to their slaves. Tucker suggested that the Virginia legislature pass a law which would free all female slaves born in the future. This, he argued, would guarantee the ultimate extinction of slavery and still not work an undue hardship on slaveholders.[7]

The provision in the Northwest Ordinance of 1787 which prohibited slavery in the federal territory north of the Ohio River met no serious opposition in the nation's first few decades. In 1808 Congress struck another blow against slavery when it barred the importation of slaves into the United States. Stimulated by natural rights sentiments, several northern states outlawed slavery. The 1777 Vermont constitution abolished slavery on the grounds that it was inconsistent with the state's commitment to the principle that every man enjoyed an equal right to life, liberty, and the pursuit of happiness. Despite the fact that the Massachusetts constitution did not specifically abolish slavery, the Massachusetts Supreme Court in 1782 ruled that the natural rights statement in the state's bill of rights in effect denied the legality of slave property in Massachusetts. In 1783 the lower house of the legislature passed a bill to compensate anyone who might have lost "property" as a result of the court's decision, but because the senate refused to concur, the ex-slaveholders of Massachusetts received no compensation for their loss. New Jersey, Pennsylvania, Connecticut, Rhode Island, and New York followed a more moderate course and declared free any slave born after a certain date and upon their reaching a specified age of adulthood. In every instance the northern state courts backed up their legislature's right to destroy a slaveowner's claim to the offspring of his slaves as long as the legislature did not abridge the owners' claim to existing slaves. There is also evidence that some courts recognized the owners' right to existing slaves, not to protect their property rights, but to make sure that owners did not use emancipation as a means of evading their legal responsibility to care for and support aging and helpless slaves.[8]

Following the Revolution, slavery remained an important economic interest in the South, an interest which most southern political leaders went to great length to protect. In 1793, under the urging of southern politicians, Congress enacted a fugitive slave law which made the federal government responsible for the return of escaped slaves. Further, southern states gradually dissociated themselves from natural rights ideas. By 1830 only one southern state, Virginia, retained in its bill of rights the phrase affirming all men's inalienable rights to life, liberty, and property. The other southern states either had no bill of rights or they altered the natural rights statement from "all men" to "all freemen." Additionally, the writers of nearly every southern constitution took the precaution to deny to their legislatures the right to emancipate slaves without compensating the owners.[9] It was not until after the Civil War, when the Radical Republicans reconstructed the South, that southern constitutions uniformly acknowledged the liberty and equality of "all men."

The task of trying to reconcile the natural rights assertion of the Declaration of Independence with the Federal Constitution's sanction of slavery fell especially heavy on American courts. Their most important guide was Lord Mansfield's 1772 *Somerset* decision. In this classic test of the legitimacy of slavery in England, Mansfield argued that when an act or claim violated natural law the courts had to assume its illegitimacy unless there was a clear positive law to the contrary. "The state of slavery is of such a nature," declared the English justice, "that it is incapable of being introduced for any reason, moral or political. . . . It is so odious, that nothing can be suffered to support it, but positive law." Fortunately for Mansfield, there was no such positive law in England, so he was able to free James Somerset without risking the charge of judicial legislation.[10]

As a rule, American courts, state and federal, followed Mansfield's precedent. John Marshall's 1825 decision in *The Antelope* case represents a fairly typical example of how American judges sought to resolve the conflict between their personal objection to slavery and their constitutional obligation to enforce the law. The lawyers for the owners of *The Antelope*, a Spanish slave ship captured by the United States Navy, argued that the court should return the slaves to their owners, since slavery was legal under Spanish law. Further, the owners had not tried to sell the slaves in the United States but in Surinam, where slavery and the slave trade were legal. Marshall ruled that while ownership was a universally recognized right which the Supreme Court would honor, property in men was not. "That it [slavery] is contrary to the law of nature will scarcely be denied," said Marshall, "that every man has a natural right to the fruits of his own labor, is generally admitted; and that no other person can rightfully deprive him of those fruits and appropriate them against his will seems to be the necessary result of this admission." Marshall freed the captured slaves and ruled that, except in the case of fugitive domestic slaves, the court would recognize property in men only in those areas where local law and custom legitimatized the unnatural relationship.[11]

Marshall's tactic became the accepted practice of American courts. But this position presented logical difficulties, as Joseph Story's views on slavery and property illustrate. Story had always insisted that all legitimate property rights derived from nature, not social convention, and therefore were not subject to destruction by society. According to Story, only under the most extreme circumstances, such as a hostile invasion or natural disaster, could a society justify the destruction of a legally vested claim without fully compensating the owner for all value lost no matter what the origin, amount, or nature of the possession. Even so, Story did not extend the sanctions of property to slaveowning because he believed that slavery violated the slave's natural right to liberty. Nonetheless, he accepted the compromise of 1787 as legally and morally binding and refused to question the legitimacy of slaveowners' titles to their slaves. Since slavery depended on constitutional guarantees, argued Story, the slaveowners' claims could not be rightfully extinguished except by constitutional amendment. Despite his agile juggling of natural and constitutional rights, Story could not keep the two from eventually colliding. For if some natural rights, the rights of the slave to exercise liberty and own property, could be abridged by social convention or by constitutional action, there was no reason why other natural rights, such as a person's right to own land, could not also be abridged.[12]

Slavery first became a subject of open political discussion during the 1820 debates over the admission of Missouri as a state. The Missouri debates revealed three distinct antislavery positions. The most numerous antislavery group reaffirmed the assumptions underlying the federal constitutional settlement. Slavery was immoral, but men must regulate their lives according to practical necessity, not abstract theory. Therefore southern property in slaves had to be honored. Those advocating the second position accepted the idea that government had no right to interfere with private property, but they denied that slavery was property and thus recommended legislation to regulate it according to the best interests of society. But because of the federal nature of the Union, Congress could only regulate slavery in the District of Columbia and the territories. Those who held to the final antislavery position broke with a natural rights conception of property. They accepted slaves as a legitimate form of property, but they denied that any right of property enjoyed absolute immunity from social control. According to this view, all rights of ownership derive from society. Thus, when a society feels it advantageous to abolish such rights, it can do so with no obligation to compensate owners. This group came close to disavowing the doctrine of natural rights in all areas, but they usually limited their assault to property holding. In fact, all the antislavery spokesmen united in their avowed loyalty to the moral philosophy expressed in the Declaration of Independence.[13]

The defenders of slavery in the Missouri debates showed more theoretical unanimity than had their antislavery adversaries. Still, there appeared two somewhat different defenses of slavery. One might be labeled the constitutional-natural rights argument and the other a positive law position. Both groups denied any fundamental difference between slaves and other forms of private property. The constitutional-natural rights advocates insisted that all property rights were inalienable and no government, state or federal, had any right to regulate slavery or any other form of property without compensating the owners for the reduced value. In order to justify the enslavement of some men and not others, these defenders of slavery, who retained a commitment to natural rights, implicitly accepted the notion of the inherent inferiority of Negroes.[14]

Rejecting any claims to natural and inalienable rights, the positive law advocates rested their entire case on the constitutional compromise of 1787. They argued that all property rights depended on constitutional sanction and could only be abridged by constitutional amendment. They denied any legal standing to the Declaration of Independence, and argued that no right or privilege existed independent of specific law. They described the assertion of the abstract natural rights of all men as at best an affirmation of unrealizable goals which in no way morally bound society. Thus, as early as 1820, apologists for slavery had already begun to divide into two groups—those who sought to assimilate slavery into an orthodox natural rights framework and those who accepted the incompatibility of slavery with a liberal value system and therefore rejected the theoretical assumptions which Americans had traditionally associated with individual liberty.[15]

The inchoate theoretical positions expressed during the Missouri debates reappeared again and again in more refined and developed form throughout the pre–Civil War period. The nonnatural rights positions, for or against slavery, were particularly well represented at the 1829–1830 Virginia constitutional convention and in the 1831–1832 Virginia legislative debate over slavery. Virginia was politically divided along geographical lines with the western mountainous half primarily peopled by small, nonslaveholding freehold farmers and the eastern tidewater region

controlled by large slaveholding planters. Reapportionment
was the crucial issue in the 1829–1830 constitutional convention. If the eastern tidewater counties retained control
of the legislature, they would be able to block any legislative efforts to bring an end to slavery. If the western
counties could gain a majority in the legislature through
reapportionment, they might be able to end slavery in Virginia.[16]

Despite the great diversity of opinion expressed in the
convention, Abel P. Upshur, a justice of the Virginia Supreme Court and later Secretary of State under John Tyler,
dominated the proceedings. Upshur denied that individuals
could claim any rights which did not derive from constitutional or legislative sanction. Since governments were established to protect property, said Upshur, political power
should be based on property, which for him meant land
and slaves. When he advocated a government controlled
by property holders, Upshur did not mean that all freeholders should enjoy an equal influence on government.
He meant that aggregate wealth should determine political
power. According to Upshur's reasoning, a county with 100
units of property and 25 freeholders would be entitled to
100 units of political power which the 25 freeholders would
share; while a county with 10 units of property and 100
freeholders would qualify for only 10 units of political
power to be shared by the 100 freeholders.[17]

Upshur's defense of the prerogatives of wealth did not
even pay lip service to libertarian theory with its emphasis
on the rights of individuals. Determined to protect slaveholders' interests, he completely abandoned the traditional
arguments in favor of political control by men of property
—that property restrictions insured that those entrusted
with political power had a stake in society and that only
persons of property possessed the economic independence
necessary to act virtuously. Instead, he urged the Virginia
constitutional convention to grant the slaveholding coun-

ties additional representation for no other reason than it would insure that Virginia's slaveholders continued to exercise power in proportion to their wealth.

The freeholders of western Virginia countered Upshur's speech with an almost equally nonlibertarian argument. Henry Ruffner presented a moderate version of this view in "An Address to the People of West Virginia." Ruffner held to a limited natural rights position. "By nature all men are free and equal, and human laws can suspend this law of nature only so long as the public welfare requires." Therefore, said Ruffner, since slaveholding, like all other property rights, rested "solely on human law," the Virginia legislature could abolish or regulate slavery in any way it wished if the "public good" required it. For reasons of equity, Ruffner believed slaveholders should be compensated for their losses. Not all western Virginians were so considerate. James Faulkner argued that the "great right of society" determined the rightness of a law, and if slavery threatened the well-being of society, then the legislature could abolish it without any compensation. Compensation, declared Faulkner, would make the costs of emancipation prohibitive and Virginia would never be able to rid herself of slavery. Under no circumstances should the good of the whole suffer simply to protect the economic interests of the few. Western Virginians made it clear that they were more than willing to answer Upshur's argument of law based only on convention with some conventions of their own. Thus, the Hobbesian realism of Upshur became a two-edged sword which majoritarian freeholders could wield as well as class-conscious planters.[18]

As strategically risky as Upshur's defense had been, the more orthodox one of relying on a qualified natural rights argument left slaveholders in a morally vulnerable position. Thomas R. Dew, professor of political law at William and Mary College, demonstrated the futility of trying to tie slaveowning to other forms of property without first repudiating natural rights. In his influential *Review of the*

Debates in the Virginia Legislature, 1831–1832, Dew defended slavery not as a necessary evil but as a decidedly good institution. He argued that the chief end of government was to protect individuals' natural rights to property, and that the state can destroy such property rights only for public need and then with compensation for the owner. In answer to the charge that slavery was not a form of natural property, Dew insisted that not only was it legitimate but slavery was one of the first forms of property. Slavery was a humane institution which had arisen to spare prisoners of war and capital criminals from execution. Without explaining how this justified southern slavery, Dew argued that the slaveowner's legal and moral property included the slave as well as the slave's offspring. Any restriction on slavery, declared Dew with unintended irony, would force slaveholders to flee Virginia in order to find "asylum in a land where they will be protected in the enjoyment of the fruits of their industry." Dew's convoluted logic as well as his failure to recognize the inconsistency of owners claiming a right to the fruit of their slaves' labor made his strained use of natural rights extremely vulnerable. Except for setting a precedent for viewing slavery as a moral good, Dew's argument raised more questions than it answered, and it became an easy target for those antislavery spokesmen who also professed belief in all men's natural and inalienable rights.[19]

One such person was William Ellery Channing. Channing, an early organizer of the American Unitarian Association and outspoken critic of slavery, adhered to Lockean liberalism as well as to the brotherhood of all men. This led him to denounce any form of human bondage as immoral, no matter how benign or enlightened. Channing believed in the freedom of the individual, and he saw slavery as an institution which frustrated a slave's personal ambitions and denied to him any choice over how to utilize his life. Adhering closely to traditional natural rights doctrine, Channing argued that men possessed certain rights before entry into society, and that they had entered society to better secure those rights, not to give them up. Therefore when a society abridged an individual's rights, it no longer served the ends for which it had been established and its actions were illegitimate. Nothing, said Channing, could excuse the violation of an individual's rights to life, liberty, and the pursuit of happiness, even in the name of "public good." Additionally, Channing opposed slavery because the institution was based on the implicit assumption of Negro inferiority. He declared that all men were created free and enjoyed an equal and exclusive right to the fruit of their labors. A slave "cannot be property in the sight of God and justice, because created in God's image, and therefore in the highest sense his child; because created to unfold godlike faculties, and to govern himself by a Divine Law written on his heart, and republished in God's word. His whole nature forbids that he should be seized as property."[20]

Channing's opposition to slavery remained passive because he refused to condone any form of coercion even when directed against an institution such as slavery. But other men, who shared Channing's ideas of Christian brotherhood and natural rights, refused to limit their actions to moral suasion. One of these, Lysander Spooner, a lawyer and reformer, in the *Unconstitutionality of Slavery* (1853) used natural rights arguments to legitimatize coercion against slaveowners. Spooner believed that the right of property was consistent with both natural law and the Federal Constitution, but he denied that slavery was sanctioned by either. By distorting the historical evidence, Spooner "proved" to his own satisfaction that the Constitution of 1787 had never allowed slavery and that soon after ratification a southern slaveholding conspiracy had subverted it. Personally, Spooner believed that the individual had a moral obligation to oppose any civil law which violated his conception of moral order and right. But he recognized that most men could not accept such a subjective stance toward law and would not tolerate the flaunting of legal authority simply because it violated a person's private conception of justice. Therefore Spooner set out to prove that the Constitution did not sanction slavery and the founding fathers had never intended that it should. If correctly interpreted, the Constitution could become an effective instrument for destroying slavery.[21]

Spooner argued that the calculated avoidance of the word "slavery" in the Constitution indicated that the founders had no intention of giving slavery constitutional protection. Further, he said that the founders had intended to create a "national" government with plenary powers. He suggested that the idea of a federal division of powers with the national government having the right to legislate only in limited and prescribed areas had been foisted on the American public by an unholy alliance of power-hungry northern politicians and slaveholding Southerners. But now with the benefit of his research, Spooner asked Americans to accept the federal government as a consolidated entity with the full assurance that they were acting in a manner faithful to the true intent of the nation's founders. Accordingly, the federal government possessed the right to end slavery in the states, and since slaveholding did not fall under the rubric of "property," the Fifth Amendment's sanctions against federal action did not apply. Although in all likelihood few persons before the Civil War would have accepted Spooner's extreme assertion of federal power, it was only a single step from Lincoln's very popular position on the right of the federal government to abolish slavery in the territories. In December 1865 with the Thirteenth Amendment the nation took just that important step when it abolished slavery in all states without compensation.[22]

Despite the obvious utility of natural rights theory for the opponents of slavery, the defenders of the "peculiar institution" refused to concede to their foes a monopoly over a concept which enjoyed such popular appeal. Since a consistent Lockean natural rights argument undercut slavery, its apologists resorted to a pre-Lockean natural rights theory which, while it utilized much of the rhetoric, avoided its dangerous implications. The title of Samuel Seabury's *American Slavery Distinguished from the Slavery of English Theorists and Justified by the Law of Nature* indicates the extent that Lockean natural rights theory disturbed the supporters of slavery.[23]

Seabury, a New York Episcopal theologian out of sympathy with the libertarian theology of Channing, remained loyal to natural law but denied its application to individuals. A society, argued Seabury, must recognize natural law or court national disaster, but it should honor the rights of individuals only as they remain consistent with the needs and well-being of society. Seabury defined natural law not as right reason or self-evident principles of justice but as Scripture, amended and extended by the laws and customs of nations. He acknowledged that slavery might violate some men's conception of the slave's "natural rights," but since slavery was not inconsistent with Scriptures or the laws and customs of nations, a society could sanction slavery without fear of violating moral order.

Even though Seabury's natural law position sacrificed the rights of individuals on the altar of "common good," he tried to show that social expediency always dictated what rights a society allowed its citizens. He believed that if Lockean categories were examined within a historical context rather than as abstract truisms this would become obvious. First of all, Seabury argued that Locke's dichotomy between liberty and slavery failed to comprehend the actual relationship between individuals and society. All men, said Seabury, enjoyed some freedoms or rights and suffered some restraint, and the degree of liberty or restraint depended on the nature of the individual and the needs of the society. For instance, a criminal enjoyed few liberties, while a law-abiding citizen enjoyed many. In the same respect free men in the North suffered few restraints, while Negroes in the South possessed few liberties, but neither group's condition resulted from any inalienable rights they might possess; rather, it depended upon the felt needs of their respective societies.[24]

In a similar fashion Seabury defended slavery against the charge that slaveowners claimed a property in men and thereby deprived slaves of liberty and the fruits of their labor without consent. He said that the slaveholders did not own the slave's person—only God could claim a title to persons—rather they owned the slave's labor as long as the slave lived. This arrangement was not unlike any other labor contract. In return for a lifetime of labor the slave received clothing, food, and shelter—even after he had ceased to be productive. Seabury admitted that on the surface other labor contracts seemed to differ from slavery in that the laborer usually gave his direct consent to the bargain, while the slave did not. But Seabury argued that more often than not a free laborer's consent was not freely given but extorted from him because of the dire necessity to provide himself and his family with food and clothing. Besides, Seabury declared, most slaves' apparent acceptance of their situation represented as direct a consent as most governments received from their citizens. After all, in the United States no woman had ever directly consented to her subordinate legal status. Even the exceptional slave who dissented and actively sought his freedom did not disprove the rule of general acquiescence or justify the deviant's action. Seabury pointed out that even the United States government operated under the assumption that general consent bound all. Thus the disgruntled slave who violated the terms of his enslavement and attacked or tried to break out of the system should be treated like any other criminal in any civil society.[25]

As logical as Seabury's arguments often were, they failed to reconcile slavery with American libertarian assumptions —the primacy of the individual and his right to pursue his own definition of happiness. For those who retained a commitment to an individual's right to seek self-fulfill-ment, no well-reasoned argument was likely to convince them of the morality of slavery. Perhaps no one better understood this than George Fitzhugh, a Virginia lawyer and political thinker, who instead of trying to synthesize the unsynthesizable, chose to resolve the problem by re-jecting the natural rights tradition in its entirety. The individual, argued Fitzhugh, far from possessing rights independent of society, owed everything to his social con-dition. Without society individuals did not exist. Therefore individuals possessed no rights which opposed the inter-ests of society, and society had the right to use its members in any way that rebounded to the public good. Whatever rights a citizen had, said Fitzhugh, "are subordinate to the good of the whole; and he had never ceded rights to it, for he was born its slave and has no rights at all."[26]

Fitzhugh's rejection of natural rights was particularly evident in his use of the word property. He argued that men should own other men and in fact that all men should be owned by someone. A property in another person sim-ply meant that the owned owed his owner an obligation, and it was only through mutually recognized obligations that society functioned. Slavery, said Fitzhugh, merely gave legal recognition to the necessary obligations incum-bent on all members of any good society. It was true that the slave owed his master obedience and hard work, but the master in return used his managerial expertise to in-sure that the slave received a maximum return on his labor. Thus, for the slave's labor the master owed him food, clothing, and shelter whether he was well or infirm.[27]

Fitzhugh criticized Northerners for describing the slave plantation as an involuntary factory which exploited its laborers solely for the benefit of the owners. Unlike the factory owners in the North who assumed no responsibility for the well-being of their workers, slaveowners did not profit from their slaves. The slaveowner kept back from his slaves only what was necessary to provide for his own personal needs and the ongoing costs of the plantation. Instead of a factory, Fitzhugh suggested that the slave plantation was analogous to a large family where everyone worked together for the good of the whole and where no one was allowed to usurp for his own use the profits which the entire group had earned. In this way the slave system could be seen as an institution for socializing profits and property. It prevented opportunistic and selfish individuals from exploiting the weaker members of society for the sake of individual gain—a situation which Fitzhugh believed typified the northern factory system.[28]

Not content with his critique of the factory and wage system, Fitzhugh also attacked the agrarian republic of Jefferson. He argued that widespread ownership of land failed to provide the majority of the society with the stability necessary for happiness. It broke society into competing units and inhibited cooperation. The rapid turnover of landownership characteristic of a nation of small landholders disrupted society and made life emotionally precarious for those whose well-being was subject to the whim and fancy of the landowner. Rather than allow the land to be broken into small single-family farms, Fitzhugh suggested reimposing entails, primogeniture, and restrictions on land sales. This would encourage large landholdings capable of supporting 30 to 40 people. Such a system would put an end to selfish land speculation which sacrificed the welfare of those dependent on the land for the opportunity of quick gain for the owner. Fitzhugh believed that if the South discarded the outworn concepts of individual property and liberty it could, through the plantation system, provide itself a ruling class with the leisure, education, and wherewithal to govern wisely and with an eye to the common good.[29]

Fitzhugh's idyllic plantation society represented a coherent social system resting on collective labor and property held together by a hierarchal social structure. It

celebrated cooperation, not competition; security, not innovation. He made no effort to dress up slavery in the
garments of individual property and liberty. In fact, he
rejected both as inimical to his goal of providing every
member of society with the psychological and economic
security necessary for personal happiness. But he offered
small comfort for those who could not accept the permanent servile status of Negroes, or who refused to acknowl-
edge the wisdom or desirability of a semi-hereditary ruling
class, or who believed that individuals represented self-
justifying entities whom society should protect. Southern
slavery represented a threat to both the Hamiltonian and
Jeffersonian models of society, and as Fitzhugh understood
so well, it could not be rationalized within a Lockean natural-rights value system. So, as it often happens, he made
a virtue of necessity.

In 1836 the abolitionist, James Birney, published a brief
editorial in the antislavery periodical *Human Rights*. In
part it read: "Having exclusive legislation over the District
of Columbia [Congress] should see that every person
therein enjoys the *right of property*. This is the very reason Congress should abolish slavery. The right of property
is sacred. It belongs to every man. It was not given to us
by government: and it cannot, justly, be taken away by
government."[30] This classic natural rights statement of
property makes clear the basic incompatibility between
slavery and the right of property. Men such as St. George
Tucker had recognized the conflict and hoped that slavery
would die out, freeing Southerners of their moral dilemma.
But this did not happen. Instead, slavery prospered and
many southern leaders began to deny that natural rights
was a valid moral standard. These Southerners, most con-
spicuously George Fitzhugh, adopted a new social idea.
They rejected the idea that the individual had an inalienable right to control and profit from his labor and replaced it with the more congenial proposition that each
man had an obligation to serve his society in whatever

way it defined as necessary for the common good. Such persons found the natural rights basis of individual property opposed to a slave society. In following Fitzhugh, they went a long way toward repudiating the differences which separated John Locke from his feudal forebears.[31]

CHAPTER 7

❖

Private Right versus Public Good: Property and Antebellum Law

English common law qualified all property rights by public necessity. Property claims were subject to society's
residual right to levy taxes, to condemn through eminent
domain proceedings, and to regulate in the interest of public health, welfare, and morality. Moreover, the English
constitution conceded to Parliament almost unlimited
power in any conflict between private right and public
need. While pre-Civil War American jurists incorporated
these common law assumptions into American law—each
with the potential to destroy entirely an individual's claim
of ownership—American judges did not accept the idea of
unlimited governmental power. Committed to private ownership as well as popular government, American law-
makers sought to develop a body of law which protected
individual property without depriving government of its
essential powers. To accomplish this they tempered English common law restrictions on individual ownership by
infusing into American law the eighteenth-century natural
rights premise that the individual enjoyed an inalienable
right to property.[1]

In the first decades of national existence American jurists frequently turned to William Blackstone's *Commentaries on English Law* for guidance. This was particularly
true in disputes involving a conflict between public interest and property rights. Superficially, Blackstone's conception of property right adhered to natural rights ideas. He
accepted the proposition that the chief end of government

was to foster personal liberty and private property. He agreed that, morally, these were inalienable rights of all men, that the rights derived from nature, and that only a tyrannical government would deprive its citizens of them. He acknowledged that the individual's right to property had preceded the social compact and that men brought with them into society their right to property. Eventually, society so modified the rights derived from nature that it was no longer possible to distinguish natural from conventional rights. Instead of rejecting the idea of men retaining natural rights within the social context, Blackstone in effect declared that all legally vested claims enjoyed the same sanctions as those rights which derived exclusively from nature. For him it did not matter whether the original justification for a privilege continued into the future, whether it had been earned, or whether it deprived others of a similar right or opportunity. All that mattered was that, if a society had vested a right, it could not rightfully reclaim it. At this point he moved away from his natural rights premise.[2]

Blackstone's use of natural rights language obscured his practical acceptance of the supremacy of positive law. He did not deny that men possessed certain natural rights, but he insisted that on entry into society all men's natural rights became subject to the law—which in England meant Parliament. While a citizen might have a moral claim to certain property, unless that claim received parliamentary sanction the property right could not be exercised. Englishmen, according to Blackstone, had no constitutional remedy to any parliamentary enactment, even if it deprived them of their legally vested property. "So long therefore as the English Constitution lasts," he wrote, "we may venture to affirm, that the power of Parliament is absolute and without control."[3] This did not mean that Blackstone sanctioned arbitrary governmental action. Far from it. He simply recognized the ultimate power of Parliament and was unwilling to suggest any legal remedies.[4]

Blackstone's positive law assertion of parliamentary sovereignty disturbed many Americans. The English jurist's confidence that Parliament would never violate men's natural rights to property was not shared by those Americans who believed that the American Revolution had been precipitated by parliamentary tyranny. These men had grave doubts as to whether American legislators would be any more virtuous or restrained than Parliament had been. As a result, immediately following the ratification of the Federal Constitution, several jurists wrote their own brief commentaries to provide an American corrective to Blackstone.⁵

James Wilson, in his 1789 *Lectures on Law*, illustrated one American response to Blackstone. Wilson, a Supreme Court justice and probably the best legal mind in the new republic, agreed with Blackstone's definition of property right as a legal claim to anything of value. But he emphatically denied that individual property rights existed only at the sufferance of the legislature. Relying on the doctrine of popular sovereignty, Wilson argued that the right to govern derived from the people. The legislature, like all elements of government, had no right to exercise any power which the people had not specifically sanctioned. Further, it would be unreasonable to imagine, said Wilson, that individuals upon entry into society had given up the very rights which they had entered society to secure—the rights of life, liberty, and property. Therefore, even if the fundamental law of the land or constitution did not specifically prohibit government from depriving its citizens of their natural rights, no just government could assume it had such despotic power. Wilson thus believed that the courts must act as the guardian both of constitutional restriction and of natural rights against legislative encroachment.⁶

In 1795 United States Supreme Court Justice William Paterson set an important precedent for American courts when in *Vanhorne's Lessee v. Dorrance* he used natural rights to overturn a Pennsylvania statute. At issue was a tract of land claimed under a 1787 law that the Pennsylvania legislature had repealed three years later. Paterson ruled in favor of the plaintiff Dorrance and declared unconstitutional the Pennsylvania law on the grounds that the Pennsylvania constitution prohibited the state from taking personal property without compensation. By depriving the plaintiff of his land, said Paterson, the legislature had denied him the means to "enjoy the fruits of his honest labor and industry." Paterson conceded that legislatures possessed a "despotic power" to divest a person of his property, but he insisted that it could be exercised rightfully only for public need and with fair compensation to the injured person. Any other policy "would be laying a burden upon an individual which ought to be sustained by the society at large." "Omnipotence in legislation is despotism," declared Paterson. "According to this doctrine we have nothing that we can call our own, or are sure of for the moment; we are all tenants at will, and hold our landed property at the mere pleasure of the legislature." Paterson then added that the Pennsylvania statute also had impaired a contract in the form of the land title.[7]

Paterson's charge contained a number of important points which subsequent courts would utilize. First, he accepted a person's claim to land ownership as a natural right. A legislature could not deprive a person of this right, at least not after it had recognized that right by granting him a legal title. Secondly, Paterson called on the courts to refuse to recognize as law any legislation which infringed upon individual property rights. He implied that even without a constitutional limitation similar to that in the Pennsylvania constitution, courts could still hold legislatures accountable to natural law. When public need demanded the taking of private property, Paterson insisted that the legislature could do so only by exercising its power of eminent domain which required fair compensation to the injured party. Finally, Paterson's description of land titles as "contracts" linked the doctrine of natural rights to that of legislative "good faith," which opened the way for later courts to extend natural rights sanctions to a much wider range of possessions and claims.[8]

Three years later a divided Supreme Court in *Calder v. Bull* endorsed, as well as challenged, Paterson's ruling. In 1795, due to the peculiar structure of Connecticut appellate procedure, the legislature had set aside a probate court decision and then ordered a new trial in the same court. As a result, the probate court reversed its earlier decision. The plaintiff, Calder, brought suit, charging that the Connecticut legislature had deprived him of his legally vested property by interfering with the actions of the probate court. The United States Supreme Court denied his plea on the grounds that the *ex post facto* clause of the Federal Constitution applied only to criminal cases. Also, since Calder's right to the property had never been legally vested, he had no basis for claiming that the legislature had deprived him of any property. The court's refusal to interpret the *ex post facto* clause broadly to include nonpenal legislation eliminated a potential federal constitutional check on state legislative abridgment of property claims. This set the stage for a debate between Justices James Iredell and Samuel Chase over a judge's authority to honor natural rights claims in situations where no specific constitutional provision limited the power of the legislature.[9]

Iredell, a prominent North Carolina lawyer and leading Federalist, declared that although legislatures should not violate individuals' right to property without fair compensation, private rights always deferred to public necessity. He could not comprehend the assertion that any private right might be immune to public power. Iredell expressed concern that a few judges had begun to declare legislation unconstitutional for no other reason than that it violated "natural justice." The most "that a court could properly say, in such an event," argued Iredell, "would be, that the legislature, possessed of an equal right of opinion, had passed an act which, in the opinion of the judges, was inconsistent with the abstract principles of natural justice." He accepted the idea that legislatures' powers were limited by their constitutions, and when a legislature exceeded its constitutional powers, judges had no choice but to declare the acts in violation of the constitution and refuse to recognize them as binding. But he would not accede to the idea that a society could be bound by any absolute and unwritten restraints, particularly by some nebulous natural law which had no precise content. Iredell insisted that judges base their decisions on the letter of the legislation and the prevailing constitution. He believed that anything else would be an usurpation of power by the courts.[10]

Samuel Chase joined Iredell and his other colleagues on the court in denying the applicability of the *ex post facto* clause in noncriminal cases and in agreeing that Calder had never possessed a legally vested right of which he could be deprived. But he did not want his concurrence to be interpreted as a sign that the Supreme Court had compromised the sanctity of authentic property rights. In response to Iredell's comments, Chase defended a judge's duty to declare unconstitutional any legislation which violated natural law, even if no specific constitutional provision justified the action. Americans had established their governments to better insure their personal security and private property, said Chase, and the courts must assume that the sovereign people never intended the power of the legislature to include the right to destroy private property. Such action would be contrary to the very end of government. "I cannot subscribe to the omnipotence of a state legislature, or that it is absolute and without control," declared Chase, even when its authority is not "expressly restrained by the constitution, or the fundamental law of the State." Any act which threatened the vital principles of free government, he said, such as the sanctity of private contracts, personal security, and private property was not law, and the courts should not enforce it.[11]

The Chase-Iredell clash represented a classic conflict between two competing legal traditions. Iredell took a positive law stance which denied the relevance of moral theory in court adjudication. He believed that any law which a legislature passed not specifically prohibited by its prevailing constitution was legal and the courts had no business considering whether or not the law violated moral order or natural justice. Chase, on the other hand, argued that no government under the guise of law had the right to violate an individual's inalienable and natural rights, which of course included his right to property. Iredell's incisive opinion underlined the political risks a judge ran when he overruled legislation without specific, positive sanction for his action. No matter how firm his moral ground or irrefutable his logic, Chase's natural rights appeal exposed nonelective judges to charges of judicial tyranny over popularly elected legislatures, charges citizens in a predominantly majoritarian society might find compelling.

In 1810 John Marshall in *Fletcher v. Peck* expanded the meaning of the "contract" clause of the Federal Constitution in an effort to rescue property rights from the tenuous position in which Iredell had placed them. In 1795 a bribed Georgia legislature had granted a large tract of land at a bargain price to four land companies. The following year, amid charges of scandal, the voters of Georgia turned out of office all the involved legislators. Carrying out a popular mandate, the new legislature promptly voided the previous legislature's grant. In the meantime the land companies had begun to sell land titles to innocent buyers who in turn sold to others. Fletcher and Peck were two of these second and third parties to the land sales who sued to have the original land grant upheld.[12]

Marshall, speaking for a majority of the court, declared that the title of the land could be clearly deduced from the legislative grant. Georgia, said the chief justice, as a party to the transaction had no right to pronounce its own deed invalid. All titles to land ultimately rested on legislative sanction. If the court accepted Georgia's action, all land titles in the nation would be threatened as well as any other transactions which depended upon legislative sanction. Marshall insisted that legislatures, no less than individuals, must act lawfully, and they could expect the courts to hold them accountable for their actions. "If a legislature felt itself absolved from those principles of equity which are acknowledged in all courts," said Marshall, "its act is to be supported by power alone, and the same power may divest any other individual of his land, if it shall be the will of the legislature to so exert it."[13]

Marshall's defense of land titles as contracts avoided the problem of whether property rights rested on natural or positive law. He conceded that a legislature had a constitutional right to repeal the general legislation of a previous legislature, but he denied that it had any constitutional right to destroy property claims or void the terms of contracts established by a previous legislature. Marshall circumvented the issue of unauthorized judicial limitation upon legislatures. He did not base the court's invalidation of state legislation on moral principles, but upon his interpretation of the positive law and upon the principle of governmental "good faith." Now any "legally vested right" or public grant enjoyed the same immunity from state governments as private contracts. *Fletcher v. Peck* had the effect of including state legislation under the same sanctions which the Fifth Amendment applied to federal legislation.[14]

Marshall's interpretation of the "contract" clause became a favored means for owners of corporate charters to protect their franchises from a willful legislature. Many Americans of the late eighteenth and early nineteenth centuries associated private corporations with special privilege and monopoly or with devices more appropriate for an aristocratic England than a republican United States. In England the crown had used the corporate form to grant special monopolistic privileges to facilitate public projects. Because of the quasi-public and monopolistic character of corporations, English courts conceded to Parliament the right to abridge or annul corporate charters as it saw fit. Even Blackstone did not consider the destruction of a corporate charter as a violation of its owners' property rights. Many Americans shared this view. Further, many feared that such grants, if permanent, would provide the basis of a privileged class whose monopolistic grants allowed them to collect unearned profits even after they ceased to perform socially useful functions. For this reason many supported the idea that a legislature should be free to regulate or repeal any corporate charter it had created.[15]

St. George Tucker, a justice of the Virginia Supreme Court and editor of an important edition of Blackstone's *Commentaries*, was the most articulate exponent of this anticorporation viewpoint. He argued that a corporation was a legal entity created by a legislature which had the right to abolish it and take away its property. Tucker insisted that special privilege, especially in the form of corporate charters, did not provide the basis of legitimate property rights. And while he asserted the legislature's absolute power over the holdings of artificial, corporate entities, he carefully limited its power over legitimate, individual property. If a legislature granted title to a "natural person," wrote Tucker, it could not deprive him of his property no matter what the circumstances as long as the owner used the property legally. Thus, for Tucker and for those who shared his sentiments, the issue of the sanctity of corporate property came down to the problem of what qualified as natural property. To him, the holdings of legal entities did not qualify as a sacred or legally exempt form of property.[16]

Not everyone agreed with Tucker. Some persons argued that the courts should provide the owners of corporate charters the same security which Tucker extended to individual property. In a series of decisions, the Marshall Court extended the "contract" clause to encompass the rights and possessions of men acting collectively as well as individually. In *Bank of United States v. Deveaux* (1809), the Supreme Court for the first time dealt with a case involving the legal status of corporate property. Marshall, speaking for the court, did not directly confront the issue of the status of corporations and refused to call a corporation a "person," but he suggested that a good case could be made for so doing. In 1815 Marshall's colleague on the court, Joseph Story, picked up the chief justice's hint and ruled in *Terret v. Taylor* that the property rights of the owners of corporate stock were no different from the rights of individuals to noncorporate property. Story argued that once a property right had been permanently vested by a legislature, it could not be divested. If legislatures had the right to revoke corporate charters, said Story, they could revoke every land title in the country. He refused to countenance any more legislative control over corporate property than could be rightfully exercised over individual property. Story then proceeded to attach natural law sanctions to the legislatively created privileges of a corporate entity—rights traditionally restricted to natural persons.[17]

In 1819 Story in *Dartmouth College v. Woodward* reaffirmed his conviction. Story described a corporation as an "artificial person" which acted as a natural person and therefore possessed all the security of property that a natural person enjoyed. But the remainder of the Supreme Court failed to follow Story's lead. They defined corporate charters as contracts that state legislatures could not impair. In his written opinion Marshall made it clear that if state legislatures wanted to retain control over a corporation's internal policy they would have to include such a right explicitly in the corporation's charter. If legislatures chose to subsidize private corporations or to grant them special privileges, said Marshall, they did so at their own risk and with the understanding that the courts would recognize the grants as unimpairable contracts. He insisted that a corporate charter represented a mutually binding agreement between its holders and government and good faith obligated the government to abide by the terms of its charter. Only a willful and arbitrary government would renege on its promises to its citizens.[18]

In the *Dartmouth* decision the Supreme Court had not freed corporations from obstructive state legislation. By basing corporate status on the "contract" clause, the court had only freed existing corporations from retrospective legislative interference. Following the court's implied suggestion, state legislatures quickly began to include "reserve clauses" in all corporate charters which specifically gave to the legislature the right to "repeal and amend" corporate charters as the need arose. Thus the Supreme Court, instead of extending to corporate groups the property rights enjoyed by individuals, limited corporate rights to the terms of their charter-contracts which, if they included the "reserve clause," meant that corporations enjoyed no legislative immunity at all. Chancellor James Kent of New York in his influential *Commentaries on American Law* went so far as to argue that if a legislature exercised its charter prerogative of repeal to vacate a charter, the corporation's property reverted to the state, and neither the stockholders nor its creditors could claim a property in its assets. In actual practice, judges by 1860 had managed to establish as a principle of law that any "amending or repeal" of corporate charters which amounted to a "taking" of property must be done according to "due process" as overseen by the courts.[19]

American courts never defended property rights at the risk of depriving government of its necessary powers. Nowhere was this more clear than in Marshall's opinion in *Providence Bank v. Billings* (1830). Providence Bank sued Rhode Island for levying a tax on its property. Basing its argument on a previous decision of Marshall's in *New*

Jersey v. Wilson (1812), the bank argued that since its
1791 charter had not contained a specific statement giving
the state the right to tax its property and the state had
not taxed the bank prior to 1822, to tax it now would
violate an implied contract between the bank and the state
guaranteeing tax immunity to the bank's property. To tax
it without any explicit statement of right, declared the
bank's lawyers, amounted to an unconstitutional taking
of property.[20]

In an argument consistent with both natural and positive law traditions, Marshall denied the bank's situation
as analogous to *New Jersey v. Wilson* in which the plaintiff's land title contained a specific guarantee of tax immunity. "That the taxing power is of vital importance, that it
is essential to the existence of government, are truths
which it cannot be necessary to reaffirm," declared Marshall. "The power of legislation and consequently of taxation operated on all the persons and property belonging
to the body politic. However absolute the right of an individual may be," he explained, "it is still in the nature of
that right that it must bear a portion of the public burdens, and that portion must be determined by the legislature." In areas of taxation, said Marshall, individuals
must depend on the "wisdom and justice" of the legislature
not to impose "unjust and excessive taxation." Marshall
made clear that in disputes between public need and private interests the courts would interpret private rights
strictly and in the public's favor. With only occasional
exceptions Marshall's conception of the taxing power became standard in American law.[21]

The Marshall Court avoided defining the limits of eminent domain and police powers. The closest it came was
in *Barron v. Baltimore* (1833) when it ruled that the phrase
in the Fifth Amendment, "nor shall property be taken for
public use without just compensation," applied exclusively
to federal action and not state. Several of the original
state constitutions contained clauses similar to the Fifth

Amendment, but none specifically granted to states the power to condemn private property. Nonetheless, by 1820 every state court had accepted the common law principle that the power to govern implicitly included the power of eminent domain. In every state except South Carolina the courts insisted that natural law imposed on governments a moral obligation not to "take" private property except for "public use" and with "fair" and "just" compensation.[22]

No American in the first half of the nineteenth century devoted more time to the issue of public power versus private right than Chancellor James Kent of New York. Kent's views, expressed in his decisions and in his *Commentaries on American Law*, represent a classic natural rights statement of government's eminent domain and police powers versus the individual's right of private property. Kent accepted eminent domain as an inherent power of government, but he placed strict natural rights limits on its exercise. "The right of eminent, or inherent sovereign power," said Kent, "gives to the legislature the control of private property for public uses, and for public uses only." It could not be used to transfer the property of one person to another or to equalize wealth. Kent insisted that in the last resort the question of public use should be determined by the courts, not the legislature. In his most important eminent domain decision, *Gardiner v. Newburgh* (1816), Kent ruled that compensation was due, not only for property directly taken, but also for losses resulting from a public project no matter how indirect the "consequential damages." In this case New York had diverted a stream which destroyed the value of the plaintiff's property, even though the state had not directly acted upon his property. Kent ruled that the public's action had changed the nature of Gardiner's property and prevented him from pursuing his livelihood. Therefore, it must compensate him for the loss of his land's productive capacity. All costs, declared Kent, direct and indirect, for public enterprises must be distributed equally among all members of the society, and the unfortunate few whose property happened to be used or damaged should not be required to bear a disproportionate burden.[23]

Despite Kent's sensitivity to the rights of private property, he accepted the necessity of regulating private possessions in the general interest. "The government may," he wrote, "by general regulations, interdict such use of property as would create nuisances, and become dangerous to the lives, or health, or peace, or comfort of the citizens." "Every person ought to use his property as not to injure his neighbor," declared Kent, and "private interest must be made subservient to the general interest of the community." But he insisted that all regulation must fall under the traditional common law understanding of "police powers." Unless a certain property endangered the community's health, comfort, or moral well-being it was not subject to regulation under the police powers, and the burden of proof rested on the regulators, not the regulated. Regulation was to be the exception, not the rule.[24]

Pre–Civil War courts rejected many of Kent's restrictions on legislative power over property, however defined. For the most part, judges allowed legislatures to determine "public use" in eminent domain proceedings and ignored any consideration of "consequential damages." Likewise, judges interpreted police power broader than Kent and placed the burden of proof on the regulated instead of the regulator. Even so, American courts never entirely repudiated the idea that individuals possessed a natural and inalienable right to various types of property. Judges consistently refused to sanction any actual "taking" of property without "due process" as administered by the courts, and then insisted on compensation for losses.[25]

The courts' complex attitude toward property rights is well illustrated in the Supreme Court's 1837 *Charles River Bridge v. Warren Bridge* ruling. In 1785 the Massachusetts legislature had granted the Charles River Bridge Company a forty-year charter to build and operate a toll bridge across the Charles River to Boston. Later the legislature extended the charter to seventy years. In 1829, under popular pressure for a free bridge, the legislature chartered the Warren Bridge Company to build a second bridge adjacent to the first with the understanding that after six years the new bridge would become state property and toll free. The proprietors of the Charles River Bridge sued the Warren Bridge Company for destroying their property in the form of future profits which their monopoly privilege guaranteed through 1855.[26]

More than a single bridge monopoly was at stake. At the time railroads were rapidly supplanting toll roads and canals as the most efficient form of transportation. In many instances the route of the railroads ran parallel to the routes of canals and toll roads. If the courts recognized the older charter privileges of the canal and toll roads as an exclusive right of conveyance between the designated points, a community, before it could avail itself of the advantages of rapid transportation, would have to condemn the toll roads and canals and compensate the owners for their loss. In *Gardiner v. Newburgh* Kent had suggested just such a policy when he asserted that the public must assume full responsibility for public enterprises and pay for both direct and indirect damages. Such a broad definition of damages would have insured individual equity at the cost of greatly increasing the expense of adopting new forms of transportation. Many communities would not have been able to afford the costs and would have been deprived of all the advantages accruing from rail transportation.

Led by Roger Taney, appointed chief justice by Andrew Jackson, the Supreme Court ruled that the bridge company's charter did not give it an exclusive privilege to build and operate a bridge. In charter grants, ruled Taney, when the claims of private right conflict with public good "nothing passes by implication." Since the company's charter did not specifically grant an exclusive right, the court could not assume that the legislature intended exclusiveness. Taney pointed out that the company's franchise had not been revoked and its bridge remained intact. Only its claim for future income had been impaired. Inasmuch as no property had actually been taken or legal rights denied, the state of Massachusetts did not owe the bridge company compensation. "While the rights of private property are sacredly guarded," declared Taney, "we must not forget the community also have rights, and that the happiness and well-being of every citizen depends on their faithful preservation."[27]

Joseph Story disagreed with his new chief justice and dissented in favor of the bridge proprietors' claims. Story insisted that the right to private property included a public "pledge that the property will be safe; that the enjoyment will be coextensive with the grant; and that success will not be the signal of a general combination to overthrow its rights and to take away its profits." He argued that if public necessity required the destruction of the profitability of a property, the public must exercise its powers of eminent domain and grant the sufferer full monetary compensation for his loss. To do anything less would violate the owner's natural right to his property and be in conflict with "the fundamental principles of a free government."[28]

Taney and Story agreed on essentials—the sanctity of private property and the necessity of social progress—but they disagreed on priorities. Taney's reliance on a strict interpretation of the bridge company's charter allowed him to avoid the issue of damages. Since no right existed, there were no damages. Taney managed to destroy an unpopular monopoly without challenging its property rights. Story, on the other hand, like Kent, recognized that public progress frequently came at private expense, and he believed that natural justice dictated that private persons, even legislatively created persons, should be compensated for all losses caused by public actions. For the most part pre–Civil War courts accepted Taney's principle that monopolistic privileges must be interpreted narrowly and in the public interest. Still, Taney's pointed denial that his decision had destroyed property rights indicated that he, like Story, considered the vested privileges of corporations as sacred as the natural rights of individuals.

Finally, in 1848, the Supreme Court squarely faced the issue of eminent domain. In 1839 Vermont had authorized local governments to condemn any monopoly which they deemed inimical to the "public good." Consequently the West River Bridge Company had its charter revoked, but with compensation. In behalf of the company Daniel Webster argued that such action violated the "contract" clause of the Federal Constitution by impairing the company's charter contract. Justice Peter Daniel, speaking for the court, dismissed Webster's argument out of hand. Daniel, a man with a strong anticorporation bias, pointed out that Webster had made the remarkable assertion "that the right of property in a chartered corporation was more sacred and intangible than the same right could possibly be in the person of a citizen." Nonetheless, even as Daniel drew a distinction between corporate privilege and individual right, he recognized the claim of both to compensation when government found it necessary to take their property. Corporate privilege and individual right had become so intertwined by 1848 that even an anticorporation southern agrarian like Justice Daniel could only insist upon equality of status.[29]

Antebellum jurists accomplished two things in their interpretation of property rights. First, they managed to preserve in the context of rapid economic and technological change the natural rights assumptions of the early agrarian republic. Pre–Civil War judges seldom enunciated their natural law beliefs as frankly as Samuel Chase had in *Calder v. Bull* or Story in *Charles River Bridge*, but the commitment existed. Following Marshall's example, American jurists shied away from any direct confrontation between their natural law assumptions and legislative power. They preferred to protect property with the "contract" and "due process" clauses of the state and federal constitutions. Nonetheless, their interpretation of "due process" rested on natural law arguments. Likewise, judges' and legislators' acceptance of the principle of "fair" and "just" compensation in eminent domain proceedings indicated their implicit acceptance of individuals' natural right to property. Confronted with the demands of public need and the claims of private right, judges responded by interpreting narrowly the rights of private claimants. By avoiding any direct confrontation between property rights and social progress, they managed to reconcile, if imperfectly, these two frequently contending demands.

The antebellum courts' second achievement was its effort to break down the anticorporation bias so evident in the first decades of American independence. Judges' use of the "contract" clause to protect corporate property tended to merge the idea of legislative "good faith" with the idea of natural justice. Marshall refused to go as far as Story and Webster in their application of natural right sanctions to corporate stock and public franchises. Still, by defining contracts as "property" and linking the "contract" clause to public charters, Marshall contributed to the blending of the idea of legislative "good faith" with natural rights. Like Marshall, most judges prior to the Civil War continued to recognize the technical distinction between publicly derived privilege and natural right. But as a practical matter they extended the same sanctions to corporate stock and public franchises that they applied to freehold property. The pre–Civil War courts, state and federal, thus established a firm foundation for the postwar assimilation of public privilege to natural right, and at the same time legally prepared the way for the subsequent emergence in the United States of the private corporation as the most important form of private property.

PART III

THE COLLECTIVIST AGE

IN 1893 Frederick Jackson Turner argued that the end of the frontier spelled the end of an era in American life. Since the first settlement Americans had enjoyed the luxury of an almost unlimited supply of unoccupied land. Now, according to Turner, this had all ended. In respect to individual ownership of productive resources Turner was correct. Most Americans in the future could no longer expect to assume the status of an independent man of property. All the free land had been taken up and occupied. Men could not claim land as their own and still leave as much and as good for others. One man's ownership now necessarily denied another the opportunity to own.

Heretofore individual proprietors, preeminently farmers, controlled most of the nation's productive resources. No more; during the course of the nineteenth century the percentage of farmers in the total work force had declined steadily from almost 80 percent in 1820 to less than 43 percent in 1890. Outside agriculture the story was much the same. In 1889 corporations controlled 67 percent of the country's manufacturing enterprises, 75 percent of the railroads, 85 percent of the mining, and almost all banking, insurance, and public utilities. By 1930 corporations of widely divergent sizes owned an estimated 78 percent of the nation's business assets. Individual ownership or small partnerships had become the exception, not the rule. Thus as early as the beginning of the twentieth century for the majority of Americans farm ownership or ownership of any productive resource was becoming an elusive dream.[1]

Policy makers ultimately accepted the necessity, if not the desirability, of corporate ownership and control of production. Many believed that the worst attributes of large corporate enterprise could be mitigated by public regulation. After 1865 the federal Congress and various state legislatures enacted an unprecedented number of regulations covering a wide range of industrial and commercial activities. Particularly in the twentieth century expanded public supervision resulted in a rapid enlargement of governmental bureaucracy and an equally rapid narrowing of economic freedom as government regulated working conditions, quality of goods, maximum prices, and minimum wages. The gradually increased role of government eventually received general approval. Today it is orthodox. Nonetheless, the related development of large corporate enterprises and large bureaucratic governments touched off a prolonged debate over the precise meaning of property rights.

After 1865 three distinct definitions of property right developed. Neo-Jeffersonians remained loyal to older, individualistic conceptions of property which tied individual ownership to production. For neo-Jeffersonians property implied individual proprietorship in which the owner was also the laborer and manager. The defenders of capitalism or, as they preferred to call it, "free enterprise" viewed ownership of the means of production as a cooperative endeavor consisting of investors, managers, and laborers —each with a different "property right." Finally, the advocates of socialism or some form of welfare state accepted as justifiable property only certain personal goods and insisted that government control and manage production and commerce. None of the three groups repudiated entirely the notion of individual ownership. They all accepted for the near future individual control over strictly personal possessions. Their differences arose over whether productive resources fell under the rubric of legitimate "property rights" and whether the prerogatives of investors and managers should enjoy the same sanctions as worker-owner proprietorships.

CHAPTER 8

❖

Private Property and Free Enterprise: Stephen Field, William Graham Sumner, and Raymond Moley

American entrepreneurs have long been accustomed to a wide latitude of freedom. Since the eighteenth century Americans generally have viewed governmental power as potentially destructive to individual liberty. The right of the individual to use and enjoy all types of possessions free from governmental control and confiscation seemed an essential part of the idea of liberty. In the closing decades of the nineteenth century a number of persons came to view governmental economic intervention as a threat to personal liberty. They feared governmental regulation might destroy entirely individual enterprise and thereby stymie economic growth. Such persons frequently invoked the "inalienable right of property" to check what they considered unwise public policy. "Free enterprise" meant not simply an individual's right to pursue his chosen calling and to a full return on his labor, but also an investor's claim to a "reasonable return" and a corporate director's right to administer his investor's enterprise free from governmental hindrance.[1]

In the United States private enterprise and governmental power more often than not complemented one another. In the nineteenth century Americans used public power to foster enterprise as state and federal governments regularly granted private groups corporate privileges, tax exemptions, tariff protection, monopoly rights, favorable judicial decisions, and land.[2] One consequence of this policy was to blur the distinction between property rights and public power. At times it became difficult, if not impossible, to distinguish legitimate property rights from governmental privilege. For instance, a corporation's charter rights derived from legislative fiat, but its capital assets came from private investors. The meshing of public with private interest encouraged opportunistic individuals to seek out special governmental privileges and then demand that the courts in behalf of "free enterprise" recognize these claims as completely "private" property. In response to such practices several states in the 1870s and 1880s passed legislation designed to insure that private enterprises which affected the public interest also served the public interest. Legislatures drastically amended corporate charters, imposed confiscatory rate schedules on privately owned public utilities, and revoked franchises without compensation. Legislators defended their actions by claiming that since the property in question "affected the public interest" the sanctions of private property did not apply.[3]

This situation disturbed Stephen Field. Field viewed the confusion over property rights as an open invitation to corruption on one hand and legislative tyranny on the other.[4] As a justice of the United States Supreme Court, Field sought to establish clear distinctions between private property rights and governmental power. He hoped that his efforts would preserve free enterprise and private property without restricting the legitimate exercise of public power. Field based his definition of legitimate property rights on a "substantive" interpretation of the Fourteenth Amendment. Ratified in 1869, the Fourteenth Amendment stipulated that "no State shall make or enforce any law which shall abridge the privileges or immunities of citizens of the United States." The phrase had been taken directly from an 1823 Supreme Court decision, *Corfield v. Coryell*, in which the court had used the phrase "fundamental privileges and immunities" in a natural rights sense to mean citizens under any free government enjoyed the "right to acquire and possess property of every kind, and to pursue and obtain happiness and safety."[5] For this reason Field believed the drafters of the Fourteenth Amendment had intended to extend to all American citizens "substantive" rights vis-à-vis state governments and not simply procedural rights.

In 1873 the Supreme Court in the *Slaughter House Cases* first faced the issue of whether or not the Fourteenth Amendment placed natural rights limitations on state power. In 1869 the Louisiana legislature had granted to the Crescent City Livestock Landing Company a twenty-year monopoly for all butchering in and around New Orleans. The legislature had justified the monopoly as a health measure, although in fact it was a reward from the Republican-dominated legislature to some of its political friends. A number of excluded butchers sued on the basis that the monopoly violated their Fourteenth Amendment rights to pursue their "calling." The Supreme Court upheld the monopoly on the grounds that the monopoly was a legitimate exercise of the state's police powers. Field disagreed with the majority opinion. He pointed out that the "privileges or immunities" clause had derived from *Corfield v. Coryell* and therefore implied natural rights sanctions. Consequently, the Fourteenth Amendment prohibited states from abridging any citizen's "natural and inalienable" rights to life, liberty, and property. "The fundamental rights and privileges," wrote Field, "which belong to him as a free man and a free citizen, now belong to him as a citizen of the United States, and not dependent upon his citizenship of any state. There is no more sacred right of citizenship than the right to pursue unmolested a lawful employment in a lawful manner. It is nothing more or less than the sacred right of labor." No one, declared Field, can rightfully be denied entry into any ordinary profession or vocation, and no just government can exclude any citizen from any employment that is open to others of the same class, sex, or condition. He readily acknowledged that states could and should regulate any occupation that endangered the public health, good order, and general prosperity, but Field refused to condone the use of state police powers to grant special privileges to some and not to all.[6]

Field reaffirmed his natural rights interpretation of the Fourteenth Amendment in his dissent to the Supreme Court's decision in *Munn v. Illinois* (1877). In 1873 the Illinois legislature, in response to charges of monopolistic abuse, enacted rate schedules for Chicago grain elevators. The elevator operators sued the state on the grounds that such regulation deprived them of their property in the form of earnings without "due process." Chief Justice Morrison B. Waite in the majority opinion conceded that some regulation might be confiscatory and in violation of the Fourteenth Amendment, but he insisted that regulation of private enterprise in itself did not violate property rights. Any activity, Waite declared, such as the operation of grain elevators, which impinged on the public interest lost its private character. At that point private property became subject to public control. Because grain elevators affected the public interest, argued Waite, the legislature, not the courts, must determine whether such regulation was reasonable or if it violated "due process."[7]

Stephen Field disagreed. Field declared that for property to be "clothed in the public interest" it must have either been given to the public or have resulted from a public grant. The majority's definition of "public interest" destroyed any distinction between public and private property. Society, said Field, can and must regulate the use of private property so that it does not interfere with another person's enjoyment of property or endanger the community's well-being. But police powers should not be used to deprive a person of the use of his property any more than they should legitimatize special privilege. "If the constitutional guaranty extends no further than to prevent a deprivation of title and possession," asserted Field, "and allows deprivation of use, and the fruits of that use, it does not merit the encomium it has received." Since, according to Field, warehouses did not represent a nuisance, injure others, prevent anyone else from becoming a warehouseman, and had not been subsidized by public funds, they were not clothed with the public interest. If the legislature for reasons of public policy insisted on regulating the elevators, it should condemn the property and compensate the owners.

At first the Supreme Court denied Field's claim that "use" was an essential and constitutionally protected attribute of ownership. In a series of decisions in 1887 over the constitutionality of state legislation prohibiting the manufacture and sale of intoxicating beverages and oleomargarine, the Supreme Court, with Field in strong dissent, continued to define state police powers broadly. John Marshall Harlan, speaking for the court, denied that a prohibition to "use" property in the manufacture of intoxicating beverages qualified as "taking." The Fourteenth Amendment, said Harlan, did not destroy or limit the traditional police powers of the state over public health, safety, and morals. Since the state had only denied "use" and had not taken any property, the plaintiffs could not claim compensation. Any activity, Harlan argued, that threatened the public welfare could not justify compensation for damages that resulted from public regulation. The fact that a state allowed the brewing of intoxicants at the time the breweries were constructed in no way bound the state to allow the brewing of intoxicants in the future. A previous allowance or privilege, Harlan declared, did not constitute a vested right. In a similar decision, and on the same grounds, the Supreme Court also in 1887 disallowed the suit of a manufacturer of oleomargarine whose enterprise had been prohibited by the Pennylvania legislature.[8]

Field dissented vigorously to both decisions. In the Kansas decision he agreed with Harlan that the state had every right to regulate or prohibit the use of a property which it deemed socially harmful. Nevertheless, he insisted, the state was obligated to compensate owners for the existing inventory that had been acquired when brewing was legal. By not allowing owners to sell their inventories, even out of state, the legislature had violated good faith as expressed in the earlier license. Field saved his harshest criticism for the oleomargarine case. He pointed out that the Pennsylvania legislature had never proved oleomargarine to be "unhealthy." It had simply declared it "unhealthy" and then proceeded to outlaw its manufacture and sale. Field accused the Pennsylvania legislature of destroying a legitimate livelihood for no other reason than that it competed with dairying. He declared that the "right to pursue one's happiness is placed by the Declaration of Independence among the inalienable rights of men, with which all men are endowed, not by the grace of emperors or kings, or by force of legislation or constitutional enactments, but by their Creator: and to secure them, not to grant them, governments are instituted among men." Field argued that the action of the Pennsylvania legislature clearly fell under the provisions of the Fourteenth Amendment. "Under the guise of police regulations," he declared, "personal rights and private property cannot be arbitrarily invaded, and the determination of the legislature is not final and conclusive." Field hoped to halt the legislative practice of exercising power arbitrarily under the rubric of "police powers." He believed that police powers should only be used to regulate public morals and nuisances. Unless the courts limited legislatures' use of police power to its legitimate and intended purposes, argued Field, it placed all liberty and property at the sufferance of legislative majorities.[9]

Field based his substantive interpretation of the Fourteenth Amendment on his belief that a free government had an obligation to keep opportunity open for all of its citizens. To do this government should eliminate all special privileges and governmentally created monopolies not absolutely necessary for the public well-being. In 1884 in an opinion supporting a Louisiana statute which revoked the Crescent City Slaughter House's monopoly, Field clarified his idea of legitimate property rights as opposed to special privileges. He rejected the company's plea that a claim once vested could not be rightfully divested and declared that "special privilege" did not qualify as "property" under the Fourteenth Amendment. Field believed that the most important right an individual possessed was the right to a "calling" or, in his words, "the sacred right of labor." While Field argued that the right to pursue happiness transcended all other rights, particularly fatuous claims to special and unearned privilege, he limited the application of the "privileges or immunities" clause to the individual citizen's right to labor.[10]

At the same time that Field was expanding the meaning of "the privileges or immunities" clause he also extended its scope to include the "due process" clause and the rights of corporate investors. Antebellum courts had generally maintained that individual property rights were distinct from corporate privileges. While the rights of citizens derived from nature or constitutional guarantees, corporations were created by legislative enactment. In the *Dartmouth* decision the Supreme Court had tried to shield corporate property from arbitrary legislatures by defining corporate charters as "contracts." Legislatures circumvented the *Dartmouth* ruling by including in all corporate charters a "right to amend and annul" clause which the courts accepted as proper. As late as 1869 in *Paul v. Virginia* the Supreme Court reaffirmed the antebellum courts' interpretation of the contract clause. The case arose when Virginia passed several laws that discriminated against out-of-state insurance companies, making it difficult for them to compete with Virginia companies. One of these foreign companies asked the Supreme Court to overrule the Virginia statute as being in violation of the "privileges or immunities" clause of the newly enacted Fourteenth Amendment. Field, speaking for the court, denied that the phrase "privileges or immunities of citizens" applied to corporations. Unlike individuals, corporations could not claim immunity from discriminatory state action. "The corporation being the mere creation of local law," wrote Field, "can have no legal existence beyond the limits of sovereignty where created."[11]

In *Paul v. Virginia* Field appeared to deny corporate property holders any rights vis-à-vis a state legislature not specifically granted in its charter. It is possible that he had no such intention. Certainly his later decisions indicate his sympathy for investors' rights. *Paul v. Virginia* did not actually confront the issue of property rights. The Virginia legislature had only denied the corporation the right to conduct business in the state. The legislature had not destroyed or confiscated the corporation's assets. Field apparently viewed the Virginia legislature's action as a legitimate exercise of its police powers and entirely unrelated to Fourteenth Amendment property rights. Field did not address the issue of corporate property rights until the 1880s. When he did so, he chose to use the "due process" clause rather than the "privileges or immunities" clause. The significance of the shift was that while the drafters of the Fourteenth Amendment had chosen to use the word "citizen" in the "privileges or immunities" clause, in the "due process" clause they substituted the word "person."[12]

In 1882 Roscoe Conkling suggested to the Supreme Court the significance of the change. Conkling, a member of the Joint Committee of Congress which drafted the Fourteenth Amendment, told the court that the Joint Committee had intentionally substituted the word "persons" for "citizens" in order to include corporations under the protective shield of the Fourteenth Amendment. Conkling's revelations provided Field the constitutional justification he needed to protect investment property from state legislatures. In 1884 on circuit, in *Santa Clara County v. Southern*

Pacific Railroad, Field accepted Conkling's assertion and used it to strike down Santa Clara County's railroad taxes which discriminated against the Southern Pacific Railroad. Field did not deny that corporations as creatures of the law must operate within their charters and general incorporation statutes. But he argued that while reservation clauses might give to state legislatures the right to annul charters and regulate rates, such clauses did not give to states the right to confiscate corporate assets. Corporate property, which had not been created by the state, enjoyed all the sanctions of individual property. The state, Field pointed out, had only granted corporations their charters, not their tangible and visible assets. In the Santa Clara decision Field tied his substantive interpretation of the "privileges or immunities" clause to the "due process" clause. In 1886 the Supreme Court heard the *Santa Clara* case on appeal and accepted Field's opinion without comment or dissent.[13]

For the next fifty years the *Santa Clara* decision determined the courts' policy toward state regulation of corporate property. In a long series of decisions the Supreme Court held that while states could regulate corporate activities and in the case of public utilities and transportation even set rates, states could not regulate to the point of confiscation. Further, the final determination of "reasonable regulation" meant that stockholders were to be guaranteed a "fair return" on their investment as well as protected in their tangible assets. Anything less, argued the court, violated stockholders' rights to property and due process.[14]

The significance of Field's *Santa Clara* decision was not that his use of the Fourteenth Amendment protected otherwise helpless corporations from state regulation. He could have achieved this just as easily through the "commerce" clause. And, as Field acknowledged, the decision was not intended to limit states' exercise of their legitimate police powers. Field only denied to states the right to destroy the property of corporate investors. The significance of the decision lay in Field's association of the natural rights of a citizen to pursue a calling with an investor's claim to a "reasonable profit." This marked an important change in attitude toward investment property. Field was correct in pointing out that corporate stockholders were natural persons as much as freehold farmers. But he did not add or, probably, did not even think significant that investors, unlike freehold farmers, in many cases neither managed nor labored in the enterprises they owned. They invested their money and profited from other persons' labor and entrepreneurial skills. In the case of investment property "substantive due process" did not protect individuals in their "calling" or their "sacred right of labor."

Despite this important change in the use of "natural rights" Field's application of "substantive due process" to investment property grew out of a genuine concern for traditional liberties. While he recognized that governmental power might be necessary to protect disadvantaged social groups as well as to administer a complex national economy, Field believed that government could easily become an instrument of bureaucratic tyranny and unearned privilege. Historically, most Americans had based their arguments in favor of private property and personal liberty on natural rights assumptions. By the end of the nineteenth century such defenses ran counter to the dominant intellectual currents of scientific naturalism. But through Field's "substantive due process," American courts, in the name of private property and free enterprise, managed to withstand the tide as they successfully fulfilled older natural rights commitments by their use of the Fourteenth Amendment.

Stephen Field's genius was to take an older natural right conception of property and tie it to new, emerging forms of ownership. Even though Field considered himself a conservative, he was an instrument of change. He approved of the alterations in the American economy and sought to legitimatize them even while preserving traditional notions of liberty. William Graham Sumner, in contrast, pictured himself as a radical. Nothing delighted Sumner so much as to depict the absurdity of traditional beliefs or, as he liked to call them, "sentimentalities." No matter. Both men sought the same end. Like Field, Sumner hated with a passion individuals' manipulation of government to serve their private interests. Field called such practices "corruption"; Sumner labeled it "jobbery." Furthermore, both men believed that economic growth could only be sustained if society allowed its citizens maximum freedom to pursue their economic self-interest and protected its citizens in their earnings, savings, and investments. Both thought that worker-owner proprietorships had become inefficient and largely obsolete. Future economic development would depend on a division of labor, capital investment, and technological innovation. Finally, both men, while accepting the transformation of the American economy as necessary and desirable, hoped nonetheless to preserve individual liberty and private property.[15]

Sumner was born in 1840 in Paterson, New Jersey, attended Yale, and in 1872 received from Yale an appointment as professor of political and social science. Early in his career Sumner discovered in the writings of Herbert Spencer and Thomas Malthus what he took to be the two underlying laws of social development—(1) man's endless struggle to increase subsistence at a rate at least equal to population increases and (2) the survival of those who successfully did so. A committed rationalist, Sumner accepted a completely materialistic interpretation of human history and rejected all supranatural explanations or claims. Life, said Sumner, involves struggle, and it always will. Nature provides men the means of subsistence but in most situations, yields it only with extreme reluctance. In order to survive men must exploit to the fullest their energy and intelligence. Those unable or unwilling to do so perish.[16]

Sumner's theory of social progress was not based on biological determination through natural selection. Rather, he insisted that all social progress was a direct consequence of man's creative and willful energies—his productivity. Sumner recognized that while men were primarily self-serving, they also possessed a social sense and a rational mind. Faced with starvation, men were rarely content simply to fight it out among themselves. Instead, out of concern for themselves, their family, and their group, men as a rule searched for some remedy. Nature offered two possibilities—increased productivity or war. Seemingly war was the easiest solution, and a "solution," in Sumner's opinion, that societies adopted all too often. But he did not think war was a rational solution, and it clearly did not result in social progress since war did not increase the amount of subsistence. It only transferred, or frequently destroyed, what already existed. Very quickly the victorious society found its population exceeding the means of subsistence necessitating still another war. The only real solution, argued Sumner, was to increase production through more efficient use of labor and tools. By maximizing the returns from a successful struggle between man and nature, societies minimized the struggle between men. This led to a higher standard of living, a larger population, and a more stable and secure society. Sumner declared necessity the mother of invention and invention the mother of civilized society.

In order to survive Sumner believed that a society must constantly increase its productivity. Since there was rarely enough natural subsistence for every one and never enough for subsequent population increases, a society which expected to survive always had to be concerned with improving its productive capacity. Sumner considered economic growth a natural imperative, and he narrowed the factors of growth to hard work and self-denial. Through hard work men won from nature, not only subsistence, but a small surplus. If the individual denied himself im-

mediate gratification, he could apply his surplus to the
acquisition of technology (industrial skills and tools).
Technology made possible larger surpluses which in turn
could be used to improve technology. Sumner's formula
of economic growth and social progress was simple. Necessity forced men to labor and self-interest drove some
to save. In time the most intelligent members of society
accumulated great wealth which in the expectation of
profits they invested in improved technology.

Sumner believed that government should restrict itself
to protecting the honor of women and private property.
Any effort to interfere with the natural course of social
evolution only obstructed and delayed economic development and thereby increased human misery. Perhaps, in the
future, men would acquire the scientific knowledge to improve upon nature's evolutionary struggle for survival.
But at this time, Sumner argued, men knew so little that
their efforts to ameliorate human suffering by political
means almost always resulted in more harm than good.
Men should concentrate all of their creative energies on
what they knew best—how to organize labor and develop
new technology. For the time being governments could
best serve mankind if they limited themselves to the maintenance of civil order and the protection of laborers in
their wages and capitalists in their savings.

After an extensive study of a great variety of societies,
Sumner concluded that the most successful societies were
those which allowed liberty and therefore protected property. He defined liberty as "the security given to each man
that, if he employs his energies to sustain the struggle on
behalf of himself and those he cares for, he shall dispose
of the product as he chooses."[17] The greatest injustice
Sumner could imagine was for a society to force a person
to share his honest earnings and profits with someone else.
The essential forms of charity should be voluntary. He
thought it only right that those who had good health and
yet failed to labor industriously, or who indulged them-

selves beyond their means, be allowed to suffer for their own choices. No one should be penalized for another's sins. When government took from the industrious and gave to the profligate it destroyed the individual's most important liberty—his right to earn or inherit property. Furthermore, any policy designed to equalize wealth flew directly in the face of the necessities of the human condition. "Let it be understood," declared Sumner, "that we cannot go outside of this alternative: Liberty, inequality, survival of the fittest; not-liberty, equality, survival of the unfittest. The former carries society forward and favors all its best members; the latter carries society downward and favors all its worst members."[18]

Sumner included under the label "property" anything which an individual acquired through his own labor and self-denial. This included a laborer's wages, a farmer's land as well as a banker's money, a landlord's tenement, and an heir's legacy. Each represented labor or self-denial and the protection of each encouraged further labor and self-denial. Sumner considered all efforts to guarantee equal opportunity as sentimentally attractive, but unrealistic. He pointed out that men were unequal at birth, they were nurtured by parents of unequal abilities, and they faced unequal circumstances. Real equality seemed absurd and contrary to nature. To Sumner it seemed only proper that unequal men should be unequal in possessions.

Sumner was less concerned with the distribution of existing wealth than society's potential for producing more wealth in the future. He believed that if society denied its citizens the opportunity to accumulate wealth, to use it as they saw fit, and to pass it on to those they had affection for, there would be little incentive to save or labor. And, Sumner added, while the son of a rich man enjoyed great wealth without having to work or save, if he spent his wealth foolishly, his own children would inherit nothing. Even though all laborers could not be expected to save enough to become capitalists, many would. Their chances were not as good as those of the children of rich men. Nonetheless, even a laborer's sometimes futile effort to become a capitalist worked to the good of society as he worked harder than he might have otherwise. And even those individuals, who struggled and failed to save, at least usually enjoyed relatively high levels of consumption for their efforts.

Sumner suggested that the intensity of a society's struggle to gain subsistence from nature was relative. If only a few persons occupied a large amount of land, life could be leisurely and there would still be enough for all. Under these circumstances men struggled almost exclusively with nature. An abundance of land made it possible for a society to allow its citizens great personal leisure. Relative equality also characterized a society with an abundance of land. Few persons were willing to work for another, which made the accumulation of wealth difficult. But with easy subsistence, men had no incentive to innovate. Social progress came slowly or not at all. Due to population increases, a high land to man ratio never lasted long, and thereby the exception proved the rule. A normal scarcity intensified struggle, particularly among men. There might not be enough for everyone. The fittest ate and propagated, while the unfit starved and died. For anyone to survive, a populous society had to organize itself in the most efficient manner. This meant less equality and more industrial discipline. But it could result in a rising standard of living and social progress. According to Sumner, areas of dense population had been the cradles of civilization, while areas of low density had been centers of equality and stagnation.

The United States, said Sumner, because of its vast amount of land, comparatively few people, and an absence of strong neighbors had heretofore been spared much of this struggle. No more. The American population had begun to outstrip the available means of subsistence. Now for the first time the United States was forced to face problems the remainder of the world had long taken for granted. If Americans failed to face reality and respond intelligently to the changed circumstances, they would starve and their social bonds dissolve. A superior society, which behaved consistently with the hard, unalterable facts of social evolution, would destroy and replace the United States. Necessarily, predicted Sumner, equality and independence would have to give way to inequality and cooperation. Still, the United States enjoyed one great advantage over most other societies—its historical commitment to individual liberty. The American people possessed a tradition of economic freedom, a profound respect for private property as well as a long standing animosity towards governmental intervention. If the United States continued to honor these traditions, Sumner believed it could anticipate a prosperous future.

Thus Sumner was by no means a pessimist. He viewed the growing concentration of wealth and economic power in the United States as a sign of progress. Economic growth depended on accumulated capital as much as on disciplined labor. Wealth made possible the acquisition of complex technology and encouraged extensive economic integration and division of labor. Sumner saw a direct and unavoidable correlation between economic stratification and productivity. The more developed and prosperous the civilization, argued Sumner, the more concentrated its wealth and the greater the economic distance between men. There was no other way. A prosperous industrial society almost by definition exhibited clear distinctions of income. Those who provided capital or managerial expertise received the largest rewards. Those who contributed only unskilled labor received the least. Those who offered nothing received nothing. Nonetheless, Sumner pointed out, the difference between rich and poor was only relative. The great wealth of the few made possible the comfort and economic security of the many. For the wealthier the society, the higher its wage scales. "Every successful effort to widen the power of man over nature," Sumner declared, "is a real victory over poverty, vice, and misery" as rich and poor alike benefit from economic growth.[19]

From the 1870s until his death in 1910 William Graham Sumner tirelessly lectured Americans on what he considered the necessities of social evolution. He eschewed all appeals to sentiment and showed contempt for anyone who rejected the hard facts of reality simply because they found them too harsh. Men must accept reality as it existed and cope with it as best they could. To pretend life was benign only compounded men's already difficult struggle for existence. Sumner recognized that the leisure and wealth that made civilization valuable depended on sustained economic growth, if more than a small, privileged handful were to share the pleasures of civilized society. He believed that in the United States this growth would occur naturally as long as men did not intrude government into economic affairs. Regardless of the motives, Sumner thought governmental intervention inevitably transferred the honest earnings of producers to nonproducers. By taking from the "haves" and giving to the "have nots," government exacerbated social strife, discouraged enterprise, and denied to society's most productive members the fruit of their labor. Thus Sumner opposed governmental regulation of factory laborers' wages, hours, and working conditions. He described all political efforts to ameliorate the lot of laborers paternalistic. It demeaned laborers as well as prevented them from selling their labor freely. Labor legislation reduced the most hard-working and self-denying laborer to the level of the laziest and most self-indulgent. While Sumner endorsed factory legislation which protected women and children, he did so only because he thought that physical weakness made women and children incapable of competition with men. He saw no social advantage in the destruction of women and children. Nonetheless, Sumner insisted that every able-bodied man, rich and poor alike, make his own way on his own labor and talent without any special privilege or assist-

ance. If American society required all men to compete for
their living and protected them in their earnings, Sumner
argued, it would enjoy sustained economic growth and its
citizens happiness and security.

Sumner's arguments were far too frank and unflattering
to become widely accepted and repeated. His rejection of
orthodox Christianity, of much natural rights rhetoric, and
imperialism made his views on the whole an anathema to
American public leaders. Sumner also applied his canon of
laissez faire equally to capitalists and laborers. He considered tariff legislation, railroad subsidies, or any other publicly derived privilege as noxious to economic growth as
price and wage laws. Still, no American offered a more
sophisticated and convincing argument against governmental economic intervention than Sumner. Consequently,
as governmental controls increased in the last decades of
the nineteenth century some Americans turned, almost always selectively, to the arguments of Sumner and Field
to defend a free market economy. And for a short time, a
few of their ideas toward government and private property
became embodied in American law.[20]

During the depression of the 1930s the United States
Supreme Court abandoned "substantive due process" as a
defense of certain property rights, particularly for large
corporations. The change was a direct consequence of the
departure from the court of several faithful defenders of
laissez faire, and Franklin Roosevelt's appointment of several equally faithful defenders of the welfare state. By the
mid-1930s the ideas of William Sumner and Stephen Field,
as a matter of public policy, were in eclipse. Still, a few
Americans continued to use their arguments to criticize
the welfare state as it developed after the 1930s. Ironically,
one of the most consistent critics of the New Deal and its
various Democratic successors was one of Roosevelt's early
advisers, Raymond Moley. Moley found in Sumner's writings the basis for his defense of free enterprise. Moley's
arguments, many of which are still currently in use, indi-

cated not only the lasting appeal of Sumner, but also the impact the events of the twentieth century imposed even on an archdefender of free enterprise.[21]

Although initially infatuated by Roosevelt, Moley found himself deeply disturbed by the implications of many New Deal policies. After he left the administration, he insisted that Roosevelt had abandoned the true tenets of "progressivism" and adopted "statist" policies. Moley described "statism" as a political philosophy that advocated ever-expanding governmental intervention into economic, social, and personal activities. In contrast Moley considered himself a "progressive," which he defined as a person who accepted the necessity of some governmental regulations. Even so, a true progressive, according to Moley, retained a commitment to a free, competitive marketplace where supply and demand, not government, determined prices, wages, and production. Moley accepted as necessary labor unions, factory legislation, and public regulatory bodies. Without limited governmental control, enormous abuses and injustices might develop and lead to social chaos. As long as government restricted itself to obvious problems, Moley asserted, it posed no immediate threat to free enterprise or private property. But once policy makers began to view governmental intervention as a good in itself, rather than a necessary evil, it became dangerous and "statist" in character.[22]

Above all else Moley feared the tyranny of centralized government. He believed that bureaucratic control of the economy discouraged innovation and thereby limited productivity. Instead of responding to the rational criteria of supply and demand, governmental agents tended to impose on production their own, frequently arbitrary, values. Productivity became a secondary concern to such other ends as equality and personal security. Rather than devote their energies to increased output, businessmen found themselves compelled to cope with a plethora of governmental regulations. Moley wanted government to leave businessmen free to manage their enterprises subject to the minimal regulation of government and the marketplace. Granted this freedom, Moley contended that businessmen could provide to all Americans an abundant and secure life.

Moley offered several policies, which if followed, he thought would curb the worst abuses of a free market economy without inhibiting productivity. First, government should avoid, if possible, ownership and management of any economic enterprise. Secondly, government should impose regulations only when necessity dictated and, whenever possible, reduce or eliminate existing regulations. Additionally, legislators should levy taxes for revenue purposes only and not use taxation as an instrument of economic policy. Tax schemes designed to redistribute wealth or subsidize particular groups discouraged enterprise and disrupted the effective working of the marketplace. Finally, Moley wanted Americans to honor the constitutional division between state and federal government. Whenever possible, states should assume responsibility. Moley felt that the diversity among the states made innovation more likely even as the decentralization of governmental power checked the growth of a potentially tyrannical federal government.

Moley addressed his program to what he called the "middle interests" or "forgotten men" in American society. He argued that the vast "middle interests" held a stake in the preservation of private property and free enterprise. The United States was a classless society, said Moley, "in which one man is as good as another, that given the appropriate and due opportunity one person can achieve as much as another, and that self-reliance is the key to success."[23] He insisted that the maintenance of a free market economy was the only means to preserve Americans' property and opportunity. Like Sumner, Moley did not mean that everyone should share or share equally in the ownership and management of productive resources. He accepted wholeheartedly the collectivization of the American economy and considered large, privately owned and managed corporations necessary for maximum efficiency. Rather, Moley used the term "free enterprise" to mean the freedom of managers to control their businesses free from governmental interference. He equated detailed governmental control over management with inefficiency, socialism, and tyranny.

For most Americans, Moley envisioned enough "spending units" to guarantee a comfortable life, a home, and security. When he described the majority of Americans as "property owners," he meant that most Americans received high enough wages to assure themselves a comfortable share of the nation's production. Further, Americans were free to use their wages in any manner compatible with the public good. Even though most were precluded from managerial responsibilities, Moley suggested that American consumers actually dictated business policy through their spending habits. He asked Americans to exercise their power as consumers rather than as voters. In this way business managers could react directly to the whims of consumers rather than the dictates of bureaucrats. Voting with one's pocketbook also had the added virtue of granting to those who worked the hardest (i.e., those with the highest income) a proportionately greater impact on economic policy. While democratic government had to respond to all voters regardless of their social contribution, the free enterprise system listened only to productive members of society.[24]

Moley's acceptance of the necessity of even minimal governmental intervention placed him at odds with Sumner's far more radical theory. Moley rejected Sumner's merciless struggle for survival and offered Americans a much more benign prospect. Nonetheless, Moley shared with Sumner a commitment to unregulated enterprise, mass production, and economic growth. They each believed that production could be most efficiently managed by managerial experts free from governmental control. Furthermore, while each claimed to be the standard-bearer of economic liberty, they offered to most Americans the freedom to choose only their employer, negotiate for wages, and consume as they saw fit. Neither man believed it likely in such a system for a majority to exercise entrepreneurial liberty. Nor did they think it desirable. To them the control of production by worker-owners hearkened back to an earlier and simpler age.

On the surface Sumner, Field, Moley, and other supporters of laissez faire appear to have been prophets of a lost cause. American society has opted for governmental intervention as well as an elaborate welfare system that subsidizes everything from airplane manufacturers to dependent children. But in a more fundamental sense Sumner's vision has proven remarkably farsighted. Americans have seemingly learned to value the right to consume over the right to manage productive property; they consistently support economic growth; and they have accepted with only sentimental protest their virtual loss of entrepreneurial opportunity. Despite the increase in governmental regulation during the twentieth century, managers of private corporations still enjoy extensive leeway in their control of the nation's production. Only in agriculture, retailing, and service industries does opportunity remain open for other than a very few individual entrepreneurs. All the doomsday rhetoric aside, Americans for the most part accept the highly centralized and restrictive management of our most productive resources and tools as legitimate examples of "free enterprise."

✦

CHAPTER 9

New Individualism:
Four American Collectivists

Not all Americans viewed increased governmental control over production as inimical to individual liberty. In fact, a number of Americans, who loosely considered themselves "collectivists," viewed private ownership of production as destructive to "real" liberty, which they often defined anew as freedom from want and insecurity. They despaired of the virtual absence of economic regulation in the United States and wanted to move from an individualistic society based on private ownership of production to a cooperative commonwealth resting on communal ownership.[1]

Four men, Edward Bellamy, Thorstein Veblen, Herbert Croly, and John Dewey, exemplified the diversity as well as the consensus among American collectivists. Each viewed Americans' reverence for certain forms of property rights as a primary cause of much of the nation's social problems. They believed that economic autonomy encouraged individuals to place their personal well-being before the well-being of society, frequently to the point of destroying all communal sentiment. As a result, they argued, selfishness and profit-seeking characterized American society instead of sociableness and benevolence. Society lost its cohesion as each person tended to look to himself even as he ignored the needs of others and society as a whole. For collectivists individual control over production and unregulated enterprise necessarily led to exploitive and acquisitive behavior. Bellamy, Veblen, Croly, and

Dewey agreed that only by eliminating or radically cur-
tailing traditional property rights could the United States
expect to establish a better society.

These four American collectivists were a mixed lot.
Bellamy, for instance, was unapologetically utopian, and
Veblen was just as unapologetically cynical. Croly's elitism
at times bordered on fascism, while Dewey throughout his
entire life sought to increase popular participation in policy making. Even so, they shared certain common assumptions. First of all, none was a doctrinaire Marxist. They
unanimously eschewed class conflict and supported constitutional politics. In many ways they resembled the early
followers of Robert Owen and Charles Fourier, for, except-
ing Veblen, they spoke in terms of industrial cooperation
rather than social conflict. Secondly, they each considered
economic collectivization and mass production as progressive forces which made possible the elimination of scarcity. For this reason Bellamy, Veblen, Croly, and Dewey
all agreed that private ownership and control of productive resources and tools were at best necessary and temporary evils. They thought that without public control and
planning the enormous potential of modern industry
would be wasted in chaotic and meaningless activities or
would be aggrandized by individuals. Related to their infatuation with mass production and technology was their
common aversion to individualism, which they considered
as both anachronistic and an impediment to further social
progress. Finally, again with the exception of Veblen, each
of them deemphasized or entirely ignored a labor theory
of value. Instead, they preferred to speak of social equality and personal rights without regard to individual contribution. They expected technology to replace labor, benevolence to supplant self-interest, and cooperation to
supersede individualism.

In 1888 Edward Bellamy published *Looking Backward*,
one of the most popular and influential books ever written
by an American. *Looking Backward* became an immediate

best seller. During the first two years it sold over 160,000 copies and continued to be widely read through the 1920s. There is no doubt Bellamy articulated the anxieties and hopes of large numbers of Americans. *Looking Backward* transformed Bellamy from an obscure free-lance writer and reformer into an enduring prophet of American collectivism. *Equality* (1896), the sequel to *Looking Backward*, was inferior in quality and was never as widely read. But in *Equality* Bellamy made more explicit his own views and developed more thoroughly his ideas on property and liberty. Together, the two books established a social model for subsequent American collectivists.[2]

Bellamy began his fictional story in Boston in 1887. In that year Julian West, the protagonist, became trapped while asleep in his airtight basement where he remained unconscious until the year 2000, when workmen uncovered him. West found Boston marvelously transformed. Poverty, unemployment, inequality, and violence had all disappeared, and every citizen enjoyed a life free from want and drudgery. Men worked, but for short hours in pleasant working conditions and primarily as overseers of machines. West learned to adjust to the changed circumstances and value the Boston of 2000. He came to believe that a collectivized and planned economy was a logical outgrowth of capitalism and consistent with social evolution.

Bellamy used *Looking Backward* to criticize late-nineteenth-century capitalism. In it he pictured the 1887 Julian West as a nonproductive ne'er-do-well who lived off the earnings of the corporate stock his grandfather had bequeathed him. Bellamy described dividends as taxes in perpetuity levied by stockholders on laborers. Without ever having performed an honest day's labor Julian West had lived in leisure his entire life, and inheritance laws made it possible for him to extend to his own son the same unearned privilege. Still, Bellamy made clear that he considered capital accumulation necessary to finance large-scale industry. It underwrote the costs of increased industrial efficiency which led to an increased standard of living. Bellamy entertained no romantic illusions about a precapitalist past. "The restoration of the old system with the subdivisions of capital," he wrote, "might indeed bring back a greater equality of conditions with more dignity and freedom, but it would be at the price of general poverty and the arrest of material progress."[3] Corporate stockholding, which might at first glance appear to epitomize economic injustice, actually represented a forward step in social evolution. Corporations undercut small, independent producers and consolidated economic enterprise. Bellamy foresaw economic consolidation continuing unabated until a single corporate syndicate or "trust" controlled all of the nation's industrial enterprise. At that point he believed government would step in and assume control of the "Great Trust" and divide industrial profits equally among the population. In this way everyone would become an equal stockholder in the national industrial trust, just as previously everyone had been an equal citizen in the national government.

Bellamy's ideal society allowed no private ownership of productive resources. He considered such property inconsistent with justice. Individuals, he declared, did not create wealth. Rather, wealth resulted from the collective efforts of the entire community—past and present. Consequently, all moral claims to productive resources accrued to society, not individuals. An individual working in isolation, wrote Bellamy, "would be fortunate if he could at the utmost produce enough to keep himself alive." Therefore, he asserted, "society can be the only heir to the social inheritance of intellect and discovery, and it is society collectively which furnishes the continuous daily concourse by which alone the inheritance is made effective."[4] Furthermore, the quantity of productive resources in a community was limited. Since one man's ownership of production denied another man the means to secure subsistence, private ownership of production violated the most fundamental of all rights—the right of life. Accordingly, the state was morally obligated to prevent individuals from possessing productive resources. Only through government ownership could the subsistence of present and future generations be secured and everyone be guaranteed their rightful share of society's production.

Bellamy saw no conflict between individual liberty and governmental ownership of production. He contended that, while capitalism offered everyone a wide range of theoretical liberties, in actuality most men lacked any significant freedom. Out of physical need and fear of starvation the vast majority of persons were forced to labor for long hours at tasks they did not like and for wages barely sufficient to sustain life. Only when society guaranteed all its citizens both a job and subsistence were meaningful choices possible. Economic security enabled a laborer to choose where to work, and if he offended his employer, he always had the option to leave his job and take up a new one without having to fear he and his family would starve.

While Bellamy's utopia precluded private ownership of productive resources, he warmly endorsed private ownership of personal property as well as the right of individuals to determine how to spend their income. He insisted that nationalization of production in no way threatened "legitimate" property rights. On the contrary, through nationalization government redeemed the property rights of the entire community by dispossessing those stockholders who unjustly claimed community property as their own. Bellamy reasoned that government acknowledged and enforced its citizens' property rights by giving to each person an equal share of production. In Bellamy's Boston of 2000 each individual received from government a credit card equal to one share of the gross national product. Each person's portion was equal regardless of their job, skill, or education; and each person was free to purchase from governmental stores whatever he desired. Individuals could even trade among themselves and accumulate as much personal property as they wished. Bellamy not only thought that government should recognize and protect such personal property rights, but it should also allow individuals to bequeath their personal possessions as they saw fit.

Despite his assertion that nationalization guaranteed to everyone their property rights, Bellamy did not mean each person would therefore be allowed to share in the management of production. Like Sumner, Bellamy did not think all men were capable of managerial responsibilities. For him, property rights only included a person's share of industrial production. Managerial decisions remained the exclusive prerogative of industrial executives. He suggested that production managers as well as political leaders be selected by elder, retired members of the community. These leaders would then determine how everyone else would labor. Bellamy's description of his utopian society as an "industrial army" accurately expressed its hierarchal structure. Managers gave the orders and workers obeyed. Bellamy expected everyone to work for the general welfare, and he assumed leaders would not abuse their power. As in an army each person understood his dependence on others as well as his social obligations. Each person labored conscientiously. The reward for such cooperative behavior, prophesied Bellamy, would be unprecedented wealth, personal security for all, and a society free from strife.

Bellamy affirmed a sanguine view of mankind. He assumed man was malleable and men could be made into cooperative and benevolent creatures. He blamed private ownership of productive resources for the inequitable distribution of wealth and mankind's avaricious and selfish habits. In a technologically backward society restraints and coercion might have been necessary to force men to labor at unpleasant tasks and for low wages. But now machines made it possible for society to provide for all its citizens a decent income without the restraints and coercions previously necessary. Even so, Bellamy maintained a realistic estimate of varying capabilities, and implicitly accepted the innate differences among men. While some were capable of exercising leadership, others had to be relegated to the lower ranks of his industrial army.

Bellamy valued individual choice and in his utopia he provided individuals the opportunity to choose their employment and to use their credit cards as they desired. At the same time he did not give individuals the option to choose to work or not to work, to set their own hours, or to manage their own labor. If workers exercised managerial freedom, they might jeopardize productivity and slow down social evolution. Instead, Bellamy expected industrial leaders to determine hours, tasks, and production goals. Bellamy's frequent allusion to military organization revealed the latent, if very compassionate, coercion on which his utopia rested. Order had to be maintained; men must be told what to do; and laggards were to be literally limited to a diet of "bread and water." Bellamy did not consider this coercive, because he believed that all rational and well-intentioned men would agree with his idea of a good society. He presumed that a consensus over social ends could be reached, and thus the coercion implicit in his utopia would always remain dormant. Furthermore, his belief that such a system was a consequence of the inevitable and inexorable forces of social evolution made the coercive aspects of his system appear as an imposition on society rather than an instrument of society. Human choice and responsibility were not involved but rather the laws of nature. Firm in the rightness of his ideas, Bellamy seemed willing to impose his utopia on all men or he was at least heartened by the prospect of its inevitability.

Thorstein Veblen stood in stark contrast to the idealism of Edward Bellamy. Almost a cynic, Veblen considered himself a tough-minded social scientist who, although he wanted a better society, did not really think such an expectation realistic. Born in Manitowoc, Wisconsin, in 1857 and educated at Carleton, John Hopkins, Yale, and Cornell, Veblen spent his entire life as an interested but uninvolved outsider. He disliked the American economy and Americans' obsession with consumption, but for the most part he remained aloof, seemingly content to analyze critically social behavior. Veblen accepted the idea of progress or its possibility and the desirability of mass production. Still, his unflattering appraisal of human character provided him little reason to believe that a more personally fulfilling and just society was likely.[5]

Without discounting the importance of economic factors, Veblen argued that man's need to obtain self-respect was central to understanding human behavior. And, as a rule, a person's estimate of himself depended on how he believed other people assessed him. People tended to look outward for psychic reinforcement. Since most persons in our society judged others according to their relative wealth, said Veblen, the richer the person the higher his public esteem and therefore the greater his self-respect. It was not so much a person's possession of wealth as the public's knowledge of his wealth. For this reason conspicuous display and consumption became the most effective means of acquiring the social standing necessary for self-esteem. Veblen claimed that this imperative to acquire and publicly consume was the prime motivating factor in a modern industrial society.[6]

Nonetheless, Veblen believed that self-respect could also be secured through productive and skillful labor. If a person produced something of value and he did so with skill, he could not help but feel worthy. Veblen described this feeling as the "instinct of craftsmanship." But he thought that craftsmanship was now rare and that, while almost all men labored, only a few were true craftsmen. Instead, most men labored for money or profit, not for the intrinsic rewards gained through skillful work. In fact, conspicuous consumption threatened to destroy craftsmanship altogether. Money could best be acquired by fraud, chicanery, and theft, but artistic excellence could only be secured by disciplined, conscientious, and arduous labor. Faced with such an option, most men chose to make money because it was easier and socially more rewarding. Concerned only with making money and social prestige, men lost all pride in their work and produced sloppy and inferior products. Veblen personally had great respect for workmanship and wished that most men would seek self-respect through artistic excellence, but he feared that conspicuous consumption would ultimately destroy all pride in workmanship, the only honorable means to self-respect.[7]

Veblen tied these ideas to his theories of social evolution and private property. In primitive or precivilized societies, he argued, men lacked the skills to extract a surplus from nature, and without a surplus differences between individuals were insignificant. All persons owned and consumed roughly the same things and in roughly similar qualities and quantities. Only physical prowess and beauty distinguished one person from another. In primitive society both skillful craftsmanship and conspicuous consumption were absent. But in time, men acquired the skills to manipulate nature and produce a surplus. As society accumulated material wealth through agriculture and manufacturing, social differentiation became possible, if not inevitable. Because property was easy to measure, it soon became even more prestigious than either beauty or prowess. Wealth became the measurement of human worth.

In an industrial society, Veblen reasoned, men had two ways to acquire wealth—through labor or through stealing from those who labored. More often than not, the physically strong seized the surplus which laborers produced. Thus most wealth originated in theft. As society progressed, open violence and overt theft threatened to disrupt productivity entirely. Furthermore, the predatory property holding class did not want to lose their property to some ruthless and powerful upstart. Therefore, property holders conspired to establish laws to justify and protect their ill-gotten wealth. The predatory rich succeeded in perpetuating their income and social position, not so much by protecting their personal possessions and money, but through their control over productive resources and tools. By claiming a "property right" to production, the predatory class was able either to charge producers rent for the use of "their property" or to force laborers to accept employment for low wages. Veblen believed that property rights to production were the primary means by which nonproducers enslaved the productive members of society.[8]

In Veblen's opinion, contemporary property rights were nothing more than regularized stealing. He ridiculed a caricatured version of natural rights claims to property as an ingenious effort by nonproducers to justify their exploitation of producers. He insisted that productive resources were a gift of nature to which no person could rightfully claim exclusive title. The only claim which had any semblance of right was that of a worker-owner, whose labor and productivity justified his claim. But once workmanship and ownership became separated all claims to ownership of productive resources lost their legitimacy. When an owner hired another to labor for him, exploitation began and rightful property ended. Profits, rather than workmanship, became the primary concern. Except for a few farmers and shopkeepers, Veblen believed that most ownership of productive resources in the United States had passed from workmen to absentee owners or stockholders. He contended that as long as society continued to allow nonproducers to control productive resources, it not only legalized exploitation, but it also encouraged conspicuous consumption which discouraged workmanship. In time such a process would destroy the very skills and work habits on which an industrial society depended.

Because of his cynicism, Veblen rarely offered any remedies for what he considered the gross injustice of capitalism. Unlike Marx, Veblen did not think workers would ever become alienated from their masters. The poorest class of workers would be too busy just trying to stay alive, and the more fortunate layers of society would devote all their energy toward the emulation of the next higher layers. For a person to identify with his own peers or class was an open admission of low status and made it impossible for him to pass as his better. Class consciousness undercut self-respect or, more properly, self-delusion. Consequently, only a true craftsman had the psychic self-confidence to scorn his betters. This was the source of Veblen's one small glimmer of hope. He entertained the outside chance that the engineers as a class might revolt. Engineers were occupationally committed to production and efficiency rather than to waste and display. More than any other modern occupational group they continued to honor the "instinct of craftsmanship." Moreover, they occupied a strategically essential position in an industrial society. This gave to engineers the means and the opportunity to organize a revolt against the predatory owners of production. Hopefully, once in control engineers' commitment to workmanship would compel them to impose on society an ethos of craftsmanship. Social prestige and self-respect would then be dependent exclusively on artistic excellence and productivity. In the final analysis Veblen's pessimism overshadowed his hopes. He could not bring himself to believe that engineers could resist the emoluments and flattery of owners or the almost universal human tendency to emulate one's superiors.[9]

Neither Bellamy nor Veblen gave serious consideration to the practical problems of implementing their ideas. Bellamy fixed his vision on the distant horizon, and Veblen barely bothered to hope. Herbert Croly and John Dewey, on the other hand, were less visionary than Bellamy and more hopeful than Veblen. Dewey and Croly agreed that a more just and personally fulfilling society required a radical new attitude toward the individual and certain forms of private property, and each gave serious consideration to the practical implementation of their ideas. But the two men disagreed over the role of the individual in economic and political decision making.

Born in New York City in 1869, Herbert Croly studied off and on at Harvard under Josiah Royce, William James, and George Santayana. A reformer and editor, Croly apparently influenced both Theodore Roosevelt and Woodrow Wilson. Roosevelt read approvingly Croly's important book, *The Promise of American Life* (1909), and adopted Croly's term "new nationalism" as the theme for his 1912 presidential campaign. In 1914 Croly founded the *New Republic*, which he coedited until his death in 1930. An active and forceful person attuned to the intellectual currents of his time, Croly in *The Promise of American Life* provided an early blueprint for a collectivized economy.

Croly feared that traditional American attitudes toward the individual and private property were inappropriate for a heavily industrialized and predominately urban society. He believed that individual property rights impeded industrial integration as well as political centralization thereby making impossible a truly "national consciousness." In response Croly advocated a radical, if gradual, transformation of American values away from individual liberty toward a more public-spirited and associated life which he called "new nationalism." He conceived of the nation as "an enlarged individual whose special purpose is that of human amelioration, and in whose life every individual should find some particular but essential function."[10] Americans' commitment to the concepts of individualism, equal rights, and private property threatened to pull society apart. Such ideas discouraged the adoption of policies Croly considered necessary to the national welfare. He suggested that Americans' almost religious loyalty to personal liberty had originated at a time when the United States was a republic of freehold farmers and independent artisans. He granted that in a society in which most men owned their own land or shops private ownership of production and individual liberty offered no serious threat to society. But now, only a small fraction of the population owned land, and governments had dispensed almost all of the public holdings. Men's expectations to become landowners no longer bound the nation together. Quite the opposite. By insisting that government honor their claims regardless of the public welfare, the present owners of the nation's productive resources were driving the nation to the brink of economic and social chaos.

Croly argued that out of a misplaced concern for property rights American government had failed to regulate properly public utilities, supervise financial institutions, or oversee industrial relations. Only by discarding traditional and now anachronistic definitions of property and liberty could the United States ever hope to fulfill its promise. Americans must repudiate the Jeffersonian idea that government's primary function was to guarantee to each citizen the equal opportunity to pursue their personal happiness. Instead, the national government should impose on all citizens the collective goals of an equitable distribution of wealth and "a constantly higher standard of living." By assuring the material prosperity of everyone the nation could elicit the loyalty of every class of citizens, not just a few fortunate and privileged property holders. Socially guaranteed consumption, not ownership and management of production, would be the binding force of Croly's new nation.

Even though Croly advocated greater equality and less liberty, he was neither radically egalitarian nor in principle antilibertarian. In the abstract he found such terms as "equality" and "liberty" dangerous, if not absurd, goals. Rather, he suggested that Americans accept liberty and equality only so far as they contributed to "human brotherhood," by which he meant an equitable distribution of wealth and an absence of social conflict. Croly, like Bellamy and Veblen, found intolerable the economic inequities and social tensions which unregulated, profit-oriented capitalism seemed inevitably to spawn. He preferred an "organically unified" society in which each individual worked for the general welfare and each received in return from government a guarantee of economic security.

Croly freely admitted that such a society was not immediately possible. Americans were too selfish, too individualistic, and too wedded to traditional ideas of private property and acquisition. Nonetheless, he believed that a strong national government with the power to set national goals and to control the various segments of society could transform Americans from self-centered individualists into selfless nationalists. Croly denied that his ideas were visionary or unrealistic. Democratic leaders should not assume that its citizens were motivated solely by self-interest. Such a negative view easily became a self-fulfilling prophecy. Instead, policy makers should seek to make their people better and to arouse and expand the public's latent social instincts. Popular government, declared Croly, must "stand or fall on a platform of human perfectability," and social perfection should be the goal of all democratic politicians.[11]

Croly recognized that the successful creation of a new national character would be a slow and unfolding process. Therefore, he intentionally avoided specific and rigid proposals for the future. He expected policy makers to cope with issues as they arose and as circumstances demanded. But they must always keep their eyes firmly fixed on the goal of a cooperative national commonwealth. Even so, Croly offered a few suggestions based on the circumstances which existed in 1909 when he wrote *The Promise of American Life*. Croly saw large corporations and large labor unions as the greatest immediate dangers to democratic government and national unity. As labor and capital selfishly struggled for control of American industry, the public interest suffered. No matter who won, the nation lost. Still, the large size of organized labor and capital also held the means to greater national unity. Croly endorsed the recognition of labor unions and even proposed active governmental discouragement of unorganized labor. Unions forced individual laborers to act as a group and, with the aid of employers, organized and disciplined the labor force. Likewise, Croly supported the consolidation of economic enterprise. He even urged government to use its tax policy to penalize and eliminate small, independent entrepreneurs. He believed that size and productivity were directly related and that government should ignore all claims to the means of production except those based on efficiency.

But strong national labor unions and corporate trusts necessitated an even stronger national government. Political leaders had to have the power to compel both capital and labor to act socially responsible. To guarantee the public welfare, Croly wanted governmental leaders to ignore all self-serving claims of private property. As a matter of policy, government should allow corporate managers a free hand in the direction of their enterprises. Arbitrary and frequent governmental interference would impede industrial efficiency. Nonetheless, Croly argued that the freedom of managers was to be understood as a privilege and not a right. At any time public officials retained the right to insist upon particular policies or production goals. Furthermore, once it became clear that an activity could no longer best be performed by private management, government should immediately assume control—all claims to private property and free enterprise notwithstanding.

Similarly, Croly urged that labor unions be granted limited autonomy which included the right to strike and bargain over wages, hours, and working conditions. Even so, he would specifically prohibit unions from any participation in managerial policy. Within socially defined limits and goals, Croly wanted corporate executives to exercise their special talents to organize and direct American industry in the most efficient manner possible. As long as workers received a fair wage and enjoyed good working conditions, they had no reason or justification to ask for more. Laborers were only capable of uninformed judgment which might hinder industrial production.

Croly tempered his hierarchal industrial system by subjecting political leaders to periodic popular elections. He expected public officials to execute faithfully popularly accepted goals. Indirectly, workers as voters retained control over their lives. Still, once in office public officials should enjoy the freedom to serve the public as they saw best. If the public disagreed with their leaders' actions, it was free to select another leader at the next election. Social well-being dictated that society rely on the judgment of its most intelligent and talented individuals. Croly thought that a democracy would remain prosperous and united only if it loyally and obediently followed the direction of its leaders.

To those who criticized Croly's new nationalism as an abandonment of personal liberty, he replied that traditional American concepts of freedom, equal opportunity, and private property were in fact arguments in favor of selfishness and contrary to "real" individuality. Individualism had nothing to do with the acquisition of productive resources or the accumulation of wealth, but with self-fulfillment, which he believed could only come through service to society. Croly wanted Americans to divorce the concept of liberty from economic self-interest and instead view it as the freedom of the individual to fulfill himself intellectually and morally. American society should encourage the freedom to think and serve rather than the freedom to exploit and acquire. Authentic individuals were those disinterested persons who selflessly devoted themselves to public service through such activities as politics, science, and industry. Individual economic autonomy did not encourage civic virtue; it impeded it. If freed from starvation and want, Americans in the future, no longer compelled to exploit one another, would serve their fellow citizens. Croly asked Americans to reject the individualistic and antigovernmental ideas of Jefferson and adopt the Hamiltonian goals of a cooperative nation.

John Dewey shared some, but not all, of Croly's ideas. Born in Vermont in 1859 and educated at the University of Vermont and Johns Hopkins, Dewey dominated American intellectual life in the first half of the twentieth century. Dewey agreed with Croly upon the need for a "new nationalism," the inadequacy of competitive and profit-oriented capitalism, and the necessity for some type of welfare state. But like Veblen, he found appalling the prospect of the mass of mankind condemned to live and work for no other end than consumption. Dewey did not discount the importance of material well-being to individual happiness, and he applauded efforts to provide all members of society economic security. Nevertheless, he insisted that material prosperity should be only a means to an artful and creative life and not an end in itself. Consequently, Dewey rejected many of the more elitist and hedonistic assumptions implicit in the thought of Croly.[12]

Dewey premised his social analysis on his belief that social values derived from material circumstances. Economic structure and relationships set limits within which societies must organize themselves. Thus, whatever kind of society Americans might prefer, their choice was limited to some form of collectivism. Modern industrial economies depended on aggregated capital and centralized direction. Furthermore, individuals no longer owned nor controlled production, and industrial tasks did not require individual skills or allow individual freedom. Rhetoric aside, regimentation and uniformity penetrated every facet of American life as most people labored at equally undemanding jobs, lived in similar homes and neighborhoods, and consumed nearly identical goods. Individualism as traditionally understood, Dewey contended, had become entirely submerged into a "new corporateness." To speak of individual liberty and property in such a situation was both misleading and foolish. Americans, declared Dewey, must discard their individualistic values inherited from a precollectivist past, accept the communal reality of modern life, and shape their society and values accordingly. The perpetuation of such myths as "rugged individualism" and individual ownership of production foreclosed all chance of creating a personally fulfilling society.[13]

Dewey described American society as collective in substance and individualistic in sentiment. The corporate and regimented nature of the American economy precluded all possibility of personal choice or individuality. At the same time Americans denied themselves the benefits of communal life by politically honoring as rights private claims to profit and production. Prosperity no longer derived from individual initiative and risk, but rather from scientific insight, applied technology, and the rational organization of labor. Cooperation and group action, not competition and individual enterprise, were the necessary preconditions of economic well-being. Dewey believed that the protection of private claims to profit and control over production allowed certain groups to take for their own what was in fact the product of the entire community. Moreover, private control over production allowed the almost total control of the nation's economic life by a privileged class of corporate owners and managers. By nearly monopolizing managerial prerogatives, corporations had reduced the overwhelming majority of Americans to the level of well-paid slaves. Denied control over their labor as well as access to productive resources, most Americans turned to consumption, militarism, or other emotional stimulants for psychic relief. In the entrepreneurial sense of the word, the American economy denied most of its citizens property.

Dewey asserted that Americans would continue to pursue empty lives of consumptive and emotional excess as

long as profit making remained the most important function of American industry. He wanted Americans to eliminate private ownership of production and impose on industry public, nonprofit-oriented goals. He asked that
Americans be given the opportunity to find meaning in
their work and not be limited simply to labor for high
wages. But this required a new conception of "liberty."
According to Dewey, liberty should not include the individual's right to acquire and control production. Rather,
it should mean "equal opportunity." Each person should
enjoy the same chance as everyone else to obtain his voca-
tional preference. Talent and discipline alone should determine who would do what. Liberty should also include the
right of every one to engage in meaningful labor—work
which provided individuals the opportunity to think, make
choices, and see their choices implemented. Meaningful
participation of workers in managerial decision making
would provide the mass of society the occasion to act
creatively. Workers could see their own efforts and crea-
tions put to constructive use. In this way work would
become artful, and workers would carry into all aspects
of their lives the aesthetic and creative concerns they acquired through their work. Although Dewey eschewed the
word "property," his affirmation of individuals' "right to
participate" in the management of production conformed
closely to a type of cooperative property right. Within a
collective economy, Dewey argued in favor of a Jeffersonian claim to entrepreneurial liberty.[14]

Dewey's concept of liberty did not include any implied
right of the individual to act independently. Social well-
being necessitated collective action and collective goals.
Society needed certain quantities of particular goods at
specified times and places. To eliminate waste and duplication, Dewey proposed to set production goals and allo-
cate work through a national industrial council that consisted of representatives from labor, management, and the
public. Workers' liberty would be limited to their control

over the means to accomplish their assigned tasks. Within their particular corporate structures, workers would be free to decide among themselves who would do what, when, and how. Individuals would act as a group and sublimate their selfish tendencies. For Dewey, individualism in a collective society would assume a new form. It would no longer mean self-determination by the isolated personality, but self-realization within the bounds of group action.[15]

Although Dewey rejected many of the ideas of such men as Veblen, Croly, and Bellamy, at several significant points his thought corresponded with theirs. Dewey, with Croly, Bellamy, and, to a lesser extent, Veblen, for all intents and purposes abandoned a labor theory of value. Apparently, they each considered the idea of earned acquisition incompatible with community. They preferred to describe all ownership as a social legacy established by earlier generations and enlarged by the collective efforts of the present generation to pass on to subsequent generations. Individual claims of having "created" or "earned" wealth were either deceitful or myopic. Dewey, Croly, Bellamy, and Veblen concurred that in the future prosperity would depend on technological expertise rather than individual motivation. In an economy of scarcity, societies might justifiably have felt obliged to discriminate between individuals and to reward persons according to their contribution. If some must perish, it was in society's interest for its most productive members to survive. But in a technologically advanced society which produced enough for everyone and in which machines accomplished what men had previously done, there seemed no compelling reason to make distinctions between individuals based on merit. The acknowledgment and reward of individual merit or worth only encouraged self-centeredness without improving industrial efficiency. It threatened to destroy community. In so doing all four chose to overlook or diminish the particular contributions of individuals or the varying degree to which different individuals contributed to the general welfare. This led them to conclude that economic prosperity derived entirely from communal action and to discount almost completely the constructive potential of self-interest or individual genius.

Dewey, Croly, Bellamy, but not Veblen, likewise agreed on a highly optimistic estimate of man's potential. They believed that by eliminating scarcity and private ownership mankind would transcend its selfish attitudes and develop a selfless character. Each person, out of a sense of social responsibility, would work industriously without coercion. By eliminating profit making and individual ownership of production, selfishness would not be reinforced. With the achievement of community, ownership of production as a means of individual incentive became irrelevant. Everyone would work according to his abilities and share in society's production. All three men rejected the argument that economic or spatial autonomy were essential to individual liberty or human happiness. For them, liberty and happiness had lost much of their individualistic connotations. For this reason, Dewey, Croly, and Bellamy endorsed proposals which invested public officials with enormous power. They assumed that a truly collectivized society would develop a consensus on important public policies. In a society in which private interests had been eliminated through education and public ownership of production, men were likely to agree. One person's choice would be similar to every other person's. Their collectivist definition of "freedom within community" became realizable only if such a consensus developed.

By the 1930s the promise of various forms of collectivism began to lose much of their appeal. Even a committed socialist such as John Dewey, in the face of Stalinism, Fascism, and the New Deal, raised an occasional doubt as to the wisdom of large centralized government. He wondered if largeness and centralization were not themselves at the root of failures. Dewey found in New Deal programs and agencies a tendency to use rather than serve people and to manipulate instead of liberate. Although critical of all existing versions, Dewey until his death nonetheless remained loyal to some type of collective ownership. But he never answered satisfactorily the questions he himself had raised. Dewey's uneasiness paralleled the openly expressed fears of other Americans who accepted a more traditional and individualistic definition of liberty. These persons considered a collectivized economy a menace to personal freedom, and they found little solace in Dewey's hopes for a new, selfless mankind.

CHAPTER 10

❀

Latter-Day Jeffersonians: Agrarian Republicanism in Industrial America

Following the Civil War the public debate over the nature and limits of private rights over production generally developed between proponents of either private or public collectivism. Still, many Americans continued to believe in the Jeffersonian vision of widespread, individual proprietorship. For neo-Jeffersonians, corporate capitalism and socialism presented Americans equally unpalatable alternatives. Capitalism offered prosperity and socialism security, but each threatened to destroy individual freedom and popular government. Neo-Jeffersonians rejected arguments in favor of any "new" liberalism, for they insisted that liberty entailed individual autonomy. The political programs of these neo-Jeffersonians were frequently economically naive and unworkable, and their writings were often strident and millennial in tone. Nonetheless, their ethical and aesthetic concerns were sophisticated and sensitive. In their reaffirmation of such old concepts as a labor theory of value and entrepreneurial freedom for all citizens they raised fundamental questions about the nature and direction of American society—questions other Americans, preoccupied with material progress or equality, chose to ignore.

One of the earliest and most important critics of post–Civil War economic developments was Henry George. Born in Philadelphia in 1839, George spent his early adult life traveling, reading, and looking for employment. In 1866 he secured a job as a printer and soon became managing editor of the San Francisco *Times.* George's early firsthand experience with poverty sensitized him to the apparent inequities of American society which he traced to the monopolization of productive resources by a nonproductive rentier class. Despite the fact that George repudiated formal private ownership of land and instead substituted long-term tenancy, his formulations were intended to preserve entrepreneurial opportunity for individual producers. In his classic on political economy, *Progress and Poverty* (1879), George proposed to end what he saw as the paradox of unprecedented national wealth accompanied by increased poverty and human suffering by modifying the terms of private landownership. Because of the shortage of land, he thought that existing prerogatives of private ownership allowed a relatively few persons to monopolize nature's limited bounty. It also made it possible for landowners to engross the community's wealth through high rents and unearned increments. George argued that unless society destroyed the monopolistic aspects of landownership and returned control of production to producers the United States would become a nation divided between rich, nonproducing landowners and a landless but laboring poor.[1]

George, like David Ricardo, divided the elements of production into land, labor, and capital. These accounted for the three different ways a person could acquire wealth —rents from land, wages from labor, and interest from capital. Of the three, only wages and interest represented earned income. Again following Ricardo, George believed that labor added to the net sum of a community's wealth and therefore everyone had a natural right to the product of his labor. George viewed capital as earned wealth which a person either used to buy tools to increase his productivity or lent to someone else to improve theirs. But rent was another matter. Since unimproved land and other natural resources were the free gift of nature, no one could rightfully claim exclusive ownership to what he had not created with his own labor. Rent was income derived from the ownership of unearned resources, not the rightful return from labor devoted to improvements (George followed the classic Ricardian tradition and called this "interest"). To make matters worse the rate of rent depended largely on where the land was located. Rent was high in an area of dense population and high productivity and low in an area of sparse population and low productivity. Therefore, a city lot would rent for several hundred times the price of a comparable lot in an unpopulated rural area. The difference in value reflected the labor and productivity of the residents of the city, not the owner of the lot. Landowners' control of natural resources allowed them to siphon off the wealth produced by the entire society. The more wealth a community produced the more it paid in rent which drove up all other prices. Consequently, for most men, social prosperity increased the cost of living without increasing income.[2]

To put an end to this injustice, George proposed abolishing all forms of taxation except a single *ad valorem* tax on land. This "single tax" would be equal to the "pure" rent a landowner otherwise would have charged for the use of his land. Such a single tax would force landowners either to utilize their land to pay their taxes or to rent it to someone who would. (Note that much that usually goes under the label "rent" is really interest on capital improvements, and thus not subject to George's single tax.) A tax on improvements would penalize and discourage productivity—something George wanted to avoid—as well as violate the individual's natural right to the fruit of his labor. George was convinced that his "single tax" would so lower rents and thereby the cost of living as to give more people an opportunity to exploit nature for their profit. Additionally, it would insure that all wealth that accrued from community enterprise would redound to the public.[3]

Despite George's antipathy to private ownership of land, he held fast to many of the natural rights assumptions concerning ownership. He defended private ownership as the individual's natural right to the products of his labor. He also believed owners had a right to use their possessions as they wished. Further, he wanted to insure everyone access to nature and the opportunity to manage it for their own benefit. George hoped that his "single tax" would preserve in a more densely populated society the relative equality and economic freedom which he associated with an earlier, land-rich America. Rather than accept the development of an increasingly stratified society where special privilege and inheritance instead of enterprise and talent determined opportunity, George suggested doing away with what he thought was the primary source of unearned privilege—rent. In a changed environment where free land was a thing of the past, George sought to maintain opportunity, equity, and individual autonomy.

As a matter of practical policy George's single tax oversimplified complex economic relationships. Its implementation would probably have disrupted the economy without really improving on more orthodox property taxes. Furthermore, as societies became more dependent on technology, a single tax on land and other natural resources could hardly have coped with all the possible economic inequities that might arise. The importance of *Progress and Poverty* lay rather in its moral theory. In many ways George brought full circle the discussion over private ownership. Medievalists, who accepted the idea of a fixed quantity of wealth, had denied individuals exclusive control over natural resources because in a situation of scarcity individual ownership allowed certain, privileged individuals to claim as their own what everyone needed. Aware of the existence of the largely unpopulated new world, Locke had challenged this idea of ownership and argued that individual ownership of land would encourage productivity and add to the community's wealth to the benefit of all. But in deference to Christian moral theory, Locke had conceded that individuals had a right to claim ownership in land only as long as enough remained so that everyone could assert his right to own.

Americans prior to George had never considered Locke's qualification a serious restriction to ownership. From first settlement Americans could hardly imagine a time when there would be a scarcity of land. But with the close of the frontier George invoked the old medieval-Christian condition on private ownership. George's application of the labor theory of value to late-nineteenth-century American capitalism forced into American public debate an ancient, but compelling moral standard, a standard almost no one was willing to disavow publicly. After George had written *Progress and Poverty*, it became difficult for any American public leader to ignore the moral claim of producers nor the failure of the American economy to honor that claim. Much of the private property in the United States clearly seemed in basic violation of the natural rights arguments property holders had customarily used to justify their possessions. While George offered no feasible solution, he identified a central and enduring problem of the American economy: It seemed fundamentally at odds with its own moral theory. It rarely gave to the worker control over his labor or a full return on his labor.

In 1897 George died at the peak of perhaps the most severe economic depression in American history. His worst fears seemed realized as poverty was clearly more evident than progress. Large numbers of small farmers in the plains states and the southeast were hit especially hard. Unable to sell their crops for a profit and deeply in debt many farmers sold their land or defaulted on mortgages. Thousands of formerly independent farmers faced the unhappy prospect of becoming tenants or wage earners. In desperation, tens of thousands of these farmers abandoned the two major political parties and joined the radical Populist Party. Primarily consisting of small farmers, the

Populist Party focused its attention on farm problems. Still, it did not ignore or make light of the plight of urban factory workers. Furthermore, the Populists did not simply advocate a return to a wholly agricultural economy. They recognized the benefits of increased mechanization as well as national transportation, marketing, and financial structures. But they insisted that increased productivity did not necessitate the extinction of the individual entrepreneur. The Populists believed that sympathetic policy makers could direct American economic development in a direction which encouraged individual ownership of productive resources rather than eliminated it.[4]

Fundamentally Jeffersonian, Populist spokesmen repeatedly emphasized in newspaper editorials, political speeches, pamphlets, and books their commitment to popular government and personal liberty. Neither could long survive, in their opinion, without widespread ownership of production. The Populists based their defense of individual proprietorship on a labor theory of value. They argued that all legitimate wealth was a consequence of honest labor and that all persons enjoyed an equal and inalienable claim to productive resources. Populists applied natural rights sanctions to all earned possessions but primarily concerned themselves with the security of homes and productive resources. Nearly all Populist writers agreed that the most important liberty was the individual's right of access to natural resources, along with the associated rights of management and claim to the fruit of one's labor. During the 1892 presidential campaign the Populist candidate, James B. Weaver, wrote, "The child, who is born while we are penning these thoughts, comes into this world clothed with all the natural rights which Adam possessed when he was the sole inhabitant of the earth. Liberty to occupy the soil in his own right, to till it unmolested as soon as he has the strength to do so and to live upon the fruits of his toil without paying tribute to any other creature, are among the most sacred and essential of those

rights; and any society which deprives men of those natural and inalienable safeguards is in organized rebellion
against the providence of God, a conspiracy against human
life, and a menace to the peace of the community."[5] The
1892 party platform reaffirmed this basically natural rights
position. "Wealth belongs to him who creates it," resolved
the delegates to the Omaha Convention, "and every dollar
taken from industry without an equivalent is robbery. 'If
any will not work, neither shall he eat.' "[6]

Consistent with their Jeffersonian outlook, Populist
writers preferred minimal government. For them government always possessed the potential to become a self-
serving and tyrannical bureaucracy. They feared large government and its attendant high taxes which necessarily
fell on producers thereby depriving them of their hard-
earned property. Nonetheless, Populists understood that
individuals could not always perform for themselves desirable and necessary tasks. In such cases, if a free and
competitive marketplace was unfeasible, Populist leaders
preferred governmental ownership and operation to private enterprise. As much as Populists feared bureaucratic
government, they feared powerful, privately owned monopolies even more. Again, like Jefferson, Populists identified politically derived privilege as the source of most
social inequities as well as civic corruption. They believed
that when a legislature granted an individual or corporate
person the exclusive right to perform a socially necessary
function the legislature gave to that person the privilege
to charge rates without regard to cost. Monopolistic privilege made possible unearned profits, eliminated competition, and placed the user at the mercy of the monopolist.
In short, according to the Populists, monopoly violated
the basic American commitment to equal opportunity as
well as the labor theory of value.[7]

Populists offered several proposals to thwart the efforts
of nonproducers to exploit producers—under which label
they included farmers, laborers, and small businessmen.

First, they wanted to nationalize all economically essential monopolies such as railroads, telegraph companies, grain elevators, and banks. These would be run by the government at cost. Secondly, Populist leaders endorsed governmental regulation of all large corporations. In this way government would prevent the exploitation of laborers by employers. Finally, they wanted to end all businesses which depended on speculation rather than production for profits. For this reason the Populists called for the limitation of landownership to producers. Individuals would be restricted to that land which they actually used, and a corporation would be allowed to own only the land necessary to carry on its business (i.e., railroads could own only the land necessary for tracks, rail yards, and terminals). Populists hoped that these policies would free enough land so that "each industrious individual would have the privilege of a home where he could produce and enjoy the comforts of life."[8]

The Populist program was an ambitious effort to preserve individual ownership of productive resources in a highly integrated and mechanized economy. It allowed for large-scale, privately owned enterprise in competitive industries, but demanded public ownership of socially essential monopolies. And, while Populists tried to keep open to all persons the opportunity to own and manage productive resources, they supported safeguards for those who opted for wage earning. Despite their antipathy to large government, Populists believed that individual owners without the aid of government stood no chance against large and powerful corporate enterprises. Expanded, but nonetheless limited, government seemed the only hope to preserve individual proprietorship and with it personal liberty and popular government.

By the end of 1896 the Populist Party as a national movement had collapsed. Even so, Populist values did not disappear entirely. Several of the party's less radical proposals

were later enacted by various state and national governments, and in the South many former Populists secured
positions of influence in the Democratic Party. During the
first half of the twentieth century the southern wing of
the Democratic Party became a refuge for Populist beliefs.
This residue of Populist sentiment was particularly evident
in the 1912 presidential campaign speeches of Woodrow
Wilson. Although influenced more by Louis Brandeis than
southern Populism, Wilson at least adopted Populist rhetoric and suggested that his "New Freedom" represented
a libertarian alternative to Theodore Roosevelt's program
of "New Nationalism." In his 1912 campaign Roosevelt
disavowed any intention to break up large business monopolies simply because they were large and noncompetitive. If a business were efficient and socially responsible,
Roosevelt argued, it should be allowed to operate unham-
pered. He thus accepted and endorsed the post–Civil War
economic trends towards large, collectivized enterprise.
Wilson countered that such a policy violated traditional
American attitudes toward special privilege and equal opportunity. Young and ambitious men would be denied the
chance to own and operate their own businesses. "The
truth is, we are caught in a great economic machine that
is heartless," declared Wilson. "America is not a place of
which it can be said, as it used to be, that a man may
choose his own calling and pursue it just as far as his
abilities enable him to pursue it."[9] Employees of large
corporations, wrote Wilson, have no control over corporate
policy. Instead, like servants, employees are told what to
do as their "individuality is swallowed up in the individuality and purpose of a great corporation."[10] Americans
found themselves squeezed out, deprived of entrepreneurial liberty.

  Wilson urged that trusts and monopolies be broken up.
This would prevent corporate managers from engrossing
managerial opportunity and provide young "men on the

make" a chance to seek their fortune. Wilson saw no inconsistency between his advocacy of governmental regulation and his attachment to entrepreneurial liberty or the right of private property. He dismissed the claim that either industrial regulation or "trust busting" violated stockholders' property rights. Wilson contended that once one group of men employed another group of men the relationship became a matter of legitimate public concern and subject to public regulation. As soon as a business ceased to be individually owned and became "owned by great stock companies" all claims of private property ended. At that point it became government's responsibility to insure laborers' life and welfare.[11]

As president, Wilson failed to retard or reduce business consolidation, and he made no effort to have Congress enact the more radical Populist proposals. In fact, by the end of his last term he had adopted much of Roosevelt's "New Nationalism" regulatory program. Still, for some, the old dream of a nation of sturdy yeomen did not die even if it seemed unlikely to command the attention of any major political party. Before World War I Bolton Hall, a disciple of Henry George, popularized the idea of subsistence homesteads in two books, *Three Acres and Liberty* (1908) and *A Little Land and Liberty* (1909). In 1908 William Smythe sought to realize Hall's dream as he organized the "Little Landers," who in turn founded several agricultural communities in California. Through cooperative communities the Little Landers expected to provide Americans with the chance to become independent farmers—in their words, "proprietors rather than tenants, working not for others but for themselves." The limited popularity of these and other "back to the land" schemes continued after World War I as their appeal cut across sectarian as well as regional differences. In the 1930s the movement culminated in the New Deal's subsistence homestead program. But the most uncompromising demand for a return to an agrarian, freeholding society came not from reformers or politicians but from a small, talented circle of intellectuals associated with Vanderbilt University in Nashville, Tennessee.[12]

Following World War I a handful of Nashville poets began to meet informally to read and criticize each other's work. The group included John Crowe Ransom, Allen Tate, Robert Penn Warren, and Donald Davidson. From 1922 to 1925 they published a small literary magazine entitled *The Fugitive*. As their thought matured, a faction within the "Fugitives" and other interested persons such as historian Frank L. Owsley sensed a discrepancy between their aesthetic and artistic concerns and American society. In the 1920s the United States enjoyed unprecedented prosperity, and to these Nashville Agrarians it seemed that Americans were devoting all their time and energy to the pursuit of material well-being to the exclusion of all else. Prosperity and insatiable demands for higher standards of living caused Americans to lose sight of other, traditional ends such as beauty, community, and artistic freedom. The Agrarians felt that Americans' belief in and commitment to material progress lay at the root of their otherwise aimless, materialistic obsessions. To achieve ever-higher standards of living Americans had thoughtlessly embraced industrialism on a massive scale with all its depersonalizing consequences. According to the Agrarians, the price was much too high. Massive industrialization forced individuals to deny their individuality and become mere cogs in an impersonal industrial machine. The vast majority of Americans had become wage slaves whose only freedom was the right to change employers and to consume increasing quantities of meaningless goods and services. Consumption had replaced artful or self-directed work as man's primary activity. While George had used a labor theory of value to point up the material inequities in American society, the Vanderbilt Agrarians resorted to the same concept to make clear the antilibertarian tendency as well as the aesthetic emptiness of the American economy.[13]

Rejecting simplistic notions of progress, the Agrarians turned backward to what they imagined was a more humane and spiritually fulfilling past. As they contrasted the earlier agricultural America with the industrial America of the 1920s, several of the Agrarians, most notably Tate, Davidson, and Owsley, were struck by the decency and autonomy of the independent yeoman farming class. The small farmer owned his own land, depended only on himself and his family, and kowtowed to no one. Traditional in outlook, he worked hard, honored his parents, and feared God. The Agrarians believed that landownership was central to this earlier and, to their mind, better society. Land provided a person a stake in society as well as the means to support himself. It rooted people in time and place and gave their lives purpose. It furnished individuals the material wherewithal to be individuals, to exercise freedom, and to appreciate and pursue nonmaterialistic ends. As a consequence several of the Agrarians came to believe that unless the United States regained its agrarian, freeholding character, it would inevitably become a nation of regimented, rootless, and aimless people. They asked Americans to turn their backs on industrialism and urbanization and reaffirm their agrarian past.

In the late twenties the Agrarians, with Davidson's prodding, decided to publish an agrarian manifesto. Ransom succeeded in soliciting twelve essays and published them under the title *I'll Take My Stand: The South and the Agrarian Tradition* (1930). The twelve authors of *I'll Take My Stand* argued that in the United States the South by virtue of its backwardness had escaped the destructive impact of industrialism and urbanization. They appealed to their fellow Southerners to make the most of their good fortune and to resist all further encroachments of industrial capitalists. The twelve essays were uneven in quality and reflected several somewhat different viewpoints. Even so, each writer endorsed the views set forth by Ransom in the opening essay. The South's as well as the nation's salvation, wrote Ransom, lay in the restoration of artful work. Artful work included all labor which the artisans controlled and directed. Ransom believed that ownership of land represented the means for most men to secure the autonomy necessary for artistic freedom. Universal land-holding promised to revive in American society the individual's sense of beauty and appreciation of human dignity and worth. It promised to reestablish "real" liberty for the majority of Americans by freeing them from the bondage of machines, employers, and government to pursue their own aesthetic inclinations.[14]

Despite the defiant provincialism of *I'll Take My Stand* the book appealed to like-minded persons outside the South. The most important of these was historian-journalist Herbert Agar. Earlier in England, Agar had become interested in "Distributism," a movement founded by G. K. Chesterton and Hilaire Belloc. Like the Agrarians, the Roman Catholic Distributists advocated the breakup of large corporations, the division of large landholdings, and the restoration of widespread ownership of land. On his return to the United States, Agar with Allen Tate co-edited a collection of essays entitled *Who Owns America?*, which focused on property holding in the United States and the feasibility of widening ownership of productive resources. Many of the contributors to *I'll Take My Stand* participated in the symposium, including Lyle Lanier, Frank Owsley, Donald Davidson, Robert Penn Warren, and John Wade as well as Ransom and Tate. Also included were a number of Distributists and Catholic agrarians whom Agar had recruited, such as Hilaire Belloc and John Rawe. Even though much of the material in *Who Owns America?* repeated age-old arguments, the participants refined and added new subtleties to the agrarian concept of property as they applied it to the circumstances of the

1930s. Tate's and Agar's essays are particularly note-worthy.[15]

Of the original Fugitive group, Tate remained with Davidson the most loyal to agrarianism. His "Notes on Liberty and Property" was the most original essay in *Who Owns America?* Tate based his argument on several assumptions. First, the ownership of productive resources was the only really significant form of property. Second, the ownership of productive resources without the right to "control and use" these resources was a legal fiction. Third, given the democratic character of American society, if society protected anyone's claim to property, it had a moral obligation to protect everyone's claim. Thus, if American society intended to protect private property at all, it should adopt those policies which guaranteed to each of its citizens the right not only to hold legal title to productive resources, but to control and use them as well. If government failed to fulfill this trust, contended Tate, then its efforts to protect property were simply a manifestation of class interest and government lost its moral legitimacy.

For Tate "control and use" distinguished "genuine" property from merely "exchange" property. He argued that the owner of exchange property only possessed the right to exchange his property for something else—frequently one piece of paper for another (e.g., money for corporate stock). Since exchange property failed to afford its owner control and use of productive resources, it also failed to convey to its owner economic autonomy. An individual who owned large quantities of exchange property might be wealthy, but according to Tate, he could not be free. He did not control his labor or the means of subsistence. His life as well as his liberty was at the mercy of another. In order to live he had to do what those who controlled the means of production commanded.

Tate used the criteria of "control and use" to criticize both capitalism and socialism. He defined capitalism as the ownership of productive resources by private groups and socialism as the ownership by government. In either case ownership was vested in collective (thus to Tate fictional) persons and not real individuals. Stockholders did not really "own" corporations. Stockholders could not determine corporate policy. They only possessed a claim to its profits, the right to sell their stock, and the participation in meaningless stockholder elections. Stockholding was clearly no more than a form of exchange property. Corporate directors and managers ran corporations and, consequently, were the real owners even though legally they might own nothing. Stockholders were relegated to the sidelines, forced passively to watch others act in their name. Ironically, then, the "owners" of capitalism did not in fact own the means of production. For this reason Tate considered a sham any scheme which claimed to broaden property holding through some form of stock sharing. At the most, stock-sharing plans distributed "control and use" over consumption not production.

Tate was equally critical of socialism. When he applied his test of "control and use" to public property, he found the same deficiencies that characterized corporate property. Each denied individuals control and use of productive resources. Tate asserted that it was disingenuous to say that the people "owned" public property. Actually, "the people" as a collective whole owned nothing. The public might have access to certain "public property," but no individual could determine the use of "his" property. As with corporate property, those who effectively owned public property were those who determined its use— elected officials or, more often than not, nonelected bureaucrats. The only time "the people" owned anything, reasoned Tate, was when each one as an individual owned and controlled it. For Tate, socialization of society's productive resources entailed each person's ownership and control of a portion of the means of production. It required the distribution of productive resources to all citizens or a radical decentralization of ownership—the very opposite of collectivization.

Tate felt that the semantic confusion over the word "property" had led some people to accept collectivization uncritically. He accused corporate managers and their apologists of deliberately obscuring the profound difference between corporate and personal property in an effort to deflect public criticism and accountability. Tate found such confusion doubly unfortunate. First, it caused Americans to hesitate to break up corporations or regulate them sufficiently for fear of endangering their own personal property. This had the effect of transforming in the public mind all critics of corporations into "enemies of private property" when in fact, frequently, the critics of corporate property rights wished to expand individual property rights. Second, Tate found that those persons who objected to the control of productive resources by private corporations tended to associate all "private property" with "corporate property." While Tate sympathized with socialists in their dislike of private corporations, he believed that socialists erred by foolishly throwing the baby of personal property out with the bath water of corporate property. Socialists opposed "private property" in general without making any distinctions as to the particular kinds or the purposes different kinds might serve. As a result, Tate thought that socialists unthinkingly offered Americans simply an alternate form of tyranny or theft and not true liberty.

In Tate's mind there could be no such thing as liberty without property. Individual ownership of the tools of production made it possible for a person to survive without at the same time exercising power over others. Property insured that an individual's wealth and well-being was a consequence of his own labor, not what he denied another. An economic system based on universal ownership of production made unnecessary the imposition of one person's control over another. Each individual could stand on equal footing with all others. No one would be obligated or dependent on another. While individuals would not be equal, they would be free from the exploitation and control of other men. Any other economic system, declared Tate, necessarily placed some persons under the control of others, thereby denying freedom to those who were controlled. Without universal ownership of production, social stratification and hierarchy were unavoidable, and universal freedom for all intents and purposes impossible. Freedom became the exclusive possession of the privileged policy making classes.

Herbert Agar accepted Tate's analysis and tried to give those theories practical application. "According to the American dream," wrote Agar, "the large majority should be able to count on the freedom of men who do not have to be anyone's dependent, or anybody's toady; they should be able to count on the reasonable permanence, both of residence and occupation which makes a stable family life possible; they should be able to count on having the chance to do creative work, and to enjoy responsibility; they should be able to count on living in an atmosphere of equality, in a world which puts relatively few barriers between man and man." Agar argued that "monopoly capitalism" opposed this ideal. "Freedom to them," he asserted, "is only freedom to move from one occupation or employment to another. This only frees men from their home, their neighbors, and their personal responsibilities."[16] Agar believed that in the 1920s the Republican administration had consistently pursued an economic policy which encouraged economic consolidation and destroyed individual ownership. At the same time he entertained no delusions about Franklin Roosevelt and the New Deal. Agar appreciated Roosevelt's concern for the poor, but he felt that New Deal policies fluctuated between corporate capitalism and socialism. New Deal policies made no concerted effort to restore individual control over productive resources. Still, Agar hoped that the Democratic

Party's traditional concern for the underdog as well as its Populist and libertarian heritage would make it receptive to his and Tate's ideas and that it would become a vehicle for fundamental change.

Unlike the Agrarians, Agar refused to limit his choices to an agrarian economy. He emphasized that increased individual ownership of production in no way implied a "back to the land" movement or a repudiation of technology. Agar himself believed that farm life was not always idyllic and was not for everyone. Nonetheless, he argued, government should pursue a policy which enabled those persons who currently owned farms or those who wanted to own farms to do so. Additionally, like the Populists, Agar endorsed governmental ownership or strict supervision of all industries unsuited for private ownership —that is, noncompetitive industries. Furthermore, he wanted all other industry to be geographically decentralized and whenever possible effective ownership (control and use) transferred to those persons working in the particular industry. Rather than run by hierarchal structures, Agar wanted industry to be organized as worker cooperatives or at least the opportunity to be made available for laborers to work in a cooperative if they wished. But in all cases he consistently stipulated choice rather than coercion. For this reason Agar did not advocate the immediate or complete transformation of the American economy. He recognized that all fundamental change took place slowly and immediate conversion to cooperative ownership could be as coercive for the uncommitted as immediate collectivization. For the present he suggested legislatures change tax laws, regulate corporations, restore competition, and supervise stock issues in a manner that would reverse the trend toward consolidation of ownership. Agar envisioned the decentralization of ownership to be a gradual, always incomplete, process, but one which nonetheless provided significant and increasing numbers of Americans with the opportunity to control their labor and manage productive resources.[17]

Tate and Agar hoped that *Who Owns America?* would influence American public opinion and politics. But for the most part their arguments went unheard. In the absence of a clear popular mandate Franklin Roosevelt chose the politically expedient path of least resistance. He refused to make any decisive policy choices. While Roosevelt frequently appeared sympathetic to neo-Jeffersonian ideas, he also found attractive the ideas of laissez-faire and socialist thinkers.[18] Raymond Moley, John Dewey, and Allen Tate were equally frustrated by Roosevelt's lack of clear ideological preferences. They each wanted American policy to embody their particular ideas, and they each expected Roosevelt to pursue a policy consistent with their beliefs. But he would not be pinned down. What distressed Moley, Dewey, and Tate seemed to comfort American voters. While Americans verbally held fast to their Jeffersonian natural-rights beliefs, they also demanded an enlarged welfare state even as they acquiesced in leaving the economy largely under the control of large corporations. Consequently, American society at mid-twentieth century presented a peculiar anomaly. Confronted with a choice among laissez-faire capitalism which promised prosperity or socialism which offered security and equality or individual proprietorship which tendered individual freedom and opportunity, Americans chose not to choose. They wanted them all. Logic and moral consistency be damned.

Conclusion: The Lingering World of Thomas Jefferson

In the seventeenth century Americans recognized two categories of personal freedom—freemen and freeholders. A freeman was an individual who suffered no formal obligations to another. A woman, for instance, was not considered free because of her husband's claim over her, just as a servant or a slave was not free because of his master's legal claim to his labor. Exempt of all such claims, a freeman could engage in contracts, acquire property, and enjoy a full claim to his labor. But freemanship alone did not imply full liberty. Only freeholders had the right to vote or hold public office. Americans justified the preferred status of freeholders on the grounds that formal freedom, without the means to sustain that freedom, did not guarantee full freedom. Without economic autonomy a person could not be trusted to act responsibly and independently.

At first, outside New England and Pennsylvania, only a minority of Americans managed to secure sufficient land to qualify as freeholders. But by the middle of the eighteenth century, freeholding had increased to such an extent that a sizable majority of the white adult males in all colonies qualified as freeholders. Freeholding had become so widespread that American Revolutionaries described the Revolution as a struggle to preserve Americans' "liberty and estates" from imperial tyranny. Several of the new states in their bills of rights not only affirmed all men's natural and inalienable right to property, but also asserted government's obligation to guarantee to its citizens the "means of acquiring and possessing property." Thomas Jefferson hoped that such a commitment might be realized by utilizing the vast land reserves of the new republic. He believed that if the opportunity to acquire land were kept open, America would fulfill his dream of a virtuous republic—a place where a majority of the people participated in government, where men respected the rights and property of others, and where talent and industry determined a person's wealth and status.

This vision of America as a land of virtuous and autonomous freeholders was never fully realized. Before the Civil War in the southern states slavery denied most Negroes the opportunity to become either freemen or freeholders, and by the end of the nineteenth century a majority of Americans outside the South had either chosen or were forced to accept some form of employment. By the early decades of the twentieth century even the "owners" of the nation's largest economic enterprises frequently did not manage or work in their businesses. Instead, stockholders delegated their proprietorial responsibilities to boards of directors who often further delegated their responsibilities to hired corporate managers. To own this form of "property" no longer meant individual control and management of one's own labor. More often the word property now referred to corporate rights or consumer property, such as homes, automobiles, stocks, and savings accounts.

The declining importance of individual proprietorship was paralleled by several important changes in the concept of citizenship. First, by the end of the Civil War Americans finally resolved the paradox between their affirmation of a natural rights concept of government and their tolerance of Negro slavery. In the Thirteenth Amendment the United States abolished all property in persons, and in the Fourteenth Amendment it recognized the right of all persons to "life, liberty, and property." Secondly, with the expansion of the factory system following the War of 1812, a significant number of Americans challenged the idea that landless freemen could justly be denied full political liberty. Americans found these arguments compelling, and by 1860 the states had repealed all but minor property restrictions on voting and office holding. This marked an important change in American attitudes toward property. Now most Americans denied any important difference between wage earners and proprietors. On election day, at least, freemen and freeholders were presumed to be equal. These changes, combined with the growing tendency of Americans to equate stockholding with proprietary property, obscured the decline in proprietorships which occurred following the Civil War. By the middle of the twentieth century, while almost all Americans could claim the status of freemen, only a relative handful enjoyed the managerial freedom of a freeholder. Freemanship had become universal and individual rights and liberties expanded, but the freeholder's right to control productive resources and to manage his own labor had again become the privilege of a limited few.

Eighteenth-century American agrarians had thought that the absence of widespread ownership of freehold property would jeopardize their efforts to create a just and free society. They believed that no person had a right to the fruit of another's labor; that no one had a right to pursue his personal interest to the detriment of other persons; and that all men enjoyed a right to life and the means and opportunity to seek personal fulfillment. A republic of small freehold farmers seemed the best means to achieve these ends. Within fifty years of American independence a new and quite different society began to take shape. Even so, Americans did not abandon the ideal that had motivated the republic's founders. Americans today, for the most part, continue to affirm a concept of liberty and justice similar to that expressed in the Declaration of Independence. Even Americans' concept of property has remained remarkably fixed despite the fact that the oppor-

tunity for individual proprietorship is more restricted today than at any previous time in our past. Most Americans
still believe that individuals should control their own labor, even though few of us do. Whether in the future
Americans will allow the further narrowing of proprietary
opportunity or seek to broaden such liberties is an open
question.

It is clear that Americans in the twentieth century have
neither abandoned the ideas of individual liberty or opportunity. Nor have Americans failed to respond to changes
caused by the shift from proprietorship to employment.
Since World War I state and federal courts have signifi-
cantly widened the expressive and procedural liberties of
citizens. These "new" liberties have increased in a manner
that suggests their creation is in part a function of the
demise of "older" proprietorial liberties. Additionally, policy makers through a complex, if not comprehensive, welfare system have provided individuals much of the economic security which Americans historically derived from
various forms of property. Finally, state and federal governments through an equally complex series of regulations,
subsidies, and grants have tried to provide individuals
access to all employment opportunities for which they are
qualified or can qualify.

The change in emphasis from proprietorship to employment is particularly evident in the Supreme Court's recent
effort to expand economic opportunity through a reinter-
pretation of the Fourteenth Amendment. In the late nineteenth century the court under the leadership of Stephen
Field had defined "privileges or immunities" to mean every
citizen's "right to acquire and possess property of every
kind, and to pursue and obtain happiness." In the twentieth century fewer and fewer Americans pursued and
obtained happiness through the acquisition and management of productive property. By the 1930s the percentage
of Americans who were self-employed proprietors had declined so precipitously that many policy makers viewed

Field's interpretation of the Fourteenth Amendment as little more than a disingenuous defense of the "privileges or immunities" of corporate managers against public accountability. Such an interpretation seemed at odds both with the moral idealism of the Declaration of Independence and the necessities of the twentieth century. Most Americans now pursued and obtained happiness through employment, not through the management of their own labor. Equal opportunity meant the opportunity to secure the best job available. For many persons education, not ownership of productive resources, had become the key to individual success and upward mobility.

In 1954 the Supreme Court gave constitutional recognition to the new importance of education in its landmark decision *Brown v. Board of Education.* The court argued that education was essential for individual opportunity and the Fourteenth Amendment prohibited a state from denying any citizen access to the skills necessary to secure his desired livelihood. If a person were to exercise his right to "pursue and obtain happiness," government must guarantee his access to the best public education available. In *Brown v. Board of Education* the Supreme Court sought to secure individual economic opportunity by prohibiting exclusionary policies in education, even as in the nineteenth century the courts had tried to secure individual economic opportunity through the protection of entrepreneurial property rights. The difference lay not in the intent or the moral theory—both sought to increase individual opportunity and both based their arguments on a natural rights interpretation of the Fourteenth Amendment—but rather on the changed economic circumstances. In a radically altered situation the Supreme Court in 1954 defended a traditional notion of American liberty—but one divorced from property rights.

The concern of twentieth-century policy makers for civil liberties, social welfare, and employment opportunities is, in part, an effort to preserve for all Americans many of the liberties traditionally associated with property rights. Nonetheless, for those persons who value the autonomy and independence of self-employed proprietors these new liberties provide small solace. By themselves increased civil liberties, economic security, and employment opportunity do not provide individuals the means to direct and control their own labor, the means to exercise artistic freedom. At best, these new liberties are only partial substitutes for Jefferson's concept of property, the individual's right to the liberty as well as the means to pursue happiness.

Notes

PART I

1. J. Hector St. John de Crèvecoeur, *Letters from an American Farmer* (New York: New American Library, 1963), 48.

CHAPTER 1

1. Samuel E. Thorne et al., *The Great Charter* (New York: Mentor, 1965).

2. Chilton Williamson, *American Suffrage: From Property to Democracy, 1760–1860* (Princeton, N.J.: Princeton University Press, 1968); Page Smith, *John Adams* (New York: Doubleday, 1962), I, 57–58.

3. Ralph Hamor, *A True Discourse of the Present State of Virginia, 1615* (Richmond: Virginia State Library, 1957), 16–17; William Stith, *The History of the First Discovery and Settlement of Virginia* (Williamsburg, Va.: William Parks, 1747), 38–39, 131. Also see Edmund S. Morgan, *American Slavery—American Freedom: The Ordeal of Colonial Virginia* (New York: Norton, 1975).

4. Marshall Harris, *Origin of the Land Tenure System in the United States* (Ames, Iowa: Iowa College Press, 1953), 82–91, 194–199.

5. *Ibid.*, 199–236.

6. Edmund S. Morgan, ed., *Puritan Political Ideas* (Indianapolis: Bobbs-Merrill, 1965), 39.

7. Richard Schlatter, *Private Property: The History of an Idea* (London: George Allen & Unwin, 1951), chapters iii–v.

8. Max Weber first suggested the relationship between Protestantism and an entrepreneurial ethic in his famous essay

The Protestant Ethic and the Spirit of Capitalism, trans. Talcott Parsons (New York: Scribner's, 1958). R. H. Tawney further elaborated the idea in his *Religion and the Rise of Capitalism* (New York: Mentor, 1947). Weber's argument touched off a lengthy debate which still continues. For a summary of the issues and a useful bibliography see Robert W. Green, ed., *Protestantism, Capitalism, and Social Science: The Weber Thesis Controversy* (Lexington, Mass.: D. C. Heath, 1973).

9. Stephen Foster, *Their Solitary Way: The Puritan Social Ethic in the First Century of Settlement in New England* (New Haven, Conn.: Yale University Press, 1971).

10. John Winthrop, "A Model of Christian Charity" (1630), reprinted in Morgan, *Puritan Political Ideas*, 77–93.

11. E. A. J. Johnson, *American Economic Thought in the Seventeenth Century* (New York: Russell and Russell, 1961); Morgan, *Puritan Political Ideas*, 178–182; Robert Keayne, *The Apologia of Robert Keayne* (1653), ed. Bernard Bailyn (New York: Harper and Row, 1964).

12. William Bradford, *Of Plymouth Plantation: 1620–1647*, ed. Samuel Eliot Morison (New York: Alfred A. Knopf, 1952), 120.

13. Anonymous, "Laying Out of Towns" (1634), in *Collections of the Massachusetts Historical Society*, 5th Series, I, 475.

14. John Cotton, "Christian Calling" (1641), in Perry Miller and Thomas H. Johnson, eds., *The Puritans* (New York: Harper and Row, 1963), I, 319–327.

15. Kenneth A. Lockridge, *A New England Town: The First Hundred Years* (New York: Norton, 1970), and Sumner Chilton Powell, *Puritan Village: The Formation of a New England Town* (New York: Anchor Books, 1965), provide two excellent examples of this process. Also see Beverly Bond, *The Quit-Rent System in the American Colonies* (Gloucester, Mass.: Peter Smith, 1965), and Harris, *Origin of Land Tenure*.

16. Quote from "Information Concerning the Province of North Carolina, etc.," in William K. Boyd, ed., *Some Eighteenth-Century Tracts Concerning North Carolina* (Raleigh, N.C.: Edwards and Broughton, 1927), 434, 439, 450–451. The immigrant literature is voluminous but a good sample is contained in

J. Franklin Jameson, ed., *Original Narratives of Early American History* (New York: Barnes and Noble, 1959).

17. James A. Henretta, *The Evolution of American Society, 1700–1815* (Lexington, Mass.: Heath, 1973), 88–112; Williamson, *American Suffrage*, 20–61.

18. Wilcomb E. Washburn, "The Moral and Legal Justifications for Dispossessing the Indians," in James Morton Smith, ed., *Seventeenth-Century America: Essays in Colonial History* (Chapel Hill: University of North Carolina Press, 1959), and Alden T. Vaughan, *New England Frontier* (Boston: Little, Brown, 1965).

19. Winthrop, "Conclusion of the Plantation in New England" (1629 or 1630), in *Old South Leaflets* (Boston: Old South Association, 1884–1920), II, no. 50, 5–6; Winthrop, "General Observations for the Plantation of New England" (1629), in *Winthrop Papers* (Boston: The Massachusetts Historical Society, 1929–1940), II, 120; John White, "The Planters Plea" (1630), in Peter Force, ed., *Tracts and Other Papers* (Boston: P. Force, 1836–1846), II, 1–2.

20. Roger Williams, "The Bloudy Tenant of Persecution," in *Narragansett Publications* (Providence, R.I.: Narragansett Club, 1876), III, 254; *Records of the Colony of Rhode Island* (Providence, R.I.: A. C. Green, 1856–1865), I, 33–34.

21. John Cotton, "A Reply to Mr. Williams," in *Narragansett Publications*, II, 46–47; Cotton, "God's Promise to his Plantations" (1630), in *Old South Leaflets*, III, no. 53, 6.

22. Williams, "A Key into the Language of America," in *Narragansett Publications*, I, 120; *Records of the Colony of Rhode Island*, I, 33–34.

23. Solomon Stoddard, *Answer to Some Cases of Conscience* (Boston, 1722), 12–13. See particularly footnotes. Also J. M. [Joseph Morgan], *The Original Rights of Mankind* (Boston: 1722).

24. Morgan, *Original Rights*, preface, 2, 4, 4–11, 15–22.

25. *Ibid.*, 7, 9–11, 17–19.

26. Irving Mark, *Agrarian Conflicts in Colonial New York, 1711–1775* (New York: Columbia University Press, 1940).

27. Cadwallader Colden, "The State of the Lands in the Province of New York, in 1732," in *Documentary History of the*

State of New York (Albany, N.Y.: Weed, Parsons, 1849), I, 377–386.

28. Letter printed in *The New York Post Boy,* reprinted in *New Jersey Archives* (Paterson, N.J.: Press Printing, 1895), Series I, XII, 308–309.

29. Assembly to Governor (August 20, 1755), in Benjamin Franklin, *The Papers of Benjamin Franklin,* ed. Leonard W. Labaree (New Haven: Yale University Press, 1959–), VI, 162; Assembly to Governor (September 29, 1755), *Papers,* VI, 196–197; Assembly to Governor (September 23, 1756), *Papers,* VI, 523, 525, 529.

30. Assembly to Governor (June 24, 1760), *Papers,* VI, 133–134; Labaree, "Editorial Note," *Papers,* IX, 196–203.

31. Benjamin Franklin, *The Political Thought of Benjamin Franklin,* ed. Ralph Ketcham (Indianapolis: Bobbs-Merrill, 1965), 358.

32. *Ibid.,* 244.

33. *Ibid.,* 364–365.

CHAPTER 2

1. Bernard Bailyn, *The Ideological Origins of the American Revolution* (Cambridge, Mass.: Harvard University Press, 1967).

2. Charles Blitzer, *An Immortal Commonwealth: The Political Thought of James Harrington* (New Haven, Conn.: Yale University Press, 1960). J. G. A. Pocock in two very important essays "Civic Humanism and Its Role in Anglo-American Thought" and "Machiavelli, Harrington, and English Political Ideologies in the Eighteenth Century," both published in *Politics, Language, and Time* (New York: Atheneum, 1973), has developed at length the classical and renaissance sources of Harrington's notion of "civic virtue" and its influence on eighteenth-century American politics. Also see Pocock's *Machiavellian Moment* (Princeton, N.J.: Princeton University Press, 1975) and *The Ancient Constitution and the Feudal Law* (Cambridge: Cambridge University Press, 1957), as well as Caroline Robbins, *The Eighteenth-Century Commonwealthman* (New York: Atheneum, 1968).

3. James Harrington, *The Oceana of James Harrington and His Other Works*, ed. John Toland (Dublin: R. Riley, 1737), 37.

4. *Ibid.*, 41.

5. Caroline Robbins, *The Pursuit of Happiness* (Washington, D.C.: American Enterprise Institute, 1974).

6. Harrington, *Oceana*, 170–171.

7. John Dunn, *The Political Thought of John Locke* (Cambridge: Cambridge University Press, 1969). Also see Peter Laslett's introduction to his edition of John Locke, *Two Treatises of Government* (New York: Mentor Books, 1965); C. B. Macpherson, *Theory of Possessive Individualism* (Oxford: Clarendon Press, 1962); and Karl Olivecrona, "Appropriation in the State of Nature: Locke on the Origin of Property," *Journal of the History of Ideas*, XXXV (1974), 221–230.

8. Locke, *Two Treatises*, 399.

9. *Ibid.*, 324.

10. *Ibid.*, 1–4, 23–24, 66–69, 365–366.

11. *Ibid.*, 327–344.

12. *Ibid.*, 393.

13. *Ibid.*, 401–402, 403.

14. *Ibid.*, 374–376, 393–409. Also see Willmoore Kendall, *John Locke and the Doctrine of Majority Rule* (Urbana: University of Illinois Press, 1941).

15. Locke, *Two Treatises*, 408.

16. *Ibid.*, 476–477.

CHAPTER 3

1. Stephen Hopkins, *The Rights of Colonies Examined* (Providence: 1765), 19.

2. John Adams, "A Defense of the Constitution of Government of the United States," in *Works of John Adams*, ed. Charles Francis Adams (Boston: Little, Brown, 1850–1856), V, 453. Also see Bernard Bailyn, *Ideological Origins of the American Revolution* (Cambridge, Mass.: Harvard University Press, 1967); Caroline Robbins, *The Eighteenth-Century Commonwealthman* (New York: Atheneum, 1968); H. Trevor Colbourn, *The Lamp of Experience: Whig History and the Intellectual Origins of the American Revolution* (Chapel Hill: University

of North Carolina Press, 1965); Gordon S. Wood, *The Creation of the American Republic, 1776–1787* (Chapel Hill: University of North Carolina Press, 1969); J. G. A. Pocock, *The Machiavellian Moment: Florentine Political Thought and the Atlantic Republican Tradition* (Princeton, N.J.: Princeton University Press, 1975) and *Politics, Language and Time: Essays on Political Thought and History* (New York: Atheneum, 1973). The best survey and analysis of the philosophical basis of American revolutionary thought is Paul Conkin's *Self-Evident Truths* (Bloomington: Indiana University Press, 1974).

3. Washington to Bryan Fairfax (August 24, 1774), in *Writings of George Washington*, ed. John C. Fitzpatrick (Washington, D.C.: Government Printing Office, 1931–1947), III, 242.

4. James Otis, "The Rights of the British Colonies Asserted," in *The Political Writings of James Otis*, ed. Charles F. Mullit, in *The University of Missouri Studies*, IV (1929), 51–53, 62–63, 72–73, 94.

5. Otis, "A Vindication of the British Colonies," in *ibid.*, 135–140. There are several excellent collections of revolutionary pamphlets and tracts. Among some of the better and more accessible collections are Edmund S. Morgan, ed., *Prologue to Revolution* (Chapel Hill: University of North Carolina Press, 1959); Merrill Jensen, ed., *Tracts of the American Revolution, 1763–1776* (Indianapolis: Bobbs-Merrill, 1967); Bernard Bailyn, ed., *Pamphlets of the American Revolution: 1750–1776* (Cambridge, Mass.: Harvard University Press, 1965); Hezekiah Niles, ed., *Principles and Acts of the Revolution* (Baltimore: Niles, 1822) and Samuel E. Morison, ed., *The American Revolution: Sources and Documents: 1764–1788* (New York: Oxford University Press, 1929).

6. Samuel Adams, *The Writings of Samuel Adams*, ed. H. A. Cushing (New York: Octagon Books, 1968), I, 190–191.

7. *Ibid.*, I., 137–138.

8. *Ibid.*, II, 246–247.

9. Locke had a particularly strong influence on Adams's views toward property rights. See *Writings*, II, 298–300, and volumes I and II.

10. See for example Daniel Dulany, "Considerations on the Propriety of imposing Taxes in the British Colonies" (1765), in Bailyn, *Pamphlets*, I, 598–658; John Adams, "Novangulus"

(1775) in *Works of John Adams*, IV; John Adams, "Disserta-
tion on Canon and Feudal Law," in *Works of John Adams*,
III; Alexander Hamilton, "The Farmer Refuted," in *The Papers
of Alexander Hamilton*, ed. Jacob E. Cooke and Harold Syrett
(New York: Columbia University Press, 1961–1967), I; Samuel
Adams, *Writings*, II, 433–435, 441–442; William Samuel John-
son, in Thomas Jefferson, *Papers*, ed. Julian P. Boyd (Prince-
ton: Princeton University Press, 1950–   ), I, 495. Also see Louis
Hartz, *The Liberal Tradition in American Politics* (New York:
Harcourt, Brace and World, 1955); and Rowland Berthoff and
John M. Murrin, "Feudalism, Communalism, and the Yeoman
Freeholder: The American Revolution Considered as a Social
Accident," in Stephen G. Kurtz and James H. Hutson, eds.,
Essays on the American Revolution (Chapel Hill: University
of North Carolina Press, 1973).

   11. Martin Howard, *A Letter from a Gentleman in Halifax
to his Friend in Rhode Island* (New Port: 1765), and *A Defense of the Letter from a Gentleman at Halifax* (New Port:
1765).

   12. Jefferson, "Summary View," *Papers*, I; Pendleton to Jefferson (August 3, 1776, and October 14, 1776), in *Papers*, I, 484,
559; Jefferson to Pendleton (August 13, 1776), in *Papers*, I, 492.

   13. John Adams, "Dissertation on Canon and Feudal Law"
and "Novangulus." When Americans began to make public
land grants, they did so in a nonfeudal, fee simple title. See
Thomas Donaldson, *The Public Domain: Its History* (Washington, D.C.: Government Printing Office, 1884), I, 146–159.

   14. John Adams, *Works*, IX, 376–377.

   15. Ben Perley Poore, ed., *The Federal and State Constitutions, Colonial Charters and State Constitutions* (Washington,
D.C.: Government Printing Office, 1878), 1859.

   16. *Ibid., passim.* Also see Virginia's resolution on confisca-
tion of Loyalists' property in James Madison, *The Papers of
James Madison*, ed. William T. Hutchinson and William M. E.
Rachal (Chicago: University of Chicago Press, 1962), V, 409.

   17. Caroline Robbins in *The Pursuit of Happiness* (Washington, D.C.: American Enterprise Institute, 1974) convincingly
argues that the phrase "pursuit of Happiness" was in common
usage in eighteenth-century political discourse and came out
of the tradition of "civic humanism." François Quesnay, the

Physiocrat, in his 1765 essay "Natural Right" used a similar phrase: "The natural right of man can be defined loosely: the right that each man has to the things proper to his happiness." It seems likely that Jefferson drew from both traditions. For a discussion of the influence of Quesnay and other Physiocrats on Jefferson see Adrienne Koch, *The Philosophy of Thomas Jefferson* (Chicago: Quadrangle, 1964).

18. Jefferson to Madison (October 28, 1785), in *Papers*, VIII, 681–682.

19. "Committee Draft of 'Declaration of Rights'" in George Mason, *Papers of George Mason*, ed. Robert A. Rutland (Chapel Hill: University of North Carolina Press, 1970), I, 283; Jefferson, *Papers*, I, 358–363, 484, 560; II, 139–140. For final draft of Declaration of Rights see Poore, *Constitutions*, 1908–1909.

20. Jefferson, *Writings of Thomas Jefferson*, ed. Andrew A. Lipscomb and Albert E. Bergh (Washington, D.C.: Thomas Jefferson Memorial Association, 1903–1905), XVIII, 45–49, 108–112; *Papers*, I, 315–316, 560; X, 368; XV, 392–397, 412; XVI, 406–408; *The Correspondence of Jefferson and Dupont de Nemours*, ed. Gilbert Chinard (Baltimore, Md.: Johns Hopkins University Press, 1931), 259–260. Also see Jefferson's first inaugural address in James D. Richardson, ed., *A Compilation of the Messages and Papers of the Presidents, 1789–1897* (Washington, D.C.: Government Printing Office, 1896–1899), I, 323.

21. John Jay to Jefferson (October 27, 1786), in *Correspondence and Public Papers of John Jay*, ed. Henry P. Johnston (New York: G. P. Putnam and Sons, 1890–1893), III, 212–213. Examples of other Americans who shared Jay's opinion are Oliver Ellsworth, "Letters of a Landowner," in *Essays on the Constitution*, ed. Paul L. Ford (Brooklyn: Historical Printing Club, 1892), 159–160; Abigail Adams to Jefferson (January 29, 1787), in *The Adams-Jefferson Letters*, ed. Lester J. Cappon (Chapel Hill: University of North Carolina Press, 1959), I, 168; Noah Webster to James Bowdoin (March 15, 1787), in *Massachusetts Historical Collections*, 7th Series, VII, part 2, 181; John Adams to Henry Marchant (August 18, 1789), in John Adams, *Works*, IX, 560; Adams to James Sullivan (September 17, 1789), in *ibid.*, IX, 526. Also see James Madison, *Notes on the Debates of the Federal Convention of 1787*, ed. Adrienne

Koch (New York: Norton, 1969), 13, 38–39, 131, 144, 202, 321, 475.

22. Madison, "Observations on Jefferson's Draft of the Virginia Constitution," in Jefferson, *Papers*, VI, 310–311; Jefferson to Madison (October 28, 1785), *Papers*, VIII, 681–682.

23. Madison to Jefferson (June 19, 1786), in Madison, *Papers*, II, 362–368. Madison, Hamilton, and Jay, *The Federalist*, ed. Benjamin F. Wright (Cambridge, Mass.: Harvard University Press, 1961), #10, #14, #37, #39, and #s 41–48.

24. Jonathan Elliot, ed., *The Debates in the Several State Conventions on the Adoption of the Federal Constitution as Recommended by the General Convention at Philadelphia, in 1787* (Philadelphia: Lippincott, 1896), *passim*; Madison, *Notes*, *passim*; Max Farrand, ed., *The Records of the Federal Convention of 1787* (New Haven, Conn.: Yale University Press, 1911), *passim*.

25. Merrill Jensen, *New Nation* (New York: Vintage, 1950) and Forrest McDonald, *Formation of the Republic* (Baltimore, Md.: Penguin Books, 1965).

26. Farrand, *Records*, I, 398–401, 562; II, 116–117, 121–123, 151, 202–207, 248; III, 182; Elliot, *Debates*, II, 192–193, 237; III, 185, 208–209; IV, 321–322; Madison, *Notes*, 181, 386, 215, 401–406.

27. George Mason (August 7, 1787), *Papers of Mason*, III, 949; Madison, *Notes*, 425–430. Also see William Blackstone, *Commentaries on the Laws of England* (Oxford: Clarendon Press, 1765), 117–141; and Daniel Boorstin, *The Mysterious Science of the Law: An Essay on Blackstone's Commentaries* (Boston: Beacon, 1958).

28. Elliot, *Debates*, IV, 322.

29. Melancton Smith, "An Address to the People of the State of New York," in Paul L. Ford, ed., *Pamphlets on the Constitution of the United States* (Brooklyn: Historical Printing Club, 1892); Pennsylvania Minority, "The Address and Reasons of Dissent," in Cecelia Kenyon, ed., *The Antifederalists* (Indianapolis: Bobbs-Merrill, 1966); Richard Henry Lee, "Letters of a Federal Farmer," in Ford, *Pamphlets*; Luther Martin, "Letter to the Maryland Legislature," in Elliot, *Debates*, I, 376–377. Also see Kenyon, "Men of Little Faith: The Antifederalists on

the Nature of Representative Government," *William and Mary Quarterly*, 3d Series, XII (1955), 3–43; and Jackson Turner Main, *The Antifederalists: Critics of the Constitution, 1781–1788* (Chapel Hill: University of North Carolina Press, 1961).

30. Bernard Swartz, ed., *The Bill of Rights: A Documentary History* (New York: McGraw Hill, 1971) contains an excellent collection of the basic documents pertaining to the Bill of Rights. Also see Edward Dumbard, *Bill of Rights* (Norman: University of Oklahoma Press, 1957); Robert A. Rutland, *Birth of the Bill of Rights, 1776–1791* (Chapel Hill: University of North Carolina Press, 1955); and Kenneth R. Bowling, "Politics in the First Congress, 1789–1791" (Ph.D. thesis, University of Wisconsin, Madison, 1968).

CHAPTER 4

1. Thomas Paine, "Common Sense," in Merrill Jensen, ed., *Tracts of the American Revolution, 1763–1776* (Indianapolis: Bobbs-Merrill, 1967), 403.

2. Nathaniel Chipman, *Sketches of the Principles of Government* (Rutland, Vt.: 1793), introduction, 67–68, 75, 128–129, 174–179, 272–273.

3. *Ibid.*, 177–182.

4. John Taylor, *Tyranny Unmasked* (Washington City: Davis and Force, 1822), 23–24, 41, 100, 115–117, 123, 139, 195–198, 253. Taylor, *Arator* (Georgetown: Carter, 1813), 25, 42–46, 277–288; Taylor, *An Inquiry into the Principles of Government of the United States* (New Haven, Conn.: Yale University Press, 1950), 51, 64–68, 70–72.

5. Taylor, *Tyranny Unmasked*, 50–61, 123, 167–168, 195–196, 235, 252, 308; *Arator*, 42–56; *Principles of Government*, 51, 64–72.

6. Taylor, *Tyranny Unmasked*, 195–198.

7. Merrill D. Peterson, *Jeffersonian Image in the American Mind* (New York: Oxford University Press, 1962).

8. Jefferson, *Papers*, ed. Julian P. Boyd (Princeton, N.J.: Princeton University Press, 1950–), VII, 229, 681–682, 223; XII, 440, 228; X, 368; XIV, 387; XV, 396–397; Jefferson, *Jefferson and Dupont de Nemours Correspondence*, ed. Gilbert

Chinard (Baltimore, Md.: Johns Hopkins University Press, 1931), 162–164, 259–260.

9. Henry Nash Smith, *Virgin Land: The American West as Symbol and Myth* (New York: Vintage Books, 1950); A. Whitney Griswold, *Farming and Democracy* (New Haven, Conn.: Yale University Press, 1952); Paul W. Gates, *The Farmers' Age: Agriculture, 1815–1860* (New York: Holt, Rinehart, and Winston, 1960).

10. Thomas Hart Benton, *Thirty Years' View* (New York: Appleton, 1854–1856), I, 104. Also see Samuel Rezneck, "Depression of 1819–1822: A Social History," *American Historical Review*, XXXIX (1933), 28–47; Henry Tatter, "The Preferential Treatment of the Actual Settler in the Primary Disposition of the Vacant Lands in the United States" (Ph.D. dissertation, Northwestern University, 1932); Roy M. Robbins, "Preemption: A Frontier Triumph," *Mississippi Valley Historical Review*, XVIII (1931), 331–349.

11. Andrew Jackson, 1st Annual Message to Congress, in James D. Richardson, ed., *A Compilation of the Messages and Papers of the Presidents, 1789–1897* (Washington, D.C.: Government Printing Office, 1896–1899), II, 600–601.

12. Thomas Hart Benton, *Speeches on the Public Land* (Washington: Green and Jarvis, 1828), 8, 22; *Congressional Debates*, 23d Cong., 1st Sess. (1834), 4470–4474; Senate Committee Report (May 18, 1832), in *American State Papers*, VI, 483; House Committee Report (June 5, 1836), in *American State Papers*, VIII, 330; *Congressional Globe*, 25th Cong., 2d Sess. (1838), 136–137, 139–144, appendix, 391, 3°° 395, 493, 499; *ibid.*, 26th Cong., 2d Sess. (1841), appendix, 18–20.

13. Helen Sara Zahler, *Eastern Workingmen and National Land Policy, 1829–1862* (New York: Columbia University Press, 1941), 3–80.

14. *Working Man's Advocate*, March, 1844; March 30, 1844; April 20, 1844; May 18, 1844; August 10, 1844; Lewis Masquerier, *Sociology or the Reconstruction of Society, Government and Property* (New York: L. Masquerier, 1877), 13–15, 21; John Pickering, *The Working Man's Political Economy* (New York: Arno, 1971), 3, 16–19, 21, 31, 43–45, 66–67, 89, 100–109; Thomas A. Devyr, *Odd Book of the Nineteenth Century* (New York: T. A. Devyr, 1882), 103.

15. *Working Man's Advocate,* March 30, 1844; April 6, 1844; June 8, 1844; May 25, 1844; July 6, 1844; July 20, 1844; December 21, 1844; Masquerier, *Sociology,* 57–60, 77–78, 21, 51, 52; Devyr, *Odd Book,* 103; Pickering, *Working Man's Economy,* 15–16, 31, 46, 66–67, 82–87, 95.

16. *Working Man's Advocate,* March 30, 1844; April 6, 1844; June 8, 1844; July 20, 1844; December 21, 1844; Masquerier, *Sociology,* 13–15, 21, 57–60; Devyr, *Odd Book,* 103; Pickering, *Working Man's Economy,* 15–16, 31, 46, 65, 96, 154, 183.

17. *Working Man's Advocate,* March 30, 1844; April 6, 1844; August 10, 1844; Masquerier, *Sociology,* 13–15; Devyr, *Odd Book,* 103.

18. Pickering, *Working Man's Economy,* 15–16, 36–45.

19. *Ibid.,* 46, 3, 15–16, 16–21, 48–54, 65, 70–96, 117–143.

20. Zahler, *Eastern Workingmen and Land Policy,* 81–176; Benjamin H. Hibbard, *A History of Public Land Policy* (New York: Macmillan, 1924), 136–143, 347–385; Anonymous, "Rationale of Land Reform," *Democratic Review,* XXVI (1850), 124–132; Roy M. Robbins, "Horace Greeley: Land Reform and Unemployment," *Agricultural History,* VII (1933), 18–41.

21. Horace Greeley, *Hints Toward Reforms* (New York: Harper and Brothers, 1850), 14–15, 18–19, 312–313, 353–355.

22. *Ibid.,* 316, 20, 23–24, 313–316, 319–324.

23. *Ibid.,* 18–21, 27, 30–31, 313–317, 322–324.

24. Ben P. Poore, ed., *The Federal and State Constitutions* (Washington, D.C.: Government Printing Office, 1878), 1433, 1708, 1779–1818, 1870. States with exemption clauses in addition to Michigan were Alabama, Arkansas, Florida, Georgia, North Carolina, South Carolina, Tennessee, Texas, and Virginia.

25. George M. Stephenson, *Political History of the Public Lands* (Boston: Richard G. Badger, 1917); James Dubois and Gertrude S. Mathews, *Galusha A. Grow: Father of the Homestead Law* (Boston: Houghton, Mifflin, 1917); Patrick W. Riddleberger, "George W. Julian: Abolitionist Land Reformer," *Agricultural History,* XXIV (1955), 108–144; Robbins, "Horace Greeley: Land Reform and Unemployment"; Robert W. Winston, *Andrew Johnson: Plebeian and Patriot* (New York: H. Holt, 1928).

26. *Congressional Globe*, 32d Cong., 1st Sess. (1852), appendix, 424–428; 31st Cong., 1st Sess. (1850), 1449–1450, 1457–1467, appendix, 950–952; 32d Cong., 1st Sess. (1852), 424–428, appendix, 296–299, 424, 258–260, 730–738, 806–812; 33d Cong., 1st Sess. (1854), 1160–1670, 1702–1712, 1717–1726, 1740–1749, 1768–1779, 1811–1820, 1843–1847, appendix, 1087–1123, 1210–1214, 240–244, 424–428; 35th Cong., 1st Sess. (1860), *passim.* Also see George W. Julian, *Speeches on Political Questions* (New York: Hurd and Houghton, 1872), 51–61.

27. See 26 above and also the objections to preemption and graduation in *Congressional Globe*, 25th Cong., 2d Sess. (1838) appendix, 494–496, 500–501; 23d Cong., 1st Sess. (1834), 4479–4480.

28. See 26 and 27 above. The radicals made their differences even clearer in the debate over the homesteading of freedmen on confiscated southern land and land for railroads and corporations after the war. Julian, *Speeches*, 181–184, 212–226, 245, 365–375, 385–398; *Congressional Globe*, 38th Cong., 1st Sess. (1864), 2234, 2249–2251; 39th Cong., 1st Sess. (1866), 715–718; Andrew Johnson, "Veto Message of Land Grant to New York and Montana Iron Mining and Manufacturing Company" (June 15, 1866), in Richardson, *Messages*, VI, 416–422.

29. James Buchanan, Veto Message, in Richardson, *Messages*, V, 611–612. For best available employment statistics see David Montgomery, *Beyond Equality: Labor and the Radical Republicans* (New York: Alfred A. Knopf, 1967), appendix A.

1870 EMPLOYMENT STATISTICS

		Number	*% Work Force*
I	Proprietors		
	1. nonagricultural employers	1,108,664	8.6
	2. farmers and planters	3,127,715	24.2
	Total independent	4,236,379	32.8
II	Wage Earners		
	1. agricultural	3,722,059	28.7
	2. manufacturing	3,546,300	27.4
	3. white collar	387,559	3.0
	4. domestic	1,032,656	8.0
	Total wage earners	8,688,574	67.1

Note: Approximately one-third of wage earners were between ages 15 to 25, while nearly all self-employed persons were over age 25. Thus the relative number of wage earners to self-employed is exaggerated by these figures, since many wage earners between 15 and 25 in 1870 would eventually become self-employed or marry a self-employed person. An adjusted ratio would be about 55% to 45%. Estimate of age component derived from 1890 figures contained in Bureau of Census, *Historical Statistics of the United States* (Washington, D.C.: Government Printing Office, 1976), 132.

30. Abraham Lincoln, 1st Annual Message to Congress, in Richardson, *Messages*, VI, 57–58.

31. See 26 above. Agricultural periodicals provide additional evidence of this trend. *The Genesee Farmer* (Rochester, N.Y.: 1842–1864); *Country Gentleman* (Albany, N.Y.: 1853–1865); *American Farmer* (Baltimore: 1819–1870); *American Agriculturalist* (New York: 1842–1867), all indicated a much wider concern for productivity and labor-management problems than they did for declining freehold farming.

CHAPTER 5

1. Adam Smith, *The Wealth of Nations* (New York: Modern Library, 1965), 7, 47–54, 65–66, 78–88, 112–122, 276, 365, 627–629, 651. Also see Max Lerner's introduction to *Wealth of Nations* (Modern Library edition), and Martin Albaum, "The Moral Defenses of the Physiocrats 'Laissez-faire,'" *Journal of the History of Ideas*, XVI (1955), 179–198.

2. Smith, *Wealth of Nations*, 69–81, 119–133, 316–326.

3. Hamilton's letters, writings, and policy papers are collected in *The Papers of Alexander Hamilton*, ed. Jacob E. Cook and Harold Syrett (New York: Columbia University Press, 1961–1967). The two main popularizers of "Hamiltonian" ideas were Tench Coxe, *A View of the United States of America* (New York: Augustus M. Kelley, 1965), and Mathew Carey, *Essays on Political Economy* (Philadelphia: Carey, 1822). By far the richest and most varied source of Hamiltonian economic thought are the twelve volumes of *The American Museum, or Universal Magazine* (1787–1792), a periodical edited

and published by Carey. The subscription list found in Carey's *American Museum* contains a fairly comprehensive list of the most important American leaders who subscribed to Hamiltonian ideas. Specifically see Hamilton, *Papers*, X, 240, 256–260, 272–274, 287; VIII, 122–128; VI, 434–439; Jefferson, *Papers*, XVI, 455–462. Also see Coxe, *View of United States*, 6–7, 30–31, 193, 359–362, 366–378; Carey, *Essays*, 261, 283–284, 307–308, 376; *American Museum*, II, 119; VIII, 47–51; 181–183.

4. Hamilton, *Papers*, I, 167–170; III, 175–176; V, 123; VI, 70–76, 104, 434–439; VII, 122–124, 127–128; X, 249, 253, 272. For the arguments between Hamilton and Jefferson over the status of speculative wealth see Jefferson, *Papers*, XVI, 462–470. Julian P. Boyd has written an extended essay on the conflict in the same volume, 455–462, and in the appendix of volume XVIII, 611–688. Also see Coxe, *View of United States*, 23–24, 26, 42–43, 55, 356; Carey, *Essays*, 290, 376, 413–464; *American Museum*, I, 17–19; II, 117–119, 258; V, 460–464; VII, 24–25; XII, 167–170, 217, 221.

5. George R. Taylor, *The Transportation Revolution, 1815–1860* (New York: Harper and Row, 1968), chapters i, x, xi, xiii, xviii.

6. *Ibid.*, chapter xiii, 392–394; Stephan Thernstrom, *Poverty and Progress: Social Mobility in a Nineteenth Century City* (New York: Atheneum, 1969); David Montgomery, "The Working Classes of the Pre-Industrial American City, 1780–1830," *Labor History*, IX (1968), 3–22; Edward Pessen, "The Egalitarian Myth and the American Social Reality: Wealth, Mobility, and Equality in the 'Era of the Common Man,' " *American Historical Review*, LXXVI (1971), 989–1034.

7. Chilton Williamson, *American Suffrage from Property to Democracy, 1760–1860* (Princeton, N.J.: Princeton University Press, 1960), 139–299.

8. Merrill D. Peterson, ed., *Democracy, Liberty, and Property: The State Constitutional Conventions of the 1820's* (Indianapolis: Bobbs-Merrill, 1966), introduction.

9. *Reports of the Proceedings and Debates of the Convention of 1821, Assembled for the Constitution of the State of New York* (Albany: E. and E. Hosford, 1821), 219–223, 182–183, 196–197, 215–219; *Journal of Debates and Proceedings in the Convention of Delegates, Chosen to Revise the Constitution of*

Massachusetts (Boston: Boston Daily Advertiser, 1853), 247–248, 250–252, 253, 254, 277–278, 286, 300, 304–321.

10. See 9 above.

11. *Reports of New York Convention*, 178–179, 181–182, 234–235, 240–244; *Journal of Massachusetts Convention*, 252–253, 248, 249.

12. Arthur Schlesinger, Jr., *The Age of Jackson* (Boston: Little, Brown, 1945); Marvin Meyers, *The Jacksonian Persuasion: Politics and Belief* (New York: Vintage Books, 1960); Robert V. Remini, *Andrew Jackson and the Bank War* (New York: Norton, 1967); Lee Benson, *The Concept of Jacksonian Democracy: New York as a Test Case* (New York: Atheneum, 1965).

13. F. Byrdsall, *The History of the Loco-foco or Equal Rights Party* (New York: Clement and Packard, 1842); William Leggett, *Political Writings*, ed. Theodore Sedgwick (New York: Taylor and Dodd, 1839); Robert Rantoul, Jr., *Memoirs, Speeches, and Writings of Robert Rantoul, Jr.*, ed. Luther Hamilton (Boston: J. P. Jewett, 1854); Meyers, *Jacksonian Persuasion*, chapters ix and x; Schlesinger, *Age of Jackson*, chapters xiv, xv, and xvi; Walter Huggins, *Jacksonian Democracy and the Working Class* (Stanford University Press, 1960); John R. Commons and Helen Sumner, *History of Labour in the United States* (New York: Macmillan, 1918), I; Commons and Sumner, *The Documentary History of American Industrial Society* (Cleveland: Clark, 1910), V, VI, VII, VIII; Norman Ware, *The Industrial Worker, 1840–1860* (Chicago: Quadrangle, 1964).

14. Joseph L. Blau, ed., *Social Theories of Jacksonian Democracy: Representative Writings of the Period, 1825–1850* (Indianapolis: Bobbs-Merrill, 1954), provides an excellent sample of "Jacksonian" thought. Also see Edward Pessen, *Most Uncommon Jacksonians: The Radical Leaders of the Early Labor Movement* (Albany: State University of New York Press, 1970) for a discussion of labor radicals; and Alice Felt Tyler, *Freedom's Ferment* (New York: Harper and Row, 1962), for a survey of the utopian and religious movements of the period.

15. Arthur Bestor, *Backwoods Utopias: The Sectarian Origins and the Owenite Phase of Communitarian Socialism in America, 1663–1829* (Philadelphia: University of Pennsylvania

Press, 1970), chapters iv, v, vi, vii; Robert Owen, *The Book of the New Moral World* (New York: Augustus M. Kelley, 1970), part V, 17, 51, 56–58, 45–49.

16. Owen, *New Moral World*, part II, 22; part V, 15, 51, 56–58; part VI, 40–42, 58; Owen, *Lectures on the Entire New State of Society* (London: J. Brooks, 1830), 42–43, 50–52, 60–67, 157–158.

17. Owen, *New Moral World*, part VI, 14–15, 86; part V, 25–30, 60–65; part II, 22; *Entire New Society*, 149, 57, 64–67, 157–158.

18. Bestor, "American Phalanxes: A Study of Fourierist Socialism in the United States" (Ph.D. dissertation, Yale University, 1938); Tyler, *Freedom's Ferment*, 166–184, 217–219; Bestor, *Backwoods Utopias*, appendix, 277–285.

19. Albert Brisbane, *Social Destiny of Man: or Association and Reorganization of Society* (Philadelphia: C. F. Stollmeyer, 1840), 90–91, 110, 112–113, 331, 336–339.

20. *Ibid.*, vi, 5–6, 33–35, 328, 353–354, 378.

21. *Ibid.*, 29, 63, 353–354, 360, 378.

22. Edward Pessen, "Thomas Skidmore, Agrarian Reformer in the Early American Labor Movement," *New York History*, XXV (July 1954), 280–296.

23. Thomas Skidmore, *The Rights of Man to Property!* (New York: Burt Franklin, 1967), 125, 3–4, 54, 59–60, 100, 205–207, 241–242.

24. *Ibid.*, 137–144, 146–158.

25. *Ibid.*, 262–264.

26. *Ibid.*, 185–197, 261–262.

27. Meyer, *Jacksonian Persuasion*, chapter viii; Theodore Sedgwick, *Public and Private Economy* (New York: Arno Press, 1971), 41, 43, 51, 59, 64, 70–71.

28. Sedgwick, *Public and Private Economy*, 14, 20, 22, 26, 37, 61–63, 74–75, 77–78, 9, 220–222, 225–226. Thernstrom in *Poverty and Progress* points out that farm acquisition represented one of the prime means of upward mobility for a factory worker and also the slim odds of success.

29. Sedgwick, *Public and Private Economy*, 13, 15, 17, 61–63, 74–75.

30. Dorfman, *Economic Mind*, II, 758–770; Stow Persons, *American Minds: A History of Ideas* (New York: Holt, Rine-

hart, and Winston, 1958), 191–200; Francis Wayland, *Elements of Moral Science* (Boston: Gould and Lincoln, 1863), 230–257; Wayland, *Elements of Political Economy* (New York: Leavitt, Lord and Company, 1837), 7–9, 109–110, 111–115, 326–346.

31. Wayland, *Moral Science*, 228, 231–238, 254–257; Wayland, *Political Economy*, 111–112, 114–115.

32. Dorfman, *Economic Mind*, II, 835–843; Francis Bowen, *The Principles of Political Economy, Applied to the Condition, Resources, and the Institution of the American People* (Boston: Little, Brown, 1859), 4–5, 18–19, 28, 78, 76, 129–130, 239, 493, 499–500.

33. Bowen, *Principles of Political Economy*, 18–19, 30–31, 56.

34. *Ibid.*, 56–62, 125, 129–130, 200–201, 203, 239.

35. *Ibid.*, 494–506; Bowen, "Distribution of Property," *North American Review*, LXVII (1848), 119–160; Bowen, "Population and Property," *North American Review*, LXVII (1848), 370–419; Bowen, "French Ideas of Democracy and a Community of Goods," *North American Review*, LXIX (1849), 277–325.

36. Excellent examples of this can be seen in Francis Lieber, *Essays on Property and Labour* (New York: Harper, 1842); Edward Everett, "Accumulation, Property, Capital, Credit," (1838), in Edward Everett, *Orations and Speeches* (Boston: Little, Brown, 1860), 6th edition, II, 288–312; John Bascom, *Political Economy* (Andover: Warren and Draper, 1874); Edward Kellogg, *Labor and Other Capital* (New York: Kellogg, 1849); Henry Carey, *Essay on the Rate of Wages* (Philadelphia: Carey, Lea, and Blanchard, 1835). Also see Samuel Rezneck, "Rise and Early Development of Industrial Consciousness in the United States," in Samuel Rezneck, *Business Depressions and Financial Panics* (New York: Greenwood, 1968), 51–72, for an earlier recognition of the transition in industrial values taking place in the antebellum period.

CHAPTER 6

1. Winthrop Jordan, *White Over Black: American Attitudes Toward the Negro* (Baltimore: Penguin Books, 1969), and John Hope Franklin, *From Slavery to Freedom: A History of Negro Americans* (New York: Vintage, 1969).

2. David Brian Davis, *The Problem of Slavery in Western Culture* (Ithaca, N.Y.: Cornell University Press, 1969), 62–90, 119–120.

3. John Locke, *Two Treatises of Government*, ed. Peter Laslett (New York: Mentor Books, 1963), chapters i–iv, viii, xviii.

4. *Ibid.*, 320, 325–326, 430–433.

5. Samuel Hopkins, *A Dialogue Concerning the Slavery of Africans* (New York: 1776), 3, 37; Thomas Paine, "African Slavery in America" (1774) in *The Writings of Thomas Paine*, ed. Philip Foner (New York: Citadel Press, 1945), II, 19. Also see David B. Davis, *The Problem of Slavery in the Age of Revolution, 1770–1823* (Ithaca, N.Y.: Cornell University Press, 1975).

6. Jonathan Elliot, ed., *The Debates of the Several State Conventions on the Adoption of the Federal Constitution* (Philadelphia: Lippincott, 1896), I, 71–72, 363; II, 237, 40–41; III, 269–270, 452–459, 590–591; IV, 100–101, 283. Also see Staughton Lynd, ed., *Class Conflict, Slavery, and the United States Constitution: Ten Essays* (Indianapolis: Bobbs-Merrill, 1967).

7. St. George Tucker, *A Dissertation on Slavery* (Philadelphia: Mathew Carey, 1796). Also see David Rice, *Slavery Inconsistent with Justice and Good Policy* (Philadelphia: Gurney, 1792); Samuel Stanhope Smith, *Lectures* (Trenton, N.J.: J. J. Wilson, 1813), II, 160–179.

8. Leon Litwack, *North of Slavery: The Negro in the Free States* (Chicago: University of Chicago Press, 1961); George H. Moore, *Notes on the History of Slavery in Massachusetts* (New York: Appleton, 1866); Henry S. Cooley, *A Study of Slavery in New Jersey* (Baltimore: Johns Hopkins University Press, 1896); Edward R. Turner, *The Negro in Pennsylvania: 1639–1861* (Washington, D.C.: American Historical Association, 1911); Bernard C. Steiner, *History of Slavery in Connecticut* (Baltimore: Johns Hopkins University Press, 1893); William D. Johnstone, *Slavery in Rhode Island, 1775–1776* (Baltimore: Johns Hopkins University Press, 1896); Edgar J. McManus, *A History of Negro Slavery in New York* (Syracuse, N.Y.: Syracuse University Press, 1966). Barnett Hollander's *Slavery in America: Its Legal History* (New York: Barnes and Noble, 1963) is a good guide to legal citations.

9. For a perceptive comment on the paradoxical heritage of the Revolution see William Freehling, "The Founding Fathers

and Slavery," *American Historical Review*, LXXVII (1972), 81–93.

10. The Case of James Somerset, a Negro, 20 *State Trials* (1772–1773), 1.

11. The Antelope, 10 Wheaton (U.S.: 1825), 67–132. Also see Hollander, *Slavery in America*.

12. See Story's opinion in Society v. Wheeler, 2 Gal. (U.S.C. Ct.: 1814), for his use of natural rights and property. Also in 1830 Story wrote a short article "Natural Law" in which he viewed property rights in much more conditional terms than he did in his decisions. In the case of "contractual rights" Story retained his rigid defense of the "natural rights of property." Story's article is reprinted in James McClellan, *Joseph Story and the Study of the Constitution* (Norman: University of Oklahoma Press, 1971) appendix. For Story's comments on slave property see his *Commentaries on the Conflict of Laws* (Boston: Hillard, Gray, and Co., 1834), 92–97, and *Commentaries on the Constitution*, abridged edition (Boston: Hillard, Gray and Co., 1833), 675–676. Also see Gerald T. Dunn, *Justice Story and the Rise of the Supreme Court* (New York: Simon and Schuster, 1971), 398–403. For other legal commentators and their opinion on the status of slave property see James Kent, *Commentaries on American Law* (New York: O. Halsted, 1826–1830), II, 201–209, and Nathaniel Chipman, *Sketches on the Principles of Government* (Rutland, Vt.: 1793), 88–94.

13. *Annals of Congress*, 35th Cong., 1st Sess. (1820), 86–470, 1281–1588.

14. *Ibid.*

15. *Ibid.*

16. Merrill Peterson, ed., *Democracy, Liberty, and Property: The State Constitutional Conventions of the 1820's* (Indianapolis: Bobbs-Merrill, 1966), introduction.

17. *Proceedings and Debates of the Virginia State Convention of 1829–1830*, ed. Thomas Ritchie (Richmond, Va.: Ritchie and Cook, 1830), 68–79.

18. Henry Ruffner, *An Address to the People of West Virginia* (Lexington, Va.: R. C. Noel, 1847). For the Virginia Debates of 1832 Joseph C. Robert has included a fine sample in the appendix of his history of the debates, *Road to Monticello* (Durham, N.C.: Duke University Press, 1941), 61–112.

19. Thomas R. Dew, *Review of the Debates in the Virginia Legislature, 1831–1832*, reprinted in Chancellor Harper, ed., *The Pro-Slavery Argument* (New York: Greenwood, 1968), 300–388.

20. William Ellery Channing, "Slavery," in *The Works of William Ellery Channing*, 12th edition (Boston: Crosly, Nichols, 1853), II, 12–47, 106–110. Also see Channing's "Emancipation" in *Works*, VI.

21. Lysander Spooner, *The Unconstitutionality of Slavery* (Boston: Bella Marsh, 1853), 36–53. Also Gilbert H. Barnes, *The Antislavery Impulse, 1833–1844* (New York: Harcourt, Brace, and World, 1964); Dwight Lowell Dumond, *Antislavery Origins of the Civil War in the United States* (Ann Arbor: University of Michigan Press, 1959); Howard Jay Graham, "The Early Antislavery Backgrounds of the Fourteenth Amendment," reprinted in *Everyman's Constitution* (Madison: State Historical Society of Wisconsin, 1968), 152–240; Jacobus tenBroek, *The Antislavery Origins of the Fourteenth Amendment* (Berkeley: University of California Press, 1951).

22. Spooner, *Unconstitutionality of Slavery*, 5–20, 129–131, 270–277. For other abolitionists whose position agreed with Spooner's in his use of the Federal Constitution as an antislavery weapon see G. W. F. Mellen, *An Argument on the Unconstitutionality of Slavery* (Boston: Saxton and Pierce, 1841); William Hosmer, *The Higher Law in its Relations to Government* (Auburn, N.Y.: Derby and Miller, 1852); Frederick Douglass, "The Constitution of the United States: Is it Pro-Slavery or Anti-Slavery?", in *Life and Writings of Frederick Douglass*, ed. Philip Foner (New York: International Publishers, 1950), II, 467–480. For more moderate positions see Lincoln, "Annual Message," (Dec. 1, 1861), in James D. Richardson, *A Compilation of the Messages and Papers of the Presidents, 1789–1897* (Washington, D.C.: Government Printing Office, 1896–1899), VI, 137–141; Lincoln, *The Collected Works of Abraham Lincoln*, ed. Roy P. Basler (New Brunswick, N.J.: Rutgers University Press, 1953), II, 246, 266, 321–322, 493; III, 231; Richard Hildreth, *Despotism in America* (Boston: J. P. Jewett, 1854), 7–8, 10, 36–40, 169–172, 239–352; Francis Wayland, *The Elements of Moral Science*, ed. Joseph Blau (Cambridge, Mass.: Harvard University Press, 1963), 183–194. A number of abolitionists

challenged the antislavery interpretation of the Constitution on the grounds that Spooner had twisted the wording of the document to the point of threatening to make all law subjective. They preferred either a new constitution or the present one amended to make clear that slavery was unconstitutional. See Wendell Phillips, *Review of Lysander Spooner's Essay on the Constitutionality of Slavery* (Boston: Andrews and Prentiss, 1847); William Lloyd Garrison, "The United States Constitution," in *Selections from the Writings of William Lloyd Garrison* (Boston: R. F. Wallcutt, 1852), 302–315; William I. Bowditch, *Slavery and the Constitution* (Boston: R. F. Wallcutt, 1849), 120–121.

23. Samuel Seabury, *American Slavery Distinguished from the Slavery of English Theorists and Justified by the Law of Nature* (New York: Mason and Bros., 1861), 25, 31, 103–104. Other works with views on property and slavery similar to Seabury's are Thomas Cooper, *Lectures on the Elements of Political Economy* (Columbia, S.C.: Morris and Wilson, 1831); George W. Sawyer, *Southern Institutes* (Philadelphia: Lippincott, 1858), 12–29, 147; Thomas R. Cobb, *An Inquiry into the Law of Negro Slavery* (Philadelphia: T. and J. W. Johnson, 1858); J. K. Pauling, *Slavery in the United States* (New York: Harper and Bros., 1836); E. M. Elliott, *Cotton is King and Pro-Slavery Arguments*, 3d ed. (Augusta, Ga.: Pritchard, Abbott and Loomis, 1860). Also see W. S. Jenkens, *Pro-Slavery Thought in the Old South* (Chapel Hill: University of North Carolina Press, 1933).

24. Seabury, *American Slavery*, 31–43, 59, 76, 80–83, 170–173.

25. *Ibid.*, 80–99, 139–140.

26. George Fitzhugh, *Sociology for the South or the Failure of Free Society* (Richmond, Va.: A. Morris, 1854), 25–27, 47–48. See 23 above for the remarkable similarities between Fitzhugh's assumptions and a significant number of important southern intellectuals. The movement of Southerners away from Lockean assumptions appears to have been widespread and Fitzhugh was by no means alone. John C. Calhoun in his *Disquisition on Government*, ed. C. Gordon Post (Indianapolis: Bobbs-Merrill, 1953), anticipated the general thrust of Fitzhugh's Aristotelian arguments. Also see Eugene D. Genovese, *The Political Economy of Slavery* (New York: Vintage Books,

1965) and *The World the Slaveholders Made* (New York: Vintage Books, 1971) for the most appreciative treatment of Fitzhugh by a recent scholar.

27. Fitzhugh, *Sociology for the South,* 47–48, 68–69, 185–186, 297–298.

28. *Ibid.*

29. *Ibid.*, and "Entails and Primogeniture," *De Bow's Review,* XXVII (1859), 172–177.

30. Quoted in Graham, *Everyman's Constitution,* 220.

31. Jenkins, *Pro-Slavery Thought*; "The Constitution of the Confederate States of America," in James D. Richardson, ed., *Messages and Papers of the Confederacy* (Nashville, Tenn.: United States Publishing Co., 1905), I, 37–45.

CHAPTER 7

1. Lewis M. Simes, "Historical Background of the Law of Property," in James Casner, ed., *The American Law of Property* (Boston: Little, Brown, 1952), I, 3–71; Edward S. Corwin, "The Doctrine of Due Process of Law Before the Civil War," *Harvard Law Review,* XXIV (1911), 366–385, 460–479, and *Liberty Against Government* (Baton Rouge: Louisiana State University Press, 1948).

2. William Blackstone, *Commentaries on the Law of England* (Cambridge: Clarendon Press, 1965), I, 117–141; II, 2–21.

3. *Ibid.*, I, 157.

4. *Ibid.*, I, 48–211.

5. James Wilson, *The Works of James Wilson,* ed. Robert Green McCloskey (Cambridge, Mass.: Harvard University Press, 1967); Blackstone, *Commentaries on the Law of England,* ed. St. George Tucker (Philadelphia: W. Y. Birch and A. Small, 1803); Nathaniel Chipman, *Sketches of the Principles of Government* (Rutland, Vt.: 1793); Anonymous, *Rudiments of Law and Government* (Charleston, S.C., 1783). Also see Corwin, "The Higher Law Background of American Law," *Harvard Law Review,* XLII (1928–1929), 148–185, 365–409, and Leonard W. Levy, ed., *Judicial Review and the Supreme Court: Selected Essays* (New York: Harper and Row, 1967).

6. Wilson, *Works,* 4–14, 43, 300–331, 430, 711–719.

7. Vanhorne's Lessee v. Dorrance, 2 Dallas (U.S.: 1795) 344. Several other decisions which touched marginally on the same issue were Bayard v. Singleton, 1 Martin (N.C.: 1787); Bowman v. Middleton, 1 Bay (S.C.: 1792); Cooper v. Telfair, 4 Dallas (U.S.: 1800).

8. Vanhorne's Lessee v. Dorrance, 2 Dallas (U.S.: 1795) 344.

9. Calder v. Bull, 3 Dallas (U.S.: 1798) 386.

10. *Ibid.*

11. *Ibid.* Also see Chase's opinion in Cooper v. Telfair. Chase's argument became an important citation in most subsequent property decisions. Kent referred to it in Gardiner v. Newburgh, 2 Johns Ch. (N.Y.: 1816), and in Dash v. Van Kleek, 7 Johns (N.Y.: 1811). Also see Town of Pawlet v. Clark, 9 Cranch (U.S.: 1818), and Wales v. Stetson, 2 (Mass. 1806).

12. Peter C. Magrath, *Yazoo: Land and Politics in the New Republic* (Providence, R.I.: Brown University Press, 1966) covers the case thoroughly and also reprints a number of hard to find and important documents relevant to Fletcher v. Peck.

13. Fletcher v. Peck, 6 Cranch (U.S.: 1810) 87.

14. *Ibid.* Also see Marshall's ruling on the Fifth Amendment in Barron v. Baltimore, 7 Peters (U.S.: 1833) 243.

15. Blackstone, *Commentaries*, I, 466–485. Also see Stewart Kyd, *A Treatise on the Law of Corporations* (London: 1793–1794); E. Merrick Dodd, *American Business Corporations until 1860* (Cambridge, Mass.: Harvard University Press, 1954), parts I and III; Samuel Williston, "History of the Law of Business Corporations before 1900," *Harvard Law Review*, II (1888), 105–124, 149–160.

16. Turpin v. Locket, 6 Call (Va.: 1804) 113; Blackstone, *Commentaries,* ed. Tucker, I, appendix. Spencer Roane, Tucker's colleague on the Virginia Supreme Court, supported Tucker in Turpin v. Locket. Roane took a more defiant position than Tucker, but he lacked Tucker's logical consistency. Also see Currie's Adm'r v. Mutual Assurance Society, 4 Henry and Mumford (Va.: 1909).

17. Bank of United States v. Deveaux, 5 Cranch (U.S.: 1809) 61; Terret v. Taylor, 9 Cranch (U.S.: 1815) 43; Elliot v. Marshall (Mass.: 1807) and Wales v. Stetson, 2 (Mass.: 1806) 146. Also see Gerald T. Dunne, *Joseph Story and the Rise of the*

Supreme Court (New York: Simon and Schuster, 1971), 389–398.

18. Dartmouth College v. Woodward, 4 Wheaton (U.S.: 1819) 603. Timothy Farrar, *The Case of the Trustees of Dartmouth College Against William H. Woodward* (Boston: 1819) contains an almost complete collection of the court decisions and legal briefs for the Dartmouth case, state and federal.

19. Dodd, *American Business Corporations*, 27–41, 127–143, 158–163, 181–187; James Kent, *Commentaries on American Law* (New York: O. Halsted, 1826–1830), II, 246–247. Many of these changes were first advanced by state courts and the federal decisions were often simply ratifications of the interpretation of the state courts. I have emphasized federal decisions because the federal decisions indicated that these interpretations by that time had become acceptable to a national constituency.

20. Providence Bank v. Billings, 4 Peters (U.S.: 1830) 514; New Jersey v. Wilson, 7 Cranch (U.S.: 1812) 164. Also see R. Kent Newmyer, *The Supreme Court Under Marshall and Taney* (New York: Thomas Y. Crowell, 1968), chapter iii; Benjamin F. Wright, *The Contract Clause of the Constitution* (Cambridge, Mass.: Harvard University Press, 1938), chapter ii; Stanley I. Kutler, *Privilege and Creative Destruction: The Charles River Bridge Case* (Philadelphia: Lippincott, 1971), chapters i–iii, x, xi; Morton J. Horwitz, "The Transformation in the Conception of Property in American Law, 1780–1860," *University of Chicago Law Review*, XL (1973), 248–290.

21. Barron v. Baltimore, 7 Peters (U.S.: 1833) 243; Kutler, *Creative Destruction*, 142–145. James Kent was a prominent dissenter to Marshall's interpretation of the taxing power. Kent insisted that taxation was justified only so much as it protected and enhanced property and thus a taxpayer should receive an equivalent in service for his taxes. See his *Commentaries on American Law*, II, 324–333.

22. J. A. C. Grant, "The 'Higher Law' Background of the Law of Eminent Domain," *Wisconsin Law Review*, VI (1930–1931), 67–85. The most recent and thorough work on pre-Civil War eminent domain is Harry N. Scheiber's "Road to Munn: Eminent Domain and the Concept of Public Purpose in the State Courts," *Perspectives in American History*, V (1971), 329–403.

Also see Frank I. Michelman, "Property, Utility, and Fairness: Comments on the Ethical Foundations of 'Just Compensation' Law," *Harvard Law Review*, LXXX (1966–1967), 1165–1258, and Joseph L. Sax, "Takings and the Police Power," *Yale Law Journal*, LXXXIV (1964–1965), 36–76.

23. Kent, *Commentaries*, II, 338–339; Gardiner v. Newburgh, 2 Johns Ch. (N.Y.: 1816) 162.

24. Kent, *Commentaries*, II, 340–347.

25. Corwin, "Due Process"; Kutler, *Creative Destruction*, chapter x; Scheiber, "Road to Munn"; Grant, "Higher Law." Also see the eminent domain decisions: The Mohawk Bridge Co. v. Utica and Schenectady Railroad Co., 6 Paige (N.Y.: 1837) 555; Tuckahoe Canal Co. v. Tuckahoe and James R.R. Co., 11 Leigh (Va.: 1840) 42; Mills v. County of St. Clair, 8 Howard (U.S.: 1850) 569; Bridge Proprietors v. Hoboken Company, 1 Wallace (U.S.: 1864) 116. The most important pre-Civil War cases in which courts emphasized natural rights arguments were Hoke v. Henderson, 2 Dev (N.C.: 1833) 1; Taylor v. Porter, 4 Hill (N.Y.: 1843) 140; and Wynehamer v. State of New York, 13 (N.Y.: 1856) 378.

26. Kutler, *Creative Destruction*.

27. Charles River Bridge Company v. Warren Bridge Company, 11 Peters (U.S.: 1837) 420.

28. Also see Story's opinions in Terret v. Taylor and Dartmouth v. Woodward. In 1835 Story wrote a revealing essay "Natural Law" reprinted in James McClelland, *Joseph Story and the American Constitution* (Norman, Okla.: University of Oklahoma Press, 1971), appendix I, in which he gave a lengthy statement of his views on the nature of private property and its limitations.

29. West River Bridge v. Dix, 6 Howard (U.S.: 1848) 507. Also see Kutler, *Creative Destruction*, 145–146.

PART III

1. Adolf A. Berle, Jr., and Gardiner C. Means, *The Modern Corporation and Private Property* (New York: Macmillan, 1932), parts I and IV.

CHAPTER 8

1. Sidney Fine, *Laissez Faire and the General Welfare State* (Ann Arbor: University of Michigan Press, 1956).

2. James Willard Hurst, *Law and the Conditions of Freedom in the Nineteenth-Century United States* (Madison: University of Wisconsin Press, 1956).

3. Benjamin F. Wright, *American Interpretations of Natural Law* (Cambridge, Mass.: Harvard University Press, 1931).

4. Charles W. McCurdy in a very important essay, "Justice Field and the Jurisprudence of Government-Business Relations: Some Parameters of Laissez Faire Constitutionalism, 1863–1897," *Journal of American History* (1975), LXI, 970–1005, makes an argument in substance similar to my own and which helped clarify my own thoughts.

5. Corfield v. Coryell, Cir. Ct. (U.S.: 1823) 371. Also see Howard Jay Graham, *Everyman's Constitution* (Madison: State Historical Society of Wisconsin, 1968), 23–97, 152–265; Edward S. Corwin, *American Constitutional History*, ed. Alpheus T. Mason (New York: Harper and Row, 1964), 46–98; and Jacobus tenBroek, *The Antislavery Origins of the Fourteenth Amendment* (Berkeley: University of California Press, 1951), 113–224.

6. Slaughter House Cases, 16 Wallace (U.S.: 1873) 461.

7. Munn v. Illinois, 94 (U.S.: 1877) 113.

8. Mugler v. Kansas, 123 (U.S.: 1887) 623; Powell v. Pennsylvania, 127 (U.S.: 1887) 678.

9. Powell v. Pennsylvania, 691–692, 696.

10. Butcher's Union Slaughter House v. Crescent City Livestock Landing Company, 11 (U.S.: 1884) 746.

11. Paul v. Virginia, 8 Wallace (U.S.: 1869) 168.

12. Also see the Supreme Court opinions in Bartmeyer v. Iowa, 18 Wallace (U.S.: 1873) 129, and Loan Association v. Topeka, 20 Wallace (U.S.: 1875) 655. Graham has written an important essay on Field, "Justice Field and the Fourteenth Amendment," in *Everyman's Constitution*, 98–151. For a revision of Field's role in late nineteenth-century law see McCurdy, "Justice Field and the Jurisprudence of Government-Business Relations."

13. In a series of articles Graham has convincingly challenged Conkling's claim that the Joint Committee intentionally inserted the word "person" to include corporations, although Graham argues that the committee included the phrase "privileges or immunities" to give the Fourteenth Amendment natural rights meaning. All of Graham's articles are reprinted in *Everyman's Constitution*. In the same volume Graham has also included Conkling's statement to the court. Also see San Mateo County v. Southern Pacific Railroad, 116 (U.S.: 1882) 138; Santa Clara County v. Southern Pacific Railroad, 18 Cir. Ct. (U.S.: 1884) 345 and 118 (U.S.: 1886) 394.

14. Railroad Commission Cases, 116 (U.S.: 1886) 307; Chicago, Milwaukee, and St. Paul Ry v. Minnesota, 134 (U.S.: 1890) 418; Wabash, St. Louis and Pacific Ry v. Illinois, 118 (U.S.: 1886) 557; Smyth v. Ames, 169 (U.S.: 1898) 466; ICC v. Cincinnati, New Orleans and Texas Pacific Ry, 167 (U.S.: 1897) 479; ICC v. Illinois Central Ry, 215 (U.S.: 1910) 452; Minnesota Rate Case, 230 (U.S.: 1913) 352; Northern Pacific Ry v. No. Dakota, 236 (U.S.: 1915) 585.

15. A good introduction to Sumner's social thought is William Graham Sumner, *What the Social Classes Owe to Each Other* (Caldwell, Idaho: Caxton Printers, 1952).

16. Sumner's essays are contained in *War and Other Essays* (1911), *Earth Hunger and Other Essays* (1913), *The Forgotten Man and Other Essays* (1919), and *The Challenge of Facts and Other Essays* (1914). Albert B. Keller edited all four volumes and Yale University Press published the entire collection. Stow Persons edited a representative sample of those essays published under the title *Social Darwinism: Selected Essays of William Graham Sumner* (Englewood Cliffs, N.J.: Prentice-Hall, 1963).

17. Sumner, *Social Darwinism*, 75.

18. *Ibid.*, 76–77.

19. *Ibid.*, 24.

20. Benjamin F. Wright, *The Growth of American Law* (Chicago: University of Chicago Press, 1967) and Roscoe Pound, "Liberty of Contract," *Yale Law Journal*, XVIII (1909), 454–487.

21. Raymond Moley, *After Seven Years* (New York: Harper and Row, 1939), and *How to Keep Our Liberty: A Program for*

Political Action (New York: Alfred A. Knopf, 1952). Also see Moley's editorials in *Newsweek* magazine, in particular those in the May 29, 1950 and June 5, 1950 issues. For an opinion very close to Moley's see Milton Friedman, *Capitalism and Freedom* (Chicago: University of Chicago Press, 1962).
22. Moley, *How to Keep Our Liberty*, 1–12.
23. *Ibid.*, 19.
24. *Ibid.*, 39–61.

CHAPTER 9

1. James Gilbert, *Designing the Industrial State: The Intellectual Pursuit of Collectivism in America, 1880–1940* (Chicago: Quadrangle Books, 1972).
2. Edward Bellamy, *Looking Backward 2000–1887*, ed. John L. Thomas (Cambridge, Mass.: Harvard University Press, 1967); *Equality* (New York: Appleton, 1897).
3. Bellamy, *Looking Backward* (New York: Modern Library, 1951), 40.
4. *Ibid.*, 88.
5. Douglas Dowd, *Thorstein Veblen* (New York: Washington Square Press, 1964).
6. Veblen, *The Theory of the Leisure Class* (New York: Mentor, 1953).
7. Veblen, *The Instinct of Workmanship and the State of the Industrial Arts* (New York: B. W. Huebsch, 1922), 187–204; *The Vested Interests and the State of the Industrial Arts* (New York: B. W. Huebsch, 1919), 85–113.
8. Veblen, *The Theory of Business Enterprise* (New York: Mentor, 1953); *Absentee Ownership and Business Enterprise in Recent Times* (New York: Huebsch, 1923), 48–68.
9. Veblen, "Beginnings of Ownership," *American Journal of Sociology*, IV (1898), 352–365.
10. Herbert Croly, *The Promise of American Life* (New York: Macmillan, 1909), 414.
11. *Ibid.*, 400.
12. Paul K. Conkin, *Puritans and Pragmatists* (New York: Dodd, Mead, 1968), 345–404.
13. John Dewey, *Individualism Old and New* (New York: Capricorn Books, 1962).

14. Dewey, *Liberalism and Social Action* (New York: Capricorn Books, 1963); *Freedom and Culture* (New York: G. P. Putnam's Sons, 1939).

15. Dewey, *Ethics* (New York: Henry Holt, 1932).

CHAPTER 10

1. See John L. Thomas, "Utopia for an Urban Age: Henry George, Henry Demoarest Lloyd, Edward Bellamy," in *Perspective in American History*, VI (1972), 135–136; and Charles A. Barker, *Henry George* (New York: Oxford University Press, 1955). Henry George, *Progress and Poverty* (New York: Robert Schlakenbach Foundation, 1937), 6–12, 167, 188, 242–252, 294–296, 328–367.

2. Henry George, *Progress and Poverty*, 81–162, 242–252, 294–296, 328–367.

3. *Ibid.*, 397–453.

4. See John D. Hicks, *The Populist Revolt* (Minneapolis: University of Minnesota Press, 1931), for a narrative history of the Populist Party; Norman Pollack, *The Populist Response to Industrial America* (New York: W. W. Norton, 1966), and Lawrence Goodwyn, *Democratic Promise: The Populist Moment in America* (New York: Oxford University Press, 1976), for studies of Populist ideas. Also see Pollack, ed., *The Populist Mind* (Indianapolis: Bobbs-Merrill, 1967).

5. James B. Weaver, *A Call to Action* (Des Moines: Iowa Printing Company, 1892), quoted from excerpt in Pollack, *Populist Mind*, 155–156.

6. Omaha Platform reprinted in Pollack, *Populist Mind*, 63–64.

7. *Ibid.*, 13–19, 52–53, 58–59, 63–64, 155–156, 205–218.

8. James H. Davis, *A Political Revolution* (Dallas, Tex.: The Advance Publishing Company, 1894), excerpt reprinted in Pollack, *Populist Mind*, 205.

9. Woodrow Wilson, *New Freedom*, ed. William E. Leuchtenburg (Englewood Cliffs, N.J.: Prentice-Hall, 1961), 22–24.

10. *Ibid.*, 20.

11. *Ibid.*, 25–29, 51–64, 102–109, 114–132, 153–160.

12. Paul K. Conkin, *Tomorrow a New World* (Ithaca, N.Y.: Cornell University Press, 1959), 11–36; Gabriel Davidson, *Our*

Jewish Farmers (New York: L. B. Fischer, 1943); Raymond P. Witte, *Twenty-five Years of Crusading: A History of the National Catholic Rural Life Conference* (Des Moines, Iowa: National Catholic Rural Life Conference, 1948).

13. John L. Stewart, *The Burden of Time: The Fugitives and Agrarians* (Princeton, N.J.: Princeton University Press, 1965), 3–205.

14. Twelve Southerners, *I'll Take My Stand: The South and the Agrarian Tradition* (New York: Harper and Row, 1962).

15. Edward S. Shapiro has written extensively on the subject. See Shapiro's "Decentralist Intellectuals and the New Deal," *Journal of American History*, LVIII (1972), 938–957, and "The Southern Agrarians and the Tennessee Valley Authority," *American Quarterly*, XXII (1970), 791–806. Also see Conkin, *Tomorrow a New World*, 25–27; Stewart, *Burden of Time*, 177–203; R. Alan Lawson, *The Failure of Independent Liberalism, 1930–1941* (New York: Capricorn Books, 1972), 135–147; Herbert Agar and Allen Tate, eds., *Who Owns America?* (Boston: Houghton Mifflin, 1936); Hilaire Belloc, *The Restoration of Property* (New York: Sheed and Ward, 1936); Luigi G. Ligutti and John C. Rawe, *Rural Roads to Security* (Milwaukee, Wis.: Bruce Publishing, 1940); John C. Rawe, "Agrarian Concept of Property," *Modern Schoolman*, XIV (1936); Catholic Rural Life Conference, *Manifesto on Rural Life* (Milwaukee, Wis.: Bruce Publishing, 1939).

16. Agar, *Who Owns America?*, viii, 94–109.

17. Also see Agar, *In Pursuit of Happiness* (Boston: Houghton Mifflin, 1938), and *Land of the Free* (Boston: Houghton Mifflin, 1935).

18. Ellis W. Hawley, *The New Deal and the Problem of Monopoly* (Princeton, N.J.: Princeton University Press, 1966), as well as Paul K. Conkin, *The New Deal* (New York: Thomas Y. Crowell, 1967).

Index

Adams, John: definition of republic, 36; colonial land titles, 40; agrarian law, 41; mentioned, 6, 39, 43

Adams, Samuel: concept of ownership, 38–39

Agar, Herbert: decentralized ownership, 197–199; mentioned, 193

Agrarianism, 5–51, 53–70, 181–200

Allodial tenure, 40

American self-image, 24

Antelope decision (1825), 99–100

Antifederalist: opposition to the Federal Constitution, 48–49; Bill of Rights, 49–50; fifth amendment, 49

Articles of Confederation: reform of, 43–45. *See* Antifederalist

Barron v. Baltimore (1833): eminent domain, 125–126

Bellamy, Edward: *Looking Backward*, 159–165; mentioned, 178, 179

Belloc, Hilaire: mentioned, 193

Benton, Thomas Hart: freeholding, 58–59

Birney, James: slavery, 112–113; concept of property, 112–113

Blackstone, William: stake in society theory, 47; concept of property rights, 114–115

Bowen, Francis: ideas on political economy, 90–92; mentioned, 87

Bradford, William, 12, 13

Brandeis, Louis: mentioned, 189

Brisbane, Albert: communitarian experiment, 81–83; concept of ownership, 82–83

Brook Farm: mentioned, 82

Brown v. Board of Education (1954), 204

Buchanan, James: position on homestead legislation, 67–70

Calling (doctrine): Calvinism, 10; colonial New England, 12; fourteenth amendment, 139–140, 142–143, 146. *See* Substantive due process

Calvinism, 9–10. *See* Colonial New England

Capitalism: agrarian criticism, 194–195; mentioned, 199. *See* Factory system; Wage system; William Graham Sumner; Raymond Moley; Alexander Hamilton; Thorstein Veblen

Channing, William Ellery: slavery, 105–106; concept of liberty, 105–106

Chase, Samuel: natural rights conception of property, 118–119

Chesterton, G. K.: mentioned, 193

Chipman, Nathaniel: concept of property rights, 54–55

Civil War: mentioned, 201, 202

Colden, Cadwallader: land reform, 19

Colonial New England, 8–23

Common law: concept of property, 114
Common socage, 40. *See* Feudal concept of ownership
Connecticut: slave policy, 98
Conkling, Roscoe: substantive due process, 144–145
Contract: *Vanhorne's Lessee v. Dorrance* (1795), 116–117; *Calder v. Bull* (1798), 118–119; *Fletcher v. Peck* (1810), 120–122; agrarian criticism, 122; William Blackstone, 122; *Bank of United States v. Deveaux* (1809), 123; *Terret v. Taylor* (1815), 123; *Dartmouth v. Woodward* (1819), 123–124; antebellum courts, 131–132. *See* Corporation
Corporation: contract clause, 121–122; agrarian criticism, 122; Joseph Storey, 123; legal definition, 123–124, 130, 131, 137–146. *See* Contract
Cotton, John: quoted, 13; Indian land policy, 16–17
Crèvecoeur, de, St. John: quoted, 2; mentioned, 35
Croly, Herbert: 159–160; New Nationalism, 170–174; mentioned, 178–179

Daniel, Peter: eminent domain, 129
Davidson, Donald: mentioned, 191, 192, 193
Declaration of Independence: quoted, 36; mentioned, 41, 96, 202. *See* Thomas Jefferson; Natural rights
Dew, Thomas: concept of ownership, 104–105; slavery, 104–105
de Crèvecoeur, St. John. *See* Crèvecoeur, de, St. John
Dewey, John, 159–160, 169–170; New Liberalism, 175–178; mentioned, 178–180, 199
Dickinson, John: mentioned, 39
Distributism: mentioned, 193

Economic regulation: colonial New England, 11
Eminent domain: colonial New England, 11; legal definition, 125–131
European images: colonial America, 14
Evans, George Henry: National Land Reform Movement, 60–63
Ex post facto clause, 118–119

Factory system: John Taylor, 56; criticism, 110–112; mentioned, 71, 201. *See* Capitalism; Alexander Hamilton; Wage system; William Graham Sumner; Thorstein Veblen; Adam Smith
Federal Constitution: convention, 45–49; concept of ownership, 45–46; debtor legislation, 46; freeholding, 46–49; suffrage restrictions, 47–48; slavery, 96–97, 99–103, 106–107. *See* Fourteenth amendment
Field, Stephen, 137–146; mentioned, 154, 158, 203
Fitzhugh, George: theory of society, 110–111; concept of ownership, 111–112
Fourier, Charles: mentioned, 81. *See* Albert Brisbane
Feudalism: concept of ownership, 5, 13, 111–112, 185; American criticism, 24, 39–40; feudal political economy, 9. *See* Just price; Calvinism
Fourteenth amendment: substantive due process, 138–146; Stephen Field, 138–146; privileges or immunities clause, 138–143; *Slaughterhouse Cases* (1873), 139–140; *Corfield v. Coryell* (1823), 138–140; *Munn v. Illinois* (1877), 140–141; mentioned, 201, 204. *See* Federal Constitution
Franklin, Benjamin: concept of ownership, 21–23; suffrage re-

quirements, 47; mentioned, 35, 39

Free and common socage: mentioned, 6. *See* Freeholding

Freeholding: colonial America, 12–14; Benjamin Franklin, 22; American Revolution, 39–40; Federal Constitution, 46–49; antebellum, 53–70; fee simple, 6; mentioned, 54, 93, 200, 202. *See* Benjamin Franklin; Thomas Jefferson; George Henry Evans; Populist; Southern agrarians; Declaration of Independence; James Harrington; Horace Greeley

Fugitives: mentioned, 191

Garhart, M. C. C. *See* Thorstein Veblen

George, Henry: *Progress and Poverty*, 181–185; unearned increment, 182–183; single tax, 183–184; entrepreneurial opportunity, 184–185; mentioned, 67

Greeley, Horace: land reform proposals, 64–67

Graduation, 59

Grow, Galusha A.: quoted, 68; support of land reform and homestead legislation, 68; mentioned, 67

Hall, Bolton: Little Landers, 190

Hamilton, Alexander: concept of ownership, 73–74; tariffs, 73; centralized banking, 73; factory system, 73–74; mentioned, 39, 112

Harlan, John Marshall: fourteenth amendment, 141–142

Harrington, James: renaissance influence, 25; concept of power, 25; English Civil War, 25–26; *Common-wealth of Oceana*, 26; civic virtue, 26–27; agrarian law, 27–28; freeholding, 27–28; mentioned, 35, 37, 41, 50, 53, 54, 58

Headrights, 7–8

Homestead legislation, 67–71; Act of 1859, 67–69; Act of 1861, 60–70

Hopkins, Samuel: slave property, 96

Howard, Martin: feudal concept of ownership, 39–40

I'll Take My Stand, 191–192

Indian land policy: colonial New England, 15–17

Inheritance, 91

International slave trade: congressional action, 97–98

Iredell, James: *Calder v. Bull* (1798), 118–119

Jackson, Andrew: freeholding, 59; land policy, 59; mentioned, 78–79

James, William: mentioned, 120

Jamestown: settlement, 6–7

Jay, John: quoted, 43

Jefferson, Thomas: definition of property rights, 41–43; concept of property, 57–58; freeholding, 57–58; agrarian republicanism, 57–58; mentioned, 35, 39, 73, 75, 76, 111, 112, 187, 199, 201, 205

Johnson, Andrew: mentioned, 67

Julian, George W.: mentioned, 67

Just price, 5: mentioned, 10. *See* Feudal concept of ownership

Keaynes, John, 11–12

Kent, James: suffrage restrictions, 76; corporations, 124; property rights, 126–128; eminent domain, 127–128

Labor theory of value: colonial New England, 12; Indian land title, 15–17; Adam Smith, 71–72; slavery, 94–113; neo-Jeffersonians, 181–199; mentioned, 5, 10, 105, 160, 177, 178, 201–205

Laissez faire, 137–158. *See* Capitalism; Adam Smith; John Taylor; Stephen Field; William Graham Sumner; Raymond Moley
Land policy: federal, 59–69
Land reform: colonial America, 18–20; antebellum, 59–69. *See* Joseph Morgan; Thomas Jefferson; George Henry Evans; Henry George; Populist
Legal concept of ownership; colonial New England, 17–18. *See* William Blackstone; Federal Constitution; Joseph Storey; Roger Taney; John Marshall
Lincoln, Abraham: image of nineteenth-century America, 70; support of Homestead Act of 1861, 70; attitude toward freeholding, 70
Locke, John: *Two Treatises of Government*, 29–35; definition of property, 29–30; definition of people, 29–30; definition of liberty, 29; natural rights, 30–35; definition of citizenship, 30; landholding, 30–35; labor theory of value, 31–34; restrictions on ownership, 31–32; theory of money, 32–33; land monopoly, 33; powers of society, 32–34; taxation, 34; right of revolution, 34–35; slavery, 94–96; mentioned, 10, 15, 24, 37, 41, 53, 60, 108, 111, 112, 113, 185
Locofocos: freeholding, 79
Loomis, Arphaxed: land reform, 60

Madison, James: theory of government, 44–45; concept of ownership, 45; constitutional reform, 44–45; idea of balanced interests, 45; suffrage requirements, 47
Mansfield, Lord: slavery, 99
Marshall, John: slavery, 99–100; contract clause, 120–125

Mason, George: suffrage requirements, 47
Masquerier, Lewis: mentioned, 62
Massachusetts: Body of Liberties of 1641, 11; constitutional convention of 1820, 75–79; slave policy, 98
Medieval theory of ownership. *See* Feudal concept of ownership
Micah: quoted, 2–3
Missouri compromise: slavery, 101–102
Moley, Raymond, 154–158; concept of property, 156–157; mentioned, 199
Morgan, Joseph: concept of need and use, 18; unearned increment, 18
Morris, Gouverneur: freeholding, 46

National Reform Association: program, 60–64; mentioned, 67
Natural rights: American legal definition, 116–122, 130–131; slavery, 94–101, 102, 103–105, 106–107, 108–109; applied to corporate property, 137–139; post-Civil War legal development, 137–146; mentioned, 53, 199. *See* John Locke; Thomas Jefferson; James Otis; Declaration of Independence; Fourteenth amendment; Populist; Labor theory of value
Need and use: colonial America, 15–21. *See* Labor theory of value; John Locke; Thomas Jefferson; Agrarianism; Joseph Morgan
New Freedom: mentioned, 189–190
New Harmony, Indiana: communitarian experiment, 80–81
New Jersey: slave policy, 98; colonial land reform, 19
New nationalism: mentioned, 189, 190

New York: colonial land reform, 18–19; constitutional convention of 1821, 75–79; slave policy, 98
Northwest Ordinance of 1787, 97

Open field system: colonial New England, 13. *See* Feudal concept of ownership
Otis, James: natural rights concept, 37–38; mentioned, 39
Owen, Robert: concept of ownership, 81
Owsley, Frank: mentioned, 191, 192, 193

Paine, Thomas: quoted, 54; slave property, 96; mentioned, 61
Paterson, William: opinion in *Vanhorne's Lessee v. Dorrance* (1795), 116–117
Penn, William: mentioned, 7–8
Pennsylvania: colonial land reform, 20–21; state constitution, 117; slave policy, 98
Perkins, William: quoted, 8
Pickering, John: agrarian political economy, 63–64
Pinckney, Charles: freeholding, 48
Plymouth, Massachusetts, 12
Police powers: fourteenth amendment, 142–146
Populist: entrepreneurial ethic, 186–187; labor theory of value, 185–189; program, 187–188
Preemption, 59
Progressivism: Raymond Moley, 155
Proprietorship. *See* Freeholding
Puritanism. *See* Colonial New England; Calvinism

Quitrent, 7. *See* Feudal concept of ownership

Radical Republicans: mentioned, 67
Ransom, John Crowe, 191–192, 193
Rawe, John: mentioned, 193

Republicanism: John Taylor, 56. *See* James Harrington; John Adams; John Taylor; Declaration of Independence; Agrarianism
Restoration, 28
Rhode Island: slave policy, 98
Rights of Englishmen, 5. *See* William Blackstone
Roosevelt, Franklin D.: mentioned, 154, 155, 199
Roosevelt, Theodore: mentioned, 170
Royce, Josiah: mentioned, 170
Ruffner, Henry: Virginia debates of 1829–1830, 104; concept of ownership, 104; slavery, 104

Saint Augustine, mentioned, 8. *See* Calvinism; Colonial New England; Puritanism
Santayana, George: mentioned, 170
Seabury, Samuel: slavery, 108–109; theory of property, 108–109; natural law, 108–109
Sedgwick, Theodore: ideas on political economy, 84–87. *See* Agrarianism
Smith, Adam: ideas on property, 71–72. *See* Capitalism; Factory system
Socialism: agrarian criticism, 195–196; mentioned, 199
Somerset decision (1772), 99
Spooner, Lysander: slavery, 106–107; Federal Constitution, 106–107; concept of ownership, 106–107
Stevens, Thaddeus: mentioned, 67
Stoddard, Solomon: concept of ownership, 17
Stoics: mentioned, 8
Story, Joseph: suffrage restrictions, 76; slavery, 100–101; concept of ownership, 100–101; eminent domain, 129–130; *Charles River Bridge v. Warren Bridge* (1837), 129–130. *See*

Story, Joseph (*cont.*)
Natural rights American legal definition
Subsistence homestead program: mentioned, 190
Substantive due process, 137–146, 203–205
Suffrage reform, 75–79
Sumner, William Graham: struggle for survival, 147–154; concept of property rights, 149–151; mentioned, 158

Taney, Roger: eminent domain, 127–129
Tariffs: mentioned, 56, 137, 153
Tate, Allen: definition of property, 194–195; theory of freedom, 195–197; capitalism, 194–195; socialism, 195–196; mentioned, 191, 192, 193, 199
Taxation, 34, 36–38, 56, 137–146
Taylor, John: concept of ownership, 55–57
Thirteenth amendment: mentioned, 201
Tucker, St. George: slave property, 97; corporations, 122; mentioned, 112
Turner, Frederick Jackson: mentioned, 133

Upshur, Abel P.: defense of slavery, 103–104; concept of ownership, 103–104
Utilitarianism: concept of ownership, 87–92

Veblen, Thorstein: instinct of craftsmanship, 166–167; conspicuous consumption, 166; theory of property, 167–168; technocracy, 169; mentioned, 159–160, 178, 179
Vermont: slave policy, 98
Virginia: Jamestown, 6–7; Declaration of Rights, 54; constitutional convention of 1829–1830, 103–105. *See* Thomas Jefferson

Wage system, 71–93. *See* Factory system; Capitalism; Adam Smith; Alexander Hamilton; William Graham Sumner; Raymond Moley; Socialism; Agrarianism
Waite, Morrison B.: fourteenth amendment, 140–141
Warren, Robert Penn: mentioned, 191, 193
Washington, George: quoted, 37
Wayland, Francis: ideas on political economy, 89–90; mentioned, 87, 92
Webster, Daniel: suffrage restrictions, 76; eminent domain, 129
Who Owns America?, 193–199
Williams, Roger: Indian land policy, 16–17
Wilson, James: concept of property rights, 116
Wilson, Woodrow, 189–190; mentioned, 170
Winthrop, John: quoted, 8, 10–11; Indian land policy, 15–16
Work ethic: mentioned, 10. *See* Calvinism; Labor theory of value; Colonial New England; William Graham Sumner